365 More Ways to Cook Chicken

Melanie Barnard

A JOHN BOSWELL ASSOCIATES BOOK

 HarperCollins*Publishers*

FIRST EDITION

Series Editor: Susan Wyler
Design: Nigel Rollings
Index: Maro Riofrancos

Library of Congress Cataloging-in-Publication Data

Barnard, Melanie.
    365 more ways to cook chicken / Melanie Barnard. — 1st ed.
      p.   cm.
    "A John Boswell Associates book."
    Includes index.
    ISBN 0-06-017139-1
    1. Cookery (Chicken) I. Title.
TX750.5.C45B3725   1996
641-6'6—dc20   96-14265

---

96 97 98 99 00 DT/HC 10 9 8 7 6 5 4 3 2 1

Contents

1   The All-American Bird   5

American classics that put our favorite poultry on the map
include Pennsylvania Dutch Chicken Noodle Soup,
Southern Fried Chicken, Buffalo Wings, Chicken à la
King, and Old-Fashioned Chicken Potpie.

2   World-Class Chicken   19

Some of the best international chicken preparations are
highlighted here, including Chicken Véronique, Basque
Chicken with Tomatoes and Olives, Grilled Tandoori
Chicken, and Jamaican Jerk Chicken.

3   Chicken Nibbles   37

For appetizers and snacks, chicken can't be bested, espe-
cially when it's prepared in irresistible ways like Tarragon
Chicken Crostini, Sesame Chicken Fingers with Apricot
Mustard Sauce, Deviled Chicken Lollipops, and Chicken
Satays with Spicy Peanut Dipping Sauce.

4   Fresh and Fabulous Chicken Salads   51

Grilled Chicken Taco Salad, Caribbean Chicken Salad,
Chicken Spinach Salad with Bacon and Buttermilk Dressing, Chicken Caesar Salad, and Spicy Sesame Noodle and
Chicken Salad are just a few of the ways to eat light and
lovely.

5   Chicken in the Middle   69

Between two slices of bread, that is, or perhaps wrapped
in flaky dough. Whatever the covering, here is an assortment of ways—Tuscan Chicken and Arugula Sandwich,
Chicken Souvlaki, Chicken and Bean Quesadillas, and
Open-Face Monterey Chicken Melt among them—to eat
chicken out of hand.

6   Soup's On and Chicken's in It   83

Sicilian Chicken Soup with Escarole and Pastina, Chicken
Soup with Matzo Balls, Thai Chicken and Lemongrass
Soup, and Ten-Minute Chicken Noodle Soup are a few of
the over two dozen ways to spoon up the flavor and nour-
ishment of the starring bird.

Introduction: When More Is Better

It's hard to get too much of a good thing. And there's not much we cook and eat that's better than chicken—in terms of taste, nutrition, convenience, and versatility. America's most popular bird is in more demand than ever these days. A trip through any local supermarket will confirm the fact that chicken, in all its many cuts and sizes, is indeed king (actually queen) of the roost in the meat case.

This reign began over ten years ago, with the climb to popularity that gave birth to the first, immensely successful *365 Ways to Cook Chicken*, a book that continues to claim a loyal audience. But while that dependable book still holds tremendous appeal for its traditional and tasty recipes, our palates and nutritional standards have changed, as has the availability of many ingredients. And for those who have cooked their way through *365 Ways to Cook Chicken* (as many as ten times), the moment seems right to give a new boost to chicken cookery with *365 **More** Ways to Cook Chicken*.

Since none of the recipes here are duplicates, you can view these two cookbooks as companion volumes. Here you'll find more contemporary trends, with some lighter recipes, a keen eye to less fat, more up-to-date and fresh ingredients, and cuisines, such as northern Italian, Thai, and Mexican, that have more recently entered our culinary repertoire.

With 365 new recipes to choose from, you'll never get bored. You can still enjoy your favorite source of lean protein with the same pleasure and ease. In case you're new to chicken cookery, however, or just want to review the benefits of this beautiful bird, here are some important facts to remember.

Chicken can satisfy an important part of today's healthy dietary recommendations. We all know by now that we should eat less fat. Chicken, especially the white meat, is one of the lowest fat sources of complete protein available. In fact, according to the National Broiler Council, a 3-ounce portion of cooked skinless, boneless chicken breast contains about 1.5 grams of fat and about 116 calories.

Chicken is versatile. Only a few years ago, chicken was available only as a whole roaster or fryer, and some markets sold cut-up chickens as a convenience to the customer. Deboning and skinning were tasks left to the cook. Now we can buy not only whole and cut-up chickens, but separate packages of all parts from breasts to wings, from livers to legs. Breasts and thighs may be preboned, or are sold bone-in but skinless. Cooked chicken, either whole from a rotisserie or in single-serve packs of roasted parts, are now commonplace.

Chicken is quick. Many of the dishes in this book cook in under 30 minutes—a testimony to the quick-cooking properties of chicken. Even a whole roasted bird cooks in about 2 hours and needs no attention at all during most of that time.

Chicken tastes terrific. Chicken has a neutral yet pleasing flavor that enhances everything from fruits to nuts and vegetables to grains. Meaty, richly flavored dark meat is every bit as satisfying as a steak, while delicate white meat is nearly indistinguishable from pricey veal.

Glossary of Chicken Labeling

If you are new to the world of chicken cookery, here is a quick glossary of chicken part terminology:

• *Broiler-fryer*—whole bird weighing 2½ to 4½ pounds, usually sold without neck or giblets. A whole broiler-fryer usually serves 4 people and yields about 3 cups of diced cooked meat.
• *Young roaster*—meaty bird weighing 4½ to 7 pounds, sold with neck and giblets
• *Cut-up chicken*—whole broiler cut into 8 pieces
• *Halves or splits*—broiler cut into 2 equal pieces
• *Quarters*—leg quarters (including drumstick, thigh, and wing) and breast quarters (including wing and breast) are usually packaged and sold separately
• *Leg*—includes drumstick and thigh
• *Thigh*—portion of leg above knee joint, also available boneless and/or skinless
• *Drumstick*—lower portion of leg, also available skinless
• *Split breast*—available bone-in or boneless and skin-on or skinless
• *Cutlets*—thinly sliced portions of skinless, boneless breasts or thighs
• *Wing*—whole wing with three sections attached
• *Drumettes*—first section of wing with tips removed
• *Ground chicken*—made from skinless, boneless meat, usually a combination of dark and white meat
• *Free-range chicken*—loose term referring to chicken that is fed a variety of feed and allowed to mature in a more old-fashioned farm environment; usually more expensive
• *Cornish game hen*—a small bird weighing between 1 and 1½ pounds

Tips on Buying and Handling Chicken

• Pay attention to the "sell by" date on the package. Chicken can be refrigerated in the original wrapper for about 2 days after the sell date before being cooked or frozen.

Nutritive Breakdown By Parts*

Cut	Whole Chicken	Breast	Wing	Thigh	Drumstick
Protein	23g	24g	23g	21g	23g
Calories	134	116	147	152	131
Total Fat	4.1g	1.5g	5.6g	6.7g	3.8g
Cholesterol	76mg	72mg	72mg	81mg	79mg
Sodium	73mg	63mg	78mg	75mg	81mg
Iron	1mg	.9mg	1mg	1.1mg	1.1mg

*Figures are for a 3-ounce baked, skinless serving.

Percentage of Recommended Daily Allowances**

Protein	51%	53%	51%	47%	51%
Calories	7%	6%	7%	8%	7%
Total Fat	6%	2%	8%	10%	6%
Cholesterol	25%	24%	24%	27%	26%
Sodium	2%	2%	2%	2%	2%
Iron	6%	5%	6%	6%	6%

**Based on 2000 calories per day (the midpoint of the recommendation of the National Academy of Sciences for women ages 23–51). A maximum of 3300 mg of sodium per day is also recommended. National Institutes of Health recommends not more than 30% of calories from fat and no more than 300 mg of cholesterol per day.

Data Source: U.S. Department of Agriculture

• Chicken can be frozen, well-wrapped in freezer paper, for several months. While freezng is safe and there is no loss of nutrients, it is my experience that previously frozen chicken has a less desirable texture than fresh chicken. Thaw chicken in the refrigerator, not on the countertop, where it is likely to foster bacterial growth. Do not refreeze raw chicken.
• After handling raw chicken, thoroughly wash your hands, utensils, and counter or cutting board. Bacteria are destroyed if chicken is well cooked, but they can be transferred to other food via surface contact with raw chicken.
• Cook chicken to the well-done stage. A thermometer should read 180°F. for whole chickens, 170° for bone-in parts, and 160° for boneless pieces. Boneless breast meat should be white throughout and, for bone-in chicken, all juices should run clear when pricked almost to the bone with a knife tip.
• Never leave cooked chicken at room temperature for more than 2 hours. If it is to be transported, do so in an insulated

container that will keep it below 40°F. or above 140° to avoid bacterial growth. Remove stuffing from cooked roast chicken and refrigerate separately.
• Chicken can be cooked in the microwave, but since the cooking is often uneven, I do not recommend it except for thinly sliced cutlets or boneless breasts that can be poached in a liquid.

To help you to select chicken to fit into your diet and lifestyle, here, from the National Broiler Council, is a chart that gives the nutritional breakdown of various chicken parts.

General Cooking Guidelines

Chicken cooking times vary according to each recipe and cooking method, but here are some general guidelines:

- *Whole broiler-fryer*—1 to 1½ hours in a 350°F. oven
- *Whole roaster*—2 to 2½ hours in a 350° to 400°F. oven
- *White meat parts*—25 to 35 minutes in all cooking methods
- *Dark meat parts*—30 to 45 minutes in all cooking methods
- *Skinless, boneless breasts*—13 to 15 minutes in all cooking methods
- *Skinless, boneless thighs*—15 to 18 minutes in all cooking methods
- *Thinly sliced breast or thigh fillets*—about 5 minutes in all cooking methods

Welcome to the new world of chicken cookery!

Chapter 1

The All-American Bird

We Americans eat a lot of chicken in a lot of different guises. Some dishes, such as the chicken Purloo of Charleston or the jambalayas of Louisiana, the chicken pot-pies of mid-America or the hot browns of Kentucky, are regional favorites. Even among the classics, there are local variations. Sunday supper roast chicken and gravy will have a different twist (and stuffing) in Oregon than it will in Maine, and there are arguments even within families on how to fry a chicken.

Chicken dishes across America reflect melting-pot eating styles that together comprise American cuisine. Many are adaptations of heritage recipes that have roots in diverse ethnic backgrounds, but others are American originals based on local specialty ingredients or tastes.

Here are just a few of the chicken dishes that call America home. The common denominator (besides chicken) is that all of them are mighty tasty.

1 CORNFLAKE CRUMB OVEN-FRIED CHICKEN

Prep: 20 minutes   Cook: 40 to 45 minutes   Serves: 4

2 eggs	½ teaspoon freshly ground
⅓ cup milk	pepper
5 cups cornflakes cereal	1 (3-pound) chicken, cut into
1 teaspoon salt	8 pieces
¾ teaspoon dried marjoram	3 tablespoons butter, melted

1. Preheat oven to 375°F. In a shallow dish, whisk together eggs and milk to blend. In a food processor, crush cereal to make 1½ cups fine crumbs. Place crumbs in a paper bag along with salt, marjoram, and pepper.

2. Dip chicken pieces into milk, then shake a few pieces at a time in seasoned cornflake crumbs to coat completely. Arrange, skin side up, in a single layer without touching, in a 10x15-inch jelly roll pan or a 9x13-inch baking dish. Drizzle melted butter over chicken.

3. Bake without turning until chicken is crispy brown outside and white throughout and juices run clear when pricked, 40 to 45 minutes.

2   JEWISH GRANDMOTHER'S CHICKEN SOUP
Prep: 5 minutes   Cook: 1 hour 35 minutes   Chill: 1 hour   Serves: 6

Rich homemade stock made from a stewing hen is the traditional cure for whatever ails you. Of course, the grandmother is the secret ingredient, which I'm afraid no cookbook can provide. If you wish, you can add noodles, vegetables, or matzo balls when you reheat the soup.

1 (4- or 5-pound) cut-up stewing hen or chicken	1 parsnip, quartered
2 large onions, quartered	½ cup parsley sprigs
2 large celery ribs with leaves, quartered	1 bay leaf
2 large carrots, quartered	1½ teaspoons salt
	¾ teaspoon whole black peppercorns

1. In a large stockpot, place all ingredients and enough water to cover by 1 inch, about 4 quarts. Bring to a boil, reduce heat to medium-low, and simmer, partially covered, 1½ hours. Add additional water if needed to keep chicken and vegetables covered.

2. Strain soup, reserving chicken but discarding vegetables and herbs. When chicken is cool enough to handle, pull meat off bones in chunks. Refrigerate broth for at least 1 hour, then spoon off congealed fat.

3. To serve, reheat broth. Add chicken meat and simmer 2 minutes, or until heated through.

3   PENNSYLVANIA DUTCH CHICKEN NOODLE SOUP
Prep: 20 minutes   Cook: 1 hour 39 minutes   Chill: 1 hour Serves: 6

Start with a stewing hen or large cut-up chicken. If you can get them, slice fresh pasta sheets into noodles or squares for an old-fashioned effect. Otherwise choose broad dried egg noodles.

1 (4- or 5-pound) cut-up stewing hen or chicken	½ teaspoon freshly ground pepper
2 medium onions, quartered	2 tablespoons chopped fresh dill or 2 teaspoons dried
2 celery ribs with leaves, quartered	½ pound fresh pasta sheets or broad egg noodles
2 carrots, quartered	2 cups frozen mixed vegetables
½ cup parsley sprigs	
1 teaspoon salt	

1. In a large stockpot, place chicken, onions, celery, carrots, parsley, salt, pepper, and enough water to cover by 1 inch, about 4 quarts. Bring to a boil, reduce heat to medium-low, and simmer, partially covered, 1½ hours. Add additional water if needed to keep chicken and vegetables covered.

2. Strain soup, reserving chicken and broth separately; discard vegetables and parsley. When chicken is cool enough to handle, pull meat off bones in chunks. Refrigerate broth for at least 1 hour, then spoon off and discard congealed fat.

3. At serving time, in a large pot, bring degreased chicken stock and dill to a boil. If using pasta sheets, cut into 3x½-inch strips. Add fresh or dried noodles and frozen vegetables to boiling broth. Boil until noodles are tender, about 2 minutes for fresh or about 7 minutes for dried. Return chicken to pot and heat through, about 2 minutes.

---

4   SUNDAY SUPPER ROAST CHICKEN WITH GIBLET GRAVY
Prep: 15 minutes   Cook: 2 to 2½ hours   Serves: 6

1 **whole roasting chicken
   (5 to 6 pounds), giblets
   reserved**
1 **tablespoon butter, softened
   Salt and freshly ground
   pepper**

1 **medium onion, quartered**
1 **bay leaf, broken in half**
2 **tablespoons flour**

1. Preheat oven to 400°F. Rinse chicken inside and out and pat dry. Rub skin with butter, then season generously with salt and pepper inside and out. Place onion in chicken cavity and tie legs together with white kitchen string. Place chicken on a rack, breast side up, in a shallow roasting pan.

2. Roast chicken for 30 minutes. Reduce oven heat to 350° and continue to roast until an instant-reading thermometer inserted into thigh registers 180°, 1½ to 2 hours longer. Add chicken liver to bottom of roasting pan about 15 minutes before chicken is done.

3. While chicken is roasting, place neck, gizzard, and bay leaf in a small saucepan and cover with about 3 cups water. Bring to a boil, reduce heat to medium-low, cover, and simmer 45 minutes. Strain and reserve 2½ cups broth. Chop giblets and liver.

4. When chicken is cooked, remove to a platter and let stand 15 minutes before carving. Pour pan juices into a measuring cup and let stand 5 minutes to allow fat to rise to the top. Return 2 tablespoons fat to the roasting pan; discard remaining fat, reserving drippings. Heat fat in roasting pan set over medium-high heat. Whisk in flour and cook, stirring, until golden, about 2 minutes. Slowly whisk in reserved broth and cook, stirring, until bubbly and lightly thickened, about 4 minutes. Stir in chopped giblets. Season with salt and pepper to taste. Carve chicken, discarding onion, and serve with giblet gravy.

5   FINGER LICKIN' BARBECUED CHICKEN
Prep: 15 minutes   Cook: 44 to 49 minutes   Serves: 6

2 tablespoons vegetable oil
1 onion, chopped
2 garlic cloves, crushed
    through a press
2 teaspoons dry mustard
¼ teaspoon cayenne
1 cup ketchup
1 cup bottled chili sauce

3 tablespoons molasses
2 tablespoons Worcestershire
    sauce
3 tablespoons cider vinegar
1 cup ginger ale
4 pounds chicken breasts,
    thighs, and/or drumsticks

1. Heat oil in a nonreactive medium saucepan. Add onion and cook over medium heat, stirring, until onion is softened, about 3 minutes. Stir in garlic, mustard, and cayenne. Cook 1 minute. Add remaining ingredients except chicken. Bring to a boil; reduce heat to medium-low and simmer, stirring often, until lightly thickened, about 15 minutes. Use immediately or refrigerate up to 2 weeks.

2. Prepare a medium fire in a charcoal or gas grill. Grill chicken, skin side down, 10 minutes. Turn skin side up and grill 5 minutes. Brush with some sauce and grill, brushing with additional sauce, until chicken juices run clear when pricked, about 10 to 15 minutes longer. (White meat parts will take less time than legs and thighs.) Boil remaining sauce and serve with grilled chicken.

6   COUNTRY CAPTAIN CHICKEN
Prep: 20 minutes   Cook: 39 to 44 minutes   Serves: 4 to 6

Some say this dish traveled to Savannah, Georgia, via the West Indies, but others insist the recipe was delivered directly by a sea captain selling spices. However it arrived, this southern American classic, distinctive because of the curry seasoning and currants, makes a great one-pot meal. Serve over steamed rice.

1 chicken (about 3 pounds),
    cut into 8 pieces
½ teaspoon salt
½ teaspoon cayenne
2 tablespoons vegetable oil or
    butter
1 medium onion, coarsely
    chopped
1 medium green bell pepper,
    coarsely chopped

1 large garlic clove, crushed
    through a press
2 teaspoons curry powder
1 teaspoon dried thyme
½ teaspoon ground mace
1 (14½-ounce) can stewed
    tomatoes with juices
½ cup dry white wine or
    chicken broth
¼ cup currants or raisins

1. Season chicken with salt and cayenne. Heat oil in a Dutch oven. Cook chicken over medium-high heat, turning once or twice, until golden brown, about 8 minutes. Remove chicken from pan.

2. Add onion, bell pepper, and garlic to drippings in pan. Reduce heat to medium and cook, stirring often, until vegetables are softened, about 5 minutes. Add curry powder, thyme, and mace. Cook, stirring, 1 minute. Stir in stewed tomatoes and juices, wine, and currants. Return chicken to pan, stirring to cover with vegetables.

3. Cover, reduce heat to medium-low, and simmer until chicken is tender and white throughout, 25 to 30 minutes.

---

7   CHICKEN DIVAN
Prep: 15 minutes   Cook: 25 to 32 minutes   Serves: 4

This is a great do-ahead dish. If you opt, however, to assemble the casserole just before serving, omit the baking and simply brown the top under a broiler.

2½ **tablespoons butter**	½ **cup grated Parmesan cheese**
2 **tablespoons flour**	**Salt and freshly ground**
¼ **teaspoon ground nutmeg**	**pepper**
½ **cup chopped or thinly sliced**	¾ **pound cooked chicken, cut**
scallions	**into ¾-inch cubes (3 cups)**
1½ **cups chicken broth**	2 **(10-ounce) packages frozen**
½ **cup light cream or half-and-**	**chopped broccoli, thawed**
half	2 **tablespoons plain dry bread**
2 **tablespoons dry sherry**	**crumbs**

1. In a large saucepan, melt 2 tablespoons of butter over medium heat. Stir in flour and cook, stirring, for 1 to 2 minutes. Add nutmeg and scallions, then slowly whisk in broth and cream. Bring to a boil, whisking constantly until sauce thickens, 1 to 2 minutes. Reduce heat to medium-low and simmer 3 minutes. Stir in sherry, ¼ cup of cheese, chicken, and broccoli. Spoon into a shallow 2-quart casserole. (Can be prepared early in day and refrigerated. Return to room temperature before baking.)

2. Preheat oven to 375°F. Melt remaining ½ tablespoon butter, and mix with bread crumbs and remaining ¼ cup cheese. Sprinkle over top of casserole.

3. Bake casserole until heated through and crumbs are browned, 20 to 25 minutes.

8 MARYLAND FRIED CHICKEN WITH MILK GRAVY

Prep: 20 minutes   Marinate: 4 hours   Cook: 29 to 32 minutes
Serves: 4

Fried chicken and gravy for ladling over biscuits is popular everywhere, but is particularly loved in Maryland. Serve with hot biscuits, whether you make them from scratch or bake them from a tube.

2½ cups milk
 1 tablespoon lemon juice
 1 (3-pound) chicken, cut into
    8 pieces
 ¾ cup flour
 1 teaspoon salt

 ½ teaspoon freshly ground
    pepper
1½ cups vegetable oil
 1 cup whole milk or light
    cream

1. In a shallow dish, combine milk and lemon juice. Add chicken and turn to coat. Cover and refrigerate 4 hours, turning 2 or 3 times.

2. In a paper bag, shake together flour, salt, and pepper. Measure and reserve 2 tablespoons seasoned flour for gravy. Remove chicken from milk but do not dry. Toss a few pieces at a time in seasoned flour to coat completely. Reserve 1 tablespoon of the seasoned flour for gravy.

3. Heat oil in a deep 12-inch frying pan or deep-fryer to 375°F. Place chicken in hot oil, skin side down. Cover pan and fry 15 minutes. Uncover and use tongs to carefully turn chicken skin side up. Fry, uncovered, until chicken is browned and juices run clear when pricked, 14 to 17 minutes longer. Drain on paper towels.

4. Pour off all but 1 tablespoon drippings from the pan. Add reserved 1 tablespoon seasoned flour and cook, stirring, for 1 minute. Add 1 cup whole milk and cook, stirring over medium heat, until smooth and bubbly, about 3 minutes. Serve chicken with gravy.

9 SOUTHERN FRIED CHICKEN

Prep: 20 minutes   Marinate: 4 hours   Cook: 29 to 32 minutes
Serves: 4

1½ cups buttermilk
 ½ teaspoon Tabasco or other
    hot sauce
 1 (3-pound) chicken, cut into
    8 pieces
 ⅔ cup flour
 ⅓ cup yellow cornmeal

 1 teaspoon salt
 ¾ teaspoon freshly ground
    pepper
1½ cups vegetable oil, lard, or
    solid vegetable
    shortening

1. In a shallow dish, combine buttermilk and Tabasco. Add chicken and turn to coat. Cover and refrigerate 4 to 8 hours, turning 2 or 3 times.

2. Place flour, cornmeal, salt, and pepper in a paper bag. Remove chicken from buttermilk but do not dry. Toss a few pieces at a time in flour to coat completely.

3. Heat oil in a deep 12-inch frying pan or deep-fryer to 375°F. Place chicken, skin side down, in hot oil. Cover pan and fry 15 minutes. Uncover and use tongs to carefully turn chicken skin side up. Fry, uncovered, until chicken is golden brown and juices run clear when pricked, 14 to 17 minutes longer. Drain on paper towels before serving.

10   KENTUCKY HOT BROWN
Prep: 20 minutes   Cook: 11 to 13 minutes   Serves: 4

Though the original recipe from the Brown Hotel in Louisville contains no bourbon, it seems like an appropriate Kentucky addition.

8 slices of bacon	⅛ teaspoon cayenne
2 tablespoons minced shallots	2 teaspoons bourbon
2 tablespoons flour	(optional)
¾ cup milk	4 slices of white or whole
⅓ cup chicken broth	wheat bread, toasted
1 cup (4 ounces) grated	¾ pound sliced cooked
Cheddar cheese	chicken breast
1 teaspoon Worcestershire	2 tablespoons grated
sauce	Parmesan cheese

1. In a large frying pan, cook bacon over medium heat until crisp, about 5 minutes. Drain on paper towels. Discard all but 2 tablespoons of drippings.

2. Add shallots to bacon drippings and cook over medium heat, stirring constantly, until softened, about 2 minutes. Add flour and cook, stirring, for 1 to 2 minutes without allowing to color. Slowly whisk in milk and broth. Bring to a boil, stirring constantly. Reduce heat to medium-low and cook, stirring, until thickened and bubbly, about 2 minutes. Remove from heat and stir in Cheddar cheese, Worcestershire, and cayenne until cheese is melted and sauce is smooth. Stir in bourbon.

3. Preheat broiler. Place toast in 4 individual gratin dishes or a single large baking dish. Arrange chicken on top of toasts, then ladle on sauce. Top with bacon slices, crisscrossed. Sprinkle with Parmesan cheese. Broil about 5 inches from the heat 1 to 2 minutes, until bubbly and sauce is flecked with brown.

11   CHICKEN À LA KING
Prep: 20 minutes   Cook: 9 to 11 minutes   Serves: 6

If you have some leftover chicken, this is a breeze to make, which is probably the reason it has remained so popular ever since its inception in the 1950s. Serve with rice or noodles or over whole wheat toast.

3 tablespoons butter
3 tablespoons minced shallots
4 ounces mushrooms, thinly sliced
½ small red bell pepper, finely diced, or ¼ cup chopped pimiento
3 tablespoons flour
1¼ cups chicken broth

1 cup half-and-half or milk
1 egg yolk, beaten
¼ cup dry sherry
¼ cup chopped parsley
Salt and freshly ground pepper
3 cups cooked and cubed chicken

1. In a large saucepan, melt butter over medium heat. Add shallots, mushrooms, and bell pepper and cook, stirring, 3 minutes. (If using pimiento, reserve to add later.) Stir in flour and cook, stirring, 1 to 2 minutes, without allowing to color. Slowly whisk in broth and half-and-half. Cook, stirring, until sauce comes to a boil and thickens, 1 to 2 minutes.

2. In a small bowl, whisk about half of hot sauce into egg yolk, then return mixture to saucepan and stir in sherry. Cook, stirring, 2 minutes. Add parsley and season with salt and pepper to taste. Add chicken and cook until heated through, about 2 minutes.

12   CHICKEN AND PARSLEY DUMPLINGS
Prep: 20 minutes   Cook: 45 minutes   Serves: 4 to 6

1 chicken (about 3 pounds), cut into 8 pieces
1 large onion, thinly sliced
4 carrots, cut into 1-inch chunks
2 celery ribs, sliced about ¼ inch thick
1 bay leaf, broken in half

1 teaspoon dried thyme
4 cups chicken broth
1 cup flour
1 teaspoon baking powder
½ teaspoon salt
⅓ cup chopped parsley
2 tablespoons vegetable oil
6 to 7 tablespoons milk

1. Pull off and discard skin from chicken. Place chicken, onion, carrots, celery, bay leaf, thyme, and broth in a large pot. Bring to a boil, reduce heat to medium-low, cover, and simmer 25 minutes.

2. For dumplings, in a mixing bowl, whisk together flour, baking powder, and salt. Stir in parsley. Make a well in center and pour in oil and 6 tablespoons milk. Stir together to make a soft biscuit dough. If dough seems too dry, stir in remaining 1 tablespoon milk.

3. Uncover pot. Dip a tablespoon into broth, then scoop up and drop dough to make 8 to 12 mounds on top of simmering chicken. Cover pot and simmer until a toothpick inserted into dumplings comes out clean, about 20 minutes.

4. Remove and discard bay leaf. Serve chicken and dumplings with broth in shallow soup bowls.

---

13   BUFFALO WINGS
Prep: 20 minutes   Cook: 16 to 24 minutes   Serves: 4 to 6

Cut up the chicken wings yourself or buy them already prepared for frying into these classic nibblers. This American original is from the Anchor Bar in Buffalo, New York.

5 **pounds chicken wings (about 30)**	**Oil for deep-frying**
5 **tablespoons butter**	**Iceberg lettuce leaves**
3 **tablespoons Durkee's Hot Red Pepper Sauce or 2 tablespoons Tabasco**	**Carrot sticks** **Celery sticks**
1 **teaspoon paprika**	1 **cup blue cheese salad dressing, bottled or homemade**

1. Use a cleaver or chef's knife to chop off wing tips. (They can be popped in a bag and frozen to be used later to make chicken stock.) Cut wings in half at joint.

2. In a small saucepan, melt butter with hot sauce. Stir in paprika. Remove from heat and set butter sauce aside.

3. In a deep-fryer, bring 1½ to 2 inches of oil to 375°F. Fry wings in 2 or 3 batches until golden brown, crisp, and cooked through, about 8 minutes per batch. Drain on paper towels, then put in a large bowl. Pour butter sauce over wings and toss to coat.

4. To serve, heap hot wings on lettuce leaves. Garnish platter with celery and carrot sticks. Place a small bowl of blue cheese dressing on platter to use as a dip.

14   OLD-FASHIONED CHICKEN POT PIE
Prep: 45 minutes   Cook: 1¾ to 2 hours   Serves: 6

1 chicken (about 3½ pounds), cut into 8 pieces
1 celery rib, cut into 1-inch chunks
1½ teaspoons dried thyme
1 teaspoon dried marjoram
3 tablespoons butter
1 large onion, chopped
2 carrots, sliced
½ pound thickly sliced mushrooms (about 2½ cups), domestic or wild

1 cup frozen green peas
Salt and freshly ground pepper
3 tablespoons flour
½ cup half-and-half or light cream
½ cup chopped parsley
Pastry for a single-crust 9-inch pie or 1 refrigerated pie crust round
1 egg yolk beaten with 2 teaspoons water

1. Place chicken (including neck and back) into a pot. Add celery, ½ teaspoon each of thyme and marjoram, and water to cover by 1 inch. Bring to a boil, reduce heat to medium-low, and simmer until chicken is very tender, 45 to 50 minutes. Remove chicken from pot and when cool enough to handle, pull off meat in chunks. Discard bones and skin. Boil broth until reduced to about 2 cups, about 10 minutes. Strain, pressing hard on solids with back of a spoon. Measure and reserve 1¾ cups broth.

2. In a large frying pan, melt 2 tablespoons of butter. Add onions and carrots and cook over medium heat, stirring often, until beginning to soften, about 3 minutes. Add mushrooms and continue to cook until mushrooms are softened, about 5 minutes longer. Remove vegetables to a bowl with a slotted spoon and add peas. Season with salt and pepper.

3. Add the remaining 1 tablespoon butter to the frying pan and heat to melt. Stir in flour and cook over medium heat, stirring, for 2 minutes. Whisk in cream and reserved broth. Cook, stirring, until thick and bubbly but not browned, about 3 minutes. Stir into vegetables along with parsley. Spoon filling into a 2-quart baking dish, such as a 9-inch square or a 7x11-inch rectangle. (Filling can be made a day ahead and refrigerated. Return to room temperature to continue.)

4. Preheat oven to 425°F. On a lightly floured surface, roll out pastry round if necessary until it is slightly larger than top of the baking dish. Lay pastry over filling in dish, folding edges under and crimping to fit rim of the dish. Cut 4 slits in pastry, then brush pastry with the egg yolk glaze.

5. Bake 5 minutes. Reduce oven temperature to 375° and bake until pastry is golden brown and filling is bubbly, 35 to 45 minutes longer. Serve hot.

15   CHICKEN AND SAUSAGE JAMBALAYA

Prep: 45 minutes   Cook: 71 to 72 minutes   Serves: 6 to 8

This is great for a party since it is a one-dish meal that can be prepared ahead and simply popped into the oven. Andouille sausage is a spicy, garlicky sausage often used in Creole and Cajun cooking.

¾ **pound garlicky smoked sausage, preferably andouille, sliced about ¼ inch thick**
2 **tablespoons vegetable oil**
¾ **pound skinless, boneless chicken thighs, cut into 1½-inch chunks**
¾ **pound skinless, boneless chicken breast halves, cut into 1½-inch chunks**
½ **teaspoon cayenne**
2 **celery ribs, chopped**
2 **medium onions, chopped**
2 **green bell peppers, chopped**

3 **garlic cloves, crushed through a press**
1 **teaspoon dried thyme**
1 **teaspoon dried marjoram**
1½ **cups converted white rice**
2 **cups chicken broth**
2 **(14½- to 15-ounce) cans diced tomatoes, drained, juices reserved**
Salt and freshly ground pepper
¼ **to ½ teaspoon Tabasco or other hot sauce**
½ **cup thinly sliced scallions**

1. In a large frying pan or Dutch oven, cook sausage in ½ tablespoon of oil over medium-high heat, turning, until lightly browned, about 5 minutes. With a slotted spoon, transfer sausage to a bowl.

2. Add remaining 1½ tablespoons oil to pan. Sprinkle chicken thigh and breast pieces with cayenne and and fry in 2 batches, turning once or twice, until golden outside and white throughout, about 5 minutes per batch. Transfer to bowl with sausage.

3. Add celery, onions, and bell peppers to drippings in pan, reduce heat to medium, and cook, stirring often, until vegetables are softened, about 5 minutes. Add garlic, thyme, and marjoram and cook 1 to 2 minutes. Add rice and stir to coat grains with oil. Spoon vegetables and rice into shallow 3-quart baking dish. Cover with foil. (Recipe can be prepared a day ahead to this point. Refrigerate chicken-sausage mixture and rice and vegetable mixture separately. Return to room temperature before cooking.)

4. Preheat oven to 350°F. Stir broth and 1 cup of water into rice mixture. Cover with foil. Bake 35 minutes. Arrange chicken and sausage and drained tomatoes over rice. If rice seems dry, add up to ½ cup reserved tomato juice or water to the dish. Cover with foil and bake until heated through, about 15 minutes longer.

5. Season with salt, pepper, and Tabasco, stirring gently to mix. Sprinkle scallions on top. Serve directly from baking dish.

16   DIRTY RICE
Prep: 20 minutes   Cook: 40 minutes   Serves: 4 to 6

This Creole chicken liver and gizzard classic is also a fine use for leftover rice.

2 cups chicken broth
1 cup converted white rice
3 tablespoons butter or
   vegetable oil
⅓ pound chicken livers
⅓ pound chicken gizzards
1 green bell pepper
1 medium onion, chopped

1 large celery rib, chopped
2 garlic cloves, crushed
   through a press
Salt and freshly ground
   pepper
½ cup thinly sliced scallion
   greens

1. Bring broth to a boil in a medium saucepan. Add rice, reduce heat to low, cover, and simmer until liquid is absorbed, about 20 minutes.

2. While rice is cooking, coarsely chop chicken livers and gizzards by pulsing in a food processor. Heat 1½ tablespoons of butter or oil in a large frying pan. Add chopped livers and gizzards and cook over medium heat, stirring often, until browned, about 10 minutes. Add bell pepper, onion, celery, and garlic to frying pan along with remaining 1½ tablespoons butter or oil. Cook, stirring often, until vegetables are very tender, about 10 minutes.

3. Gently stir together rice and chicken liver mixture. Season with salt and pepper to taste. Serve hot, sprinkled with the scallion greens.

17   CHICKEN PURLOO
Prep: 20 minutes   Cook: 36 minutes   Serves: 6

There are lots of variations and ways to spell this Charleston, South Carolina, classic. Serve it over hot cooked rice, with a side of coleslaw and corn bread if you like.

¼ pound thick-sliced bacon,
   chopped
1 medium onion, chopped
1 celery rib, chopped
1 green bell pepper, chopped
1 carrot, chopped
1 cup sliced mushrooms
1 garlic clove, crushed
   through a press
2 tablespoons flour

1 teaspoon dried thyme
½ teaspoon salt
½ teaspoon dried oregano
¼ teaspoon crushed hot red
   pepper
1 (14½-ounce) can stewed
   tomatoes
4 cups cooked chicken, cut
   into 1-inch chunks

1. In a large frying pan, cook bacon over medium heat until crisp, about 5 minutes. Remove with a slotted spoon and reserve.

2. Add onion, celery, bell pepper, carrot, mushrooms, and garlic to drippings in pan. Cook, stirring often, until vegetables are softened, about 5 minutes. Stir in flour, thyme, salt, oregano, and crushed pepper and cook 1 minute. Stir in tomatoes and juices. Cover pan, reduce heat to medium-low, and simmer 20 minutes.

3. Add chicken and reserved bacon. Cook until heated through, about 5 minutes.

18 LUNCHEON CHICKEN SALAD
Prep: 15 minutes   Cook: none   Serves: 4

This simplest and most pristine of chicken salads was made famous in the tearooms of yesterday. It is just as good today. To make into chicken salad for sandwiches, simply cut the chicken into smaller pieces.

1 cup mayonnaise
2 tablespoons milk
1½ tablespoons lemon juice
½ teaspoon salt
¼ teaspoon freshly ground
   pepper
3 cups cubed cooked chicken
   breast

½ cup chopped celery
⅓ cup thinly sliced scallions
1 head of Boston lettuce
  Paprika
  Tomato wedges and
   quartered hard-cooked
   eggs, for garnish

1. In a mixing bowl, whisk together mayonnaise, milk, lemon juice, salt, and pepper. Stir in chicken, celery, and scallions. (Can be prepared up to 6 hours ahead and refrigerated.)

2. At serving time, separate lettuce into leafy cups. Spoon salad into lettuce cups. Dust lightly with paprika. Garnish with tomato wedges and quarters of hard-cooked eggs.

Chapter 2

World-Class Chicken

Chicken plays a role in every major cuisine in the world, even in those largely based on grains and vegetables. From the revered coq au vin of France to the tandoori chicken of India and from the paellas of Spain to the kung-pao chicken of China, famous chicken dishes abound.

Here is a collection of some of the best-known classics. You will also find international chicken recipes in other chapters, as well as streamlined interpretations and other variations based on the wealth of international dishes in the chicken cookery repertoire.

That chicken is so popular throughout the world is testimony to its versatility, relatively low cost, and easy preparation.

---

19 CHICKEN BONNE FEMME
Prep: 20 minutes   Cook: 45 minutes   Serves: 4

4 chicken breast halves on the bone, skinned	1 cup frozen pearl onions, thawed
1½ teaspoon salt	1 tablespoon flour
¼ teaspoon freshly ground pepper	½ cup dry white wine
1½ teaspoons dried thyme	½ cup chicken broth
2 tablespoons butter	1 cup frozen baby peas
1 cup baby carrots	½ cup heavy cream
	2 tablespoons dry sherry

1. Season chicken with salt and pepper and half of thyme. In a large frying pan, melt butter over medium heat. Add chicken and cook, turning, until golden brown, about 10 minutes. Remove from pan.

2. Add carrots and onions to pan and cook, stirring often, until pale golden, about 8 minutes. Stir in flour and cook 1 minute. Stir in wine, broth, and remaining thyme. Return chicken to pan.

3. Cover and cook over medium-low heat until chicken is white near bone and vegetables are tender, about 20 minutes.

4. Stir in peas, cream, and sherry. Simmer, uncovered, 5 minutes. Season with additional salt and pepper to taste and serve.

20   POULET NORMANDY

Prep: 10 minutes   Cook: 22 to 24 minutes   Serves: 4

The Normandy district of France is well known for the abundance of its apples and the high quality of its dairy products and cream.

4 skinless, boneless chicken breast halves
¼ teaspoon salt
⅛ teaspoon freshly ground pepper
1 teaspoon dried thyme
2 tablespoons butter
2 small green apples, cored and sliced

2 medium leeks (white part only), sliced
½ cup apple cider
1 tablespoon cider vinegar
3 tablespoons Calvados or brandy
½ cup heavy cream

1. Season chicken with salt, pepper, and ½ teaspoon of thyme. In a large frying pan, melt butter over medium heat. Add chicken and cook, turning, until golden brown outside and white throughout, 10 to 12 minutes. Remove chicken from pan.

2. Add apples to pan. Cook, turning and stirring gently, until softened and pale golden, about 4 minutes. Remove from pan. Add leeks and cook, stirring often, until softened, about 5 minutes. Add cider, vinegar, Calvados, and remaining ½ teaspoon thyme to pan. Cook for 1 minute, stirring up browned bits from bottom of pan. Add cream and return chicken and apples to pan. Simmer 2 minutes.

3. Season sauce with additional salt and pepper to taste. Serve chicken and apples with sauce spooned on top.

21   CHICKEN CORDON BLEU

Prep: 30 minutes   Cook: 18 to 20 minutes   Serves: 6

4 skinless, boneless chicken breast halves
6 very thin slices of smoked ham or prosciutto (about 2 ounces)
6 very thin slices of Swiss or fontina cheese (about 3 ounces)
⅓ cup flour

½ teaspoon salt
¼ teaspoon freshly ground pepper
1 egg
⅓ cup dry bread crumbs
2 tablespoons vegetable oil
1 tablespoon butter
½ cup dry white wine
2 tablespoons brandy

1. Place chicken between pieces of plastic wrap and pound to ¼ to ⅛ inch thick, working from middle to edges and taking care not to pound holes in chicken. Remove plastic wrap. Lay a slice each of ham and cheese on each piece of chicken. Roll up, turning in ends so that filling is completely enclosed. Press edges to seal.

2. In a shallow dish, combine flour, salt, and pepper. Beat egg in another shallow dish and place bread crumbs in a third. Dip chicken first into seasoned flour mixture, then into egg, and finally into bread crumbs, turning to coat completely. Refrigerate 15 minutes.

3. In a large frying pan, heat oil and butter. Cook chicken rolls over medium heat, turning carefully with tongs, until golden brown, 6 to 8 minutes. Cover pan, reduce heat to medium-low, and cook 5 minutes. Uncover and cook until chicken is white throughout, about 5 minutes.

4. Remove rolls from pan. Add wine and brandy to pan and cook, stirring up browned bits on bottom of pan until lightly reduced, about 2 minutes. Spoon sauce over chicken.

---

22 COQ AU VIN
Prep: 20 minutes   Cook: 56 minutes to 1 hour   Serves: 4 to 6

This is a streamlined version of the classic. Use good wine here; it's the key ingredient.

4 slices of bacon, finely diced	2 tablespoons flour
1 (3½- to 4-pound) chicken, cut into 8 pieces	2 tablespoons tomato paste
½ teaspoon freshly ground pepper	¼ cup Cognac or brandy
2 large garlic cloves, crushed through a press	2½ cups hearty red wine, such as Burgundy
1 teaspoon dried thyme	1 bay leaf, broken in half
1 pound fresh peeled or thawed frozen small white onions	2 tablespoons butter
½ pound baby carrots	½ pound mushrooms, thickly sliced
	½ teaspoon salt
	¼ cup chopped parsley

1. In a large Dutch oven, cook bacon over medium heat until crisp, about 5 minutes. Remove bacon with a slotted spoon and reserve.

2. Season chicken with ¼ teaspoon pepper and cook in batches in pan drippings over medium-high heat, turning, until browned all over, about 7 minutes per batch. Remove chicken from pan.

3. Reduce heat to medium and add garlic, thyme, onions, and carrots to pan. Cook, stirring often, until vegetables are just softened, about 5 minutes. Stir in flour and tomato paste and cook 2 minutes. Add Cognac, wine, and bay leaf. Bring to a boil, stirring up browned bits from bottom of pan. Return chicken to pan, cover, and simmer over medium-low heat until juices run clear when pricked, 20 to 25 minutes.

4. About 10 minutes before chicken is done, melt butter in a large frying pan over medium-high heat. Add mushrooms and cook until softened, about 5 minutes. Add to chicken and simmer 5 minutes. Season with salt and remaining pepper. Remove bay leaf and sprinkle chicken with parsley before serving.

23   CHICKEN VÉRONIQUE
Prep: 10 minutes   Cook: 13 to 17 minutes   Serves: 4

4 skinless, boneless chicken breast halves	½ cup dry white wine
¼ teaspoon salt	½ cup chicken broth
⅛ teaspoon freshly ground pepper	½ cup heavy cream
¾ teaspoon dried thyme	1 teaspoon grated orange zest
2 tablespoons butter	1 cup seedless green and/or red grapes
3 tablespoons finely chopped shallots	4 thin orange slices
	4 small grape clusters

1. Season chicken with salt, pepper, and ½ teaspoon of thyme. Melt butter in a large frying pan over medium heat. Add chicken and cook, turning, until golden outside, 8 to 10 minutes. Remove chicken from pan.

2. Add shallots to pan and cook until softened, about 2 minutes, stirring often. Add wine, broth, and remaining ¼ teaspoon thyme and bring to a boil, stirring up browned bits from bottom of pan. Add cream and orange zest. Return chicken to pan. Add grapes and simmer until chicken is white throughout and sauce is slightly reduced, 3 to 5 minutes.

3. Serve garnished with orange slices and grape clusters.

24   POULET EN COCOTTE
Prep: 20 minutes   Cook: 1 hour 54 minutes   Serves: 4 to 6

This chicken, baked in a tightly closed pot, is a French classic. The results are moist and flavorful. Use a casserole or Dutch oven just large enough to hold the chicken and vegetables comfortably.

1 small roasting chicken (4½ to 5 pounds)	1 parsnip, cut into 1-inch chunks
¾ teaspoon salt	1 cup chicken broth
½ teaspoon freshly ground pepper	½ cup dry white wine
1 teaspoon dried tarragon	1 tablespoon cornstarch
2 tablespoons butter	2 tablespoons Cognac or brandy
1 large onion, sliced	
2 carrots, cut into 1-inch chunks	

1. Preheat oven to 350°F. Season chicken skin and cavity with salt, pepper, and half of tarragon. Tie legs together with string. In a Dutch oven, melt butter over medium heat. Add chicken and cook, turning, until golden brown all over, about 15 minutes. Remove from pan.

2. Add onion, carrots, and parsnip to pan and cook, stirring occasionally, until onion is softened, about 5 minutes. Sprinkle on remaining tarragon. Set chicken, breast side up, on vegetables. Cover pan tightly.

3. Roast chicken until tender and a thermometer registers 180°F or juices run clear when thigh is pricked, about 1½ hours. Remove chicken to a carving board. Skim off fat. Set Dutch oven over direct heat and add broth and wine. Boil, stirring up browned bits from bottom of pan, for 3 minutes. Dissolve cornstarch in Cognac and stir into sauce. Cook, stirring, until thickened, about 1 minute. Carve chicken and serve with sauce.

---

25   CHICKEN FRICASSEE
Prep: 15 minutes   Cook: 53 to 58 minutes   Serves: 4 to 6

A fricassee is a homey French dish that is halfway between a sauté and a stew. The name sounds fancy, but the cooking isn't.

1 **chicken (about 3½ pounds), cut into 8 pieces**	1 **bay leaf, broken**
½ **teaspoon salt**	1 **cup dry white wine**
¼ **teaspoon freshly ground pepper**	1 **cup chicken broth**
2 **tablespoons butter**	¼ **pound mushrooms, sliced (about 2½ cups)**
2 **medium carrots, thinly sliced**	¾ **cup heavy cream**
3 **medium leeks (white part only), rinsed and thinly sliced**	1 **tablespoon lemon juice**
	3 **tablespoons chopped parsley**

1. Season chicken with salt and pepper. In a large Dutch oven, cook chicken in 1 tablespoon butter in batches over medium-high heat, turning once or twice, until barely golden, about 5 minutes per batch. Remove chicken from pan.

2. Add carrots and leeks to pan, reduce heat to medium-low, and cook, stirring often, until softened, about 6 minutes. Add bay leaf, wine, and broth. Bring to a simmer, stirring. Return chicken to pan, cover, and simmer until juices run clear when thigh is pricked, 25 to 30 minutes.

3. About 10 minutes before chicken is done, cook mushrooms in a medium frying pan in remaining 1 tablespoon butter over medium-low heat until softened, about 5 minutes. Remove chicken from pan and boil juices and vegetables until reduced by about one-fourth, about 3 minutes. Remove bay leaf.

4. Add mushrooms, cream, and lemon juice. Simmer until mushrooms are just tender, about 3 minutes. Return chicken to pan to reheat for about 1 minute. Serve garnished with parsley.

26 CHICKEN PALERMO
Prep: 10 minutes   Cook: 54 minutes   Serves: 4

My family hails from Palermo in Sicily, and this is one of my earliest supper memories. The vegetables were from the garden then. Today they are frequently from the local farmstand and the tomatoes often come from a can.

1 chicken (about 3 pounds),
  cut into 8 pieces
¼ teaspoon salt
¼ teaspoon freshly ground
  pepper
¼ teaspoon cayenne
2 tablespoons olive oil,
  preferably extra-virgin
3 garlic cloves, crushed
  through a press

1 green bell pepper, sliced
1 (14½-ounce) can Italian-style
  stewed tomatoes
1 cup dry red or white wine
1 teaspoon dried marjoram
½ teaspoon fennel seeds
1 cup sliced black olives

1. Season chicken with salt, pepper, and cayenne. Heat olive oil in a large frying pan. Cook chicken in 2 batches over medium-high heat, turning, until browned, about 7 minutes per batch. Remove from pan.

2. Add garlic and bell pepper to pan and cook 5 minutes over medium-low heat, stirring often. Add tomatoes, wine, marjoram, and fennel seeds.

3. Simmer, partially covered, 30 minutes, or until chicken is tender and white throughout. Add olives and simmer, uncovered, 5 minutes longer.

27 CHICKEN CACCIATORE
Prep: 15 minutes   Cook: 38 to 49 minutes   Serves: 4 to 6

⅓ cup flour
½ teaspoon salt
¼ teaspoon freshly ground
  pepper
1 chicken (about 3½ pounds),
  cut into 8 pieces
2 tablespooons olive oil
1 large onion, chopped
2 garlic cloves, crushed
  through a press
½ pound wild or cultivated
  mushrooms, sliced (about
  2½ cups)

⅔ cup dry red or white wine
2 (14½-ounce) cans Italian-
  style stewed tomatoes
½ cup sliced black olives
1 bay leaf
1 teaspoon dried rosemary
½ teaspoon dried marjoram
1 teaspoon grated lemon zest
½ cup chopped flat-leaf
  parsley

1. Place flour, salt, and pepper in a plastic or paper bag. Add chicken a few pieces at a time and shake until coated.

2. In a large frying pan, heat olive oil over medium-high heat. Cook chicken in batches, turning once or twice, until browned all over, 5 to 7 minutes per batch. Remove from pan.

3. Add onion, garlic, and mushrooms to pan drippings and cook, stirring, until softened, 3 to 5 minutes. Add wine, tomatoes, olives, bay leaf, rosemary, marjoram, and lemon zest. Return chicken to pan. Cover and simmer over medium-low heat, stirring occasionally, until chicken is tender with no trace of pink near bone, 25 to 30 minutes. Discard bay leaf and stir in parsley before serving.

28 ARROZ CON POLLO
Prep: 30 minutes   Cook: 1 hour 22 to 24 minutes   Serves: 6

Similar to paella, this is a simple saffron-flavored chicken and rice dish that usually contains green peas and pimiento-stuffed olives for color.

1 chicken (about 3½ pounds), cut into 8 pieces
1 teaspoon salt
¼ teaspoon freshly ground pepper
3 tablespoons olive oil
¼ pound baked ham, cut into ½-inch dice
1 medium onion, chopped
1 green bell pepper, coarsely chopped
2 garlic cloves, crushed through a press
2 cups converted white rice
¾ teaspoon salt
¼ teaspoon cayenne
¼ teaspoon crushed saffron threads
2½ cups chicken broth, preferably reduced-sodium
½ cup dry sherry or white wine
1 (14½-ounce) can diced tomatoes, juices reserved
1½ cups frozen green peas
½ cup sliced pimiento-stuffed olives

1. Preheat oven to 350°F. Season chicken with ¼ teaspoon salt and pepper. Heat 2 tablespoons of olive oil in a large Dutch oven. Cook chicken in 2 batches over medium-high heat, turning once or twice, until browned all over, about 7 minutes per batch. Add ham and cook, stirring occasionally, until lightly browned, 3 to 5 minutes. Remove chicken and ham from pan with a slotted spoon.

2. Add remaining 1 tablespoon oil to pan along with onion, bell pepper, and garlic. Reduce heat to medium and cook, stirring occasionally, until onion is softened, about 5 minutes. Add rice, remaining ¾ teaspoon salt, cayenne, and saffron and stir to coat rice with oil. Add broth and sherry. Return chicken and ham to pan.

3. Cover and bake 45 minutes. Add tomatoes with their juices, peas, and olives to pan. Do not stir. Cover and bake 15 minutes longer. Stir to combine all ingredients and serve directly from pan.

29 BASQUE CHICKEN WITH TOMATOES AND OLIVES

Prep: 15 minutes   Cook: 37 to 44 minutes   Serves: 4

1 chicken (about 3 pounds), cut into 8 pieces
½ teaspoon freshly ground pepper
½ teaspoon dried thyme
½ teaspoon dried marjoram
2 tablespoons olive oil
1 medium onion, chopped

1 celery rib, sliced
½ cup chicken broth
1 (14½-ounce) can stewed tomatoes
1 tablespoon red wine or sherry vinegar
¾ cup mixed pitted black and green olives

1. Season chicken with pepper, thyme, and marjoram. In a large frying pan, heat olive oil. Add chicken and cook in 2 batches over medium-high heat, turning once or twice until browned, about 7 minutes per batch. Remove chicken from pan.

2. In drippings, cook onion and celery, stirring occasionally, until softened, 3 to 5 minutes. Stir in broth, tomatoes, and vinegar. Bring to a boil; reduce heat to medium-low. Return chicken to pan.

3. Cover and simmer 15 to 20 minutes, until chicken is tender and white throughout. Stir in olives and cook, covered, 5 minutes longer.

30 CHICKEN PAPRIKASH

Prep: 15 minutes   Cook: 37 to 44 minutes   Serves: 4 to 6

Use Hungarian paprika for the best and most authentic flavor. I like to use only dark meat here, but a cut-up chicken would work just as well. Serve with poppy seed noodles or spaetzle.

4 to 6 chicken legs with thighs attached (2½ to 3 pounds)
½ teaspoon salt
4 teaspoons Hungarian paprika
2 tablespoons vegetable oil

1 large onion, chopped
1 cup chicken broth
2 tablespoons tomato paste
¾ cup sour cream or heavy cream

1. Season chicken with salt and 1 teaspoon of paprika.

2. In a large frying pan, heat oil over medium-high heat. Cook the chicken in batches, turning once or twice, until golden brown, about 7 minutes per batch. Remove chicken from pan.

3. Add onion to drippings in pan. Cook, stirring often, until softened, 3 to 5 minutes. Add broth, tomato paste, and 2 teaspoons of paprika, stirring up any browned bits from bottom of pan. Return chicken to pan, cover, and simmer until juices run clear, 20 to 25 minutes.

4. Remove chicken from pan. Stir sour cream and remaining 1 teaspoon of paprika into sauce. Heat very gently without boiling. Spoon sauce over chicken and serve.

---

31   CHICKEN CASSOULET
Prep: 30 minutes   Stand: 1 hour   Cook: 3 hours   Serves: 8

Authentic cassoulet, based on white beans, has duck, pork, sausage, and lots of other meats and poultry in it. This is a streamlined recipe, but like the real thing, it tastes even better reheated, which makes it a wonderful do-ahead company dish.

1 **pound dried white beans**	1 **roasting chicken (about**
2 **cups chicken broth**	**5 pounds), cut into**
1 **bay leaf**	**10 pieces, skin removed if**
3 **medium carrots, cut into**	**desired**
1-inch chunks	**Salt and freshly ground**
2 **celery ribs, cut into 1-inch**	**pepper**
chunks	1 **tablespoon butter or**
3 **onions, sliced**	**vegetable oil**
3 **garlic cloves, crushed**	½ **pound kielbasa, cut into**
through a press	**1-inch chunks**
6 **parsley sprigs**	1 **(16-ounce) can whole**
2 **teaspoons dried thyme**	**tomatoes, with their**
1 **teaspoon dried marjoram**	**juices**
½ **teaspoon dried savory**	¼ **cup chopped parsley**
¼ **pound salt pork with rind**	

1. In a large saucepan, bring beans and 4 cups water to a boil; cook 2 minutes. Cover and let stand 1 hour. Do not drain. Add broth, bay leaf, and half of carrots, celery, and onions to beans along with garlic, parsley sprigs, thyme, marjoram, savory, and salt pork. Bring to a boil, reduce heat to medium-low, cover, and simmer 1 hour. Add remaining carrots, celery, and onions and simmer, covered, 30 minutes longer.

2. Meanwhile, season chicken lightly with salt and generously with pepper. Melt butter in a large frying pan over medium-high heat. Cook chicken in 3 batches, turning once or twice, until well browned all over, about 8 minutes per batch. Remove to a plate. Add kielbasa to pan and cook, turning, until browned, about 6 minutes.

3. Preheat the oven to 350°F. Spoon bean mixture into a large ovenproof casserole. Add chicken and kielbasa, pushing meats down into beans. Pour tomatoes with their juices on top. Bake, covered, 30 minutes. Remove and discard salt pork. Uncover and bake 30 minutes longer. Sprinkle with parsley and serve.

32 PAELLA

Prep: 30 minutes   Cook: 45 to 50 minutes   Serves: 6 to 8

The word *paella* refers to the traditional pan in which this dish is cooked, a shallow round casserole with 2 handles. I make my version in a large skillet. The saffron rice–based dish often contains chicken, sausage, and seafood, though there are many variations. I like to use meaty chicken thighs for paella.

2 pounds chicken thighs	¼ teaspoon crushed saffron threads
1 teaspoon salt	
½ teaspoon freshly ground pepper	3 cups chicken broth, preferably reduced-sodium
3 tablespoons olive oil	
½ pound garlicky sausage, such as chorizo or kielbasa, sliced ½ inch thick	½ cup dry white wine
	1 (14½-ounce) can stewed tomatoes
1 large onion, chopped	½ pound large shrimp, shelled and deveined
1 yellow bell pepper, coarsely chopped	12 small hard-shell clams, scrubbed
2 cups converted white rice	⅓ cup thinly sliced scallions
¼ teaspoon crushed hot red pepper	

1. Season chicken with ¼ teaspoon salt and with pepper. In a large frying pan with a lid, heat 2 tablespoons of olive oil and cook chicken in batches over medium-high heat, turning once or twice, until browned, about 6 minutes per batch. Add sausage and cook until browned, about 5 minutes. Remove chicken and sausage from pan with a slotted spoon.

2. Add remaining 1 tablespoon oil to pan along with onion and bell pepper, reduce heat to medium, and cook, stirring often, until softened, about 5 minutes. Add rice, remaining ¾ teaspoon salt, hot pepper, and saffron. Cook 1 minute, stirring to coat rice with oil. Add broth and wine and return chicken and sausage to pan. Cover, reduce heat to medium-low, and simmer 12 minutes.

3. Add tomatoes, shrimp, and clams, pushing shellfish into rice. Simmer, covered, until rice is tender, chicken juices run clear when pricked, and clams have opened, 10 to 15 minutes longer. Discard any clams that do not open. Stir to combine ingredients. Serve at once, with scallions sprinkled on top.

33 COUSCOUS
Prep: 25 minutes   Cook: 45 to 49 minutes   Serves: 6 to 8

Couscous is a delicious grain; it is also the name of a classic Middle-Eastern chicken dish. As is often the case, there are countless variations. This one is much simplified, but very tasty.

3 pounds chicken thighs and drumsticks
¾ teaspoon salt
1 tablespoon vegetable oil
1 large onion, sliced
¼ to ½ teaspoon cayenne, to taste
½ teaspoon ground cumin
½ teaspoon ground allspice
¼ teaspoon ground cinnamon
¼ teaspoon turmeric
2 medium carrots, peeled and sliced
1 medium white turnip (about 6 ounces), peeled and cut into ½-inch dice

1 (14½-ounce) can diced tomatoes, juices reserved
2 cups chicken broth
1 bay leaf
1 small eggplant (about 10 ounces), peeled and cubed
1 medium zucchini (about 6 ounces), diced
1½ cups quick-cooking couscous
1 cup drained canned chick-peas
¼ cup chopped cilantro

1. Season chicken with ¼ teaspoon of salt. In a large flameproof casserole, heat oil. Add chicken and cook over medium-high heat, turning once or twice, until lightly browned, about 6 to 8 minutes. Remove from pan.

2. Add onion to drippings and cook, stirring occasionally, until softened, 3 to 5 minutes. Stir in cayenne, cumin, allspice, cinnamon, turmeric, and remaining ½ teaspoon salt. Cook, stirring, 1 minute. Add carrots, turnip, tomatoes with their juices, broth, and bay leaf. Bring to a simmer; return chicken to pan. Simmer, partially covered, 20 minutes.

3. Add eggplant and zucchini and cook, partially covered, until chicken is tender with no trace of pink near bone, about 15 minutes longer. Remove and discard bay leaf.

4. While chicken is cooking, prepare couscous according to package directions. Stir in chick-peas and cilantro.

5. To serve, mound couscous on a platter. Spoon chicken, vegetables, and sauce into center.

34   GREEK LEMON CHICKEN

Prep: 15 minutes   Stand: 30 minutes   Cook: 43 to 48 minutes
Serves: 4

3 tablespoons olive oil
3 tablespoons lemon juice
2 teaspoons dried oregano
1 teaspoon grated lemon zest
½ teaspoon salt
½ teaspoon freshly ground
   pepper

2 garlic cloves, finely chopped
1 chicken (about 3 pounds),
   cut into 8 pieces
½ cup dry white wine
½ cup chicken broth
   Thin lemon slices

1. In a small dish, combine olive oil, lemon juice, oregano, lemon zest, salt, pepper, and garlic. Use your fingers to loosen chicken skin and rub some marinade under skin. Brush remaining marinade all over chicken. Let stand 30 minutes.

2. Preheat oven to 400°F. Place chicken, skin side down, in a shallow flameproof baking dish in a single layer. Bake 20 minutes. Turn chicken pieces over and bake, brushing occasionally with pan juices, until chicken skin is browned and juices run clear, 20 to 25 minutes longer.

3. Remove chicken from pan and skim off fat from juices. Set pan over medium-high heat and pour in wine and broth. Bring to a boil, stirring up browned bits clinging to bottom of pan. Boil until slightly reduced, about 3 minutes. Season with additional salt and pepper.

4. Pour sauce over chicken. Serve garnished with lemon slices.

35   CHICKEN IN GROUNDNUT SAUCE

Prep: 20 minutes   Cook: 57 to 64 minutes   Serves: 6 to 8

In Africa, peanuts are called groundnuts. Variations of this dish are popular throughout some of the western regions of that continent.

4 pounds chicken parts of
   choice
   Salt and freshly ground
   pepper
1 tablespoon peanut oil
1 medium onion, sliced
2 teaspoons chili powder
3 tablespoons canned
   chopped green chiles

1 tablespoon finely chopped
   fresh ginger
1 (14½-ounce) can stewed
   tomatoes
1 cup chicken broth
⅓ cup crunchy peanut butter

1. Season chicken lightly with salt and pepper. In a large frying pan, heat oil. Cook chicken in batches over medium-high heat, turning once or twice, until browned, about 7 minutes per batch. Remove chicken from pan.

2. Add onion to drippings and cook, stirring often, until softened, 3 to 5 minutes. Stir in chili powder, chiles, and ginger. Cook, stirring, 1 minute. Stir in tomatoes and broth. Bring to a boil. Return chicken to pan, reduce heat to medium-low, cover, and simmer until chicken is tender and white throughout, 30 to 35 minutes.

3. Remove chicken from pan. Skim fat off sauce. Stir in peanut butter. Return chicken to pan, simmer, uncovered, 2 minutes, and serve.

---

36 CHICKEN MOLE
Prep: 20 minutes   Cook: 2¼ hours   Serves: 6 to 8

Mole, which refers to richly spiced sauce, is a recipe with as many variations as there are Mexican cooks. This is a streamlined version. Serve with rice and warm tortillas.

1 **roasting chicken (5 to 7 pounds)**	1 **garlic clove, crushed through a press**
1 **teaspoon salt**	2 **tablespoons chili powder**
½ **teaspoon freshly ground pepper**	½ **teaspoon ground cinnamon**
	½ **teaspoon ground coriander**
1 **celery rib, sliced**	1 **(16-ounce) can whole tomatoes, juices reserved**
2 **medium onions, chopped**	
2 **cups chicken broth, preferably reduced-sodium**	1 **ounce unsweetened chocolate, chopped**
	3 **tablespoons toasted sesame seeds**
2 **tablespoons vegetable oil**	

1. Season chicken with salt and pepper. Place chicken, celery, and half of onions in a large Dutch oven. Add broth, cover, and cook over medium-low heat 1 hour. Remove chicken to a roasting pan. Boil broth until reduced to about 1 cup. Strain and reserve broth.

2. Preheat oven to 350°F. In a large frying pan, cook remaining onions and garlic in oil over medium heat until onion is softened, 3 to 5 minutes. Stir in chili powder, cinnamon, and coriander. Cook, stirring, 1 minute. Stir in reserved broth, tomatoes with their juices, and chocolate. Simmer, breaking up tomatoes with back of a spoon, until sauce is lightly thickened, about 10 minutes.

3. Pour sauce over chicken in roasting pan. Bake, uncovered, basting chicken several times with sauce, 1 hour, or until an instant-reading thermometer inserted into fleshy part of chicken (not near bone) registers 180°. Serve sprinkled with sesame seeds.

37 JAMAICAN JERK CHICKEN
Prep: 15 minutes   Stand: 4 hours   Cook: 30 to 40 minutes
Serves: 6

Jerk here refers to the marinade, not to the chicken or to the cook! If the weather is inclement, bake the chicken in a 375°F. oven.

3 tablespoons olive oil
3 tablespoons white wine vinegar
3 tablespoons orange juice
1½ tablespoons lime juice
1 tablespoon sugar
¼ cup finely chopped scallion greens
2 garlic cloves, minced
1 Scotch bonnet or jalapeño pepper, minced

1 teaspoon dried thyme
1 teaspoon dried leaf sage
½ teaspoon ground allspice
½ teaspoon ground cinnamon
½ teaspoon salt
½ teaspoon cayenne
1 chicken (about 3½ pounds), cut into 8 pieces

1. In a large shallow dish, combine all ingredients except chicken. Add chicken and turn to coat with marinade. Cover and refrigerate 4 to 8 hours.

2. Prepare a medium-hot barbecue fire or preheat a gas grill. Remove chicken from marinade, reserving marinade. Grill, turning and basting with reserved marinade occasionally, until richly browned and juices run clear when pricked, 30 to 40 minutes. (Stop basting at least 5 minutes before chicken is done.) White meat will take less time than dark meat.

38 GRILLED TANDOORI CHICKEN
Prep: 15 minutes   Marinate: 4 hours   Cook: 30 to 40 minutes
Serves: 4

A tandoor is a slow-roasting clay oven that produces tender and succulent results for yogurt-marinated foods. Grilling over indirect heat yields a similar effect.

1 cup plain yogurt
2 tablespoons lemon juice
2 large garlic cloves, minced
1 tablespoon finely chopped fresh ginger
2 teaspoons ground cardamom
2 teaspoons ground cumin

1 teaspoon paprika
½ teaspoon turmeric
½ teaspoon salt
¼ teaspoon cayenne
1 chicken (about 3 pounds), cut into 8 pieces
Lemon wedges, for garnish

1. In a large shallow dish, combine yogurt, lemon juice, garlic, ginger, cardamom, cumin, paprika, turmeric, salt, and cayenne. If desired, pull skin off chicken. Add chicken to marinade, turning to coat evenly. Cover and refrigerate 4 to 8 hours.

2. Prepare a medium-hot barbecue fire, using tongs to push coals to one side of the grill, or preheat a gas grill for an indirect fire. Remove chicken from marinade and set on grill away from coals. Grill, turning occasionally, until browned and chicken juices run clear, 30 to 40 minutes. (White meat will take less time than dark meat.)

3. Serve hot, garnished with lemon wedges.

39 CHICKEN SUKIYAKI

Prep: 20 minutes   Stand: 30 minutes   Cook: 16 minutes   Serves: 6

In Japan, this quick-cooking dish is usually prepared tableside. You can do this with an electric skillet and an attractive tray of the prepared ingredients. For beef sukiyaki, substitute thinly sliced steak and beef broth. If you can't find cellophane noodles, ladle the sukiyaki over rice.

¼ **pound cellophane noodles (bean threads)**
2 **cups chicken broth, preferably reduced-sodium**
½ **cup soy sauce**
½ **cup mirin (sweet rice wine)**
2 **teaspoons grated fresh ginger**
2 **tablespoons vegetable oil**
1 **medium onion, thinly sliced**
4 **cups sliced napa (Chinese) cabbage (about 4 ounces)**

¼ **pound fresh shiitake mushrooms, stemmed, caps sliced**
1 **pound skinless, boneless chicken breasts, thinly sliced across grain**
4 **cups sliced fresh spinach (about 6 ounces)**
6 **scallions, cut into 2-inch lengths**

1. Soak noodles in a bowl of very hot tap water to cover 30 minutes. In a small dish, combine broth, soy sauce, mirin, and ginger.

2. In a large frying pan, heat oil. Add onion and cook over medium heat, until just softened, about 4 minutes. Arrange layers of cabbage, mushrooms, chicken, spinach, and scallions in pan. Pour soy sauce mixture over all. Simmer, partially covered, until chicken is white throughout and vegetables are tender, about 10 minutes.

3. Drain cellophane noodles and add to pan. Simmer 2 minutes. Serve in shallow bowls.

40   FIVE-SPICE CHICKEN
Prep: 10 minutes   Stand: 1 hour   Cook: 35 to 40 minutes   Serves: 6

This light, aromatic chicken can be baked or grilled. I like to use skinned drumsticks, but any cut of chicken can be substituted. Five-spice powder, a Chinese blend of cinnamon, cloves, fennel, star anise, and nutmeg, is found in the spice section of most supermarkets and in Asian groceries.

12 chicken drumsticks (about 2½ pounds)
¼ cup soy sauce
¼ cup dry sherry
1 tablespoon finely chopped fresh ginger
1 garlic clove, minced
2 teaspoons Chinese five-spice powder
12 scallions, trimmed and cut into 2-inch lengths

1. Pull off and discard skin from chicken. In a shallow dish just large enough to hold chicken, combine soy sauce, sherry, ginger, garlic, and five-spice powder. Add chicken and turn to coat. Refrigerate 1 to 4 hours. Add scallions to marinade during last 30 minutes.

2. Preheat oven to 375°F. or prepare a medium-hot fire in a barbecue grill. Remove chicken from marinade. Bake chicken in a shallow pan or grill, turning occasionally. In either method, brush with marinade from time to time. Cook until juices run clear when chicken is pricked, 35 to 40 minutes. During last 10 minutes, lay scallions on top of chicken in oven or grill over coals just until softened and browned.

3. Serve chicken with scallions.

41   CHICKEN AND VEGETABLE TEMPURA
Prep: 10 minutes   Cook: 5 to 7 minutes per batch   Serves: 4 to 6

For fried food with the least grease, use a thermometer to be sure the oil stays at the correct temperature.

2 cups flour
1 teaspoon salt
¼ teaspoon baking soda
1 teaspoon sugar
1 tablespoon vegetable oil, plus oil for deep-frying
2 eggs, beaten
1⅓ cups beer
1 pound skinless, boneless chicken breasts, cut into 1-inch chunks
2 to 3 cups assorted raw vegetables, such as mushroom caps, broccoli or cauliflower florets, or zucchini chunks
Bottled tempura or teriyaki dipping sauce

1. In a mixing bowl, whisk together flour, salt, baking soda, and sugar. Whisk in 1 tablespoon oil, eggs, and beer until smooth. Batter will be thin.

2. Heat about 3 inches of oil in a deep-fryer or wok to 365°F. Dip chicken pieces and vegetables in batter to coat completely. Remove with a slotted spoon and let excess batter drip back into bowl. Fry in batches without crowding until crust is a rich golden brown and crisp and chicken is white throughout, 5 to 7 minutes. Drain on paper towels.

3. Serve immediately with dipping sauce on the side.

---

42 CHICKEN CURRY
Prep: 20 minutes   Cook: 27 minutes   Serves: 6

For a wonderful buffet party main course, serve the curry with rice and surround with dishes of as many condiments as you wish. Raisins, shredded coconut, mango chutney, chopped cucumber, and chopped peanuts are all good choices.

2 tablespoons vegetable oil	3 cups cubed cooked chicken
1 red bell pepper, chopped	1 cup canned unsweetened
1 medium carrot, chopped	coconut milk
1 cup chopped scallions	1½ cups chicken broth
2 tablespoons curry powder	½ cup heavy cream
½ teaspoon ground coriander	2 tablespoons lime juice
½ teaspoon dried mint	

1. In a large saucepan, heat oil over medium heat. Add bell pepper, carrot, and scallions and cook, stirring often, until softened, about 5 minutes.

2. Add curry powder, coriander, and mint. Cook, stirring, 1 to 2 minutes. Add chicken, coconut milk, and broth. Simmer, partially covered, 15 minutes.

3. Stir in cream and lime juice. Simmer 5 minutes.

Chapter 3

Chicken Nibbles

Appetizers do more than quell the pangs of hunger before a late dinner party or an interminable cocktail party. They set the stage and the tone of the whole event. As such, it's worth doing better than the usual dips or bowl of salted nuts.

However, spending lots of time preparing hors d'oeuvres is certainly not my culinary bag, nor is it yours, I suspect. On the other hand, I do like to nosh and nibble so much that sometimes I can happily make a meal on snacks!

For easy appetizers that are sturdy enough to become a hefty snack or even the main event, chicken is superb. The following are some of my favorite chicken appetizers. They run the gamut, but the ones I like best are the livers and the wings—parts of the bird that are rarely highlighted anywhere else but take beautifully to bite-sized portions and the assertive seasonings that are the hallmark of a memorable appetizer.

All of these are easy to make and most can be assembled in advance—a real boon if you are entertaining. But don't relegate this chapter to party time. These are some of the tastiest recipes in the book, sure to become family favorites for every day, too.

43 PESTO CHICKEN PIZZAS
Prep: 5 minutes   Cook: 5 to 7 minutes   Serves: 4

4 individual Italian bread
   shells (two 8-ounce
   packages)
1 cup pizza sauce or thick
   marinara sauce

½ cup pesto sauce
1½ cups chopped or shredded
   cooked chicken
1 cup shredded mozzarella
   cheese

1. Preheat oven to 500°F. Place bread shells on 2 baking sheets. Spread pizza sauce to within ½ inch of edges. Dollop with pesto sauce and use a spoon to swirl into pizza sauce. Sprinkle on chicken, then cheese.

2. Bake 5 to 7 minutes, until crusts are golden brown with crisp edges and cheese is melted. Cut pizzas into wedges and serve while hot.

44 TARRAGON CHICKEN CROSTINI

Prep: 20 minutes   Cook: ½ to 1 minute
Makes: about 20 tea sandwiches

Serve 3 or 4 of these tea sandwiches on a plate surrounding a delicate lettuce salad for a lovely and sophisticated luncheon main course.

1 **cup finely chopped cooked
    chicken breast**
¼ **cup finely chopped celery**
¼ **cup plus 2 tablespoons
    mayonnaise**
1 **teaspoon lemon juice**
1 **teaspoon chopped fresh
    tarragon or ¼ teaspoon
    dried**

¼ **teaspoon freshly ground
    pepper**
1 **slim French bread baguette
    (about ½ pound)**
**Fresh tarragon sprigs or
    parsley, for garnish**

1. Preheat broiler. In a small mixing bowl, gently stir together chicken, celery, ¼ cup of mayonnaise, lemon juice, tarragon, and pepper.

2. Cut bread into about 20 slices ¼ inch thick. Spread one side of bread with remaining mayonnaise, then broil until mayonnaise is bubbly and bread is lightly toasted, 30 to 60 seconds. Let cool.

3. Spoon about 1 tablespoon chicken salad onto each slice of toast. Garnish each sandwich with a small sprig of tarragon.

45 BEGGARS' PURSES

Prep: 45 minutes   Cook: 10 to 15 minutes   Makes: about 40

2 **cups finely chopped cooked
    chicken**
2 **tablespoons mayonnaise**
2 **tablespoons mango chutney**
1 **tablespoon lemon juice**
½ **teaspoon curry powder**
½ **teaspoon salt**

¼ **teaspoon freshly ground
    pepper**
⅛ **teaspoon cayenne**
4 **sheets of phyllo**
8 **to 10 tablespoons butter,
    melted**

1. Preheat oven to 375°F. In a mixing bowl, combine chicken, mayonnaise, chutney, lemon juice, curry powder, salt, pepper, and cayenne.

2. Place 1 sheet of phyllo on a flat surface. Brush generously with melted butter. Top with second sheet of phyllo. (Keep remaining phyllo covered with plastic wrap and a damp towel until needed.) With a sharp knife, cut phyllo stack into 20 (3-inch) squares. Place a rounded teaspoon of filling in center of each square. Lift the corners to center and twist to seal and form a "purse." Place on an ungreased baking sheet. Repeat with remaining phyllo, butter, and filling.

3. Bake until golden brown and crisp, 10 to 15 minutes. Serve warm. If baking ahead, reheat for a few minutes in a 350°F oven.

46   SMOKED CHICKEN AND CHUTNEY CANAPÉS

Prep: 20 minutes   Cook: none   Makes: 16 tea sandwiches

If you can't get smoked chicken, rotisserie chicken from the deli will work here as well.

3 tablespoons butter, softened
3 tablespoons finely chopped drained mango chutney
1 teaspoon lemon juice
¼ teaspoon freshly ground pepper

8 thin slices of whole wheat bread, crusts trimmed
¼ pound thinly sliced smoked chicken
1 small bunch of watercress

1. In a small bowl, combine butter, chutney, lemon juice, and pepper. Blend well. (Chutney butter can be prepared a day ahead and refrigerated; return to room temperature before using.)

2. Spread about 2 teaspoons chutney butter over each slice of bread. Divide smoked chicken among half of bread slices, filling as neatly as possible. Top with remaining bread slices to make sandwiches. Cut each sandwich into 4 pieces, either squares or triangles. Insert a small watercress sprig into each sandwich so that leaf protrudes decoratively.

3. To serve, arrange sandwiches on a plate and garnish with remaining watercress sprigs.

47   CRANBERRY CHICKEN NIBBLERS

Prep: 30 minutes   Cook: none   Makes: about 48 canapés

⅓ cup whole-berry cranberry sauce, homemade or canned
1 tablespoon prepared white horseradish
1 stick (4 ounces) butter, softened
12 thin slices of firm white bread, crusts removed

½ pound thinly sliced cooked chicken
Salt and coarsely ground pepper
Fresh cranberries and watercress sprigs, for garnish

1. In a food processor, puree cranberry sauce, horseradish, and butter until nearly smooth. Spread cranberry butter over bread. Arrange chicken on top, pressing gently so it will adhere. Season with salt and pepper to taste. Use a sharp knife to cut each bread slice into 4 pieces, either squares or triangles.

2. To serve, arrange sandwiches on a platter. Decorate platter with cranberries and watercress leaves to resemble holly sprigs.

48 SWISS CHICKEN FONDUE
Prep: 15 minutes   Cook: 7 minutes   Serves: 6 to 8

On a cold winter night, this will serve 4 as a cozy fireside supper. Add some cooked broccoli and red potatoes to dip in the cheese along with the chicken. Any cooked chicken is good here, but smoked chicken is really terrific.

1 **pound shredded Swiss cheese, such as Gruỳere or Emmentaler**	1 **large garlic clove, crushed in a press**
1 **tablespoon cornstarch**	3 **to 4 tablespoons kirsch**
¼ **teaspoon grated nutmeg**	2 **tablespoons chopped chives**
¼ **teaspoon white pepper**	1 **pound cooked chicken, cut into bite-sized chunks**
1½ **cups white wine**	

1. In a medium bowl, toss cheese with cornstarch, nutmeg, and white pepper. In a heavy, nonreactive saucepan or a fondue pot, heat wine and garlic over medium-high heat until wine is bubbly around edges, about 2 minutes. Reduce heat to low and add cheese by handfuls, stirring until each is nearly melted before adding another. Cook, stirring, until fondue is completely smooth and blended and bubbles slightly around edges, about 5 minutes. Stir in kirsch. Sprinkle with chives.

2. Place fondue pot or saucepan on a heatproof surface and surround with chicken. Provide fondue forks or wooden skewers for dipping.

49 CHINESE GARLIC CHICKEN KEBABS
Prep: 10 minutes   Stand: 30 minutes   Cook: 6 to 8 minutes
Serves: 8

Reminiscent of the "barbecue" in a good Chinese restaurant, these tidbits are pretty served on individual bamboo skewers. Be sure to soak the skewers in water for at least 30 minutes before cooking.

3 **tablespoons dry sherry**	3 **garlic cloves, minced**
2 **tablespoons soy sauce**	1 **pound skinless, boneless chicken breasts, cut into 1-inch chunks**
1 **tablespoon rice wine vinegar**	
1 **tablespoon plum sauce**	8 **to 10 scallions, trimmed to leave about 2 inches of greens**
1 **tablespoon Chinese hot chili paste or sauce**	
1 **tablespoon vegetable oil**	

1. In a shallow 2-quart dish, combine sherry, soy sauce, vinegar, plum sauce, chili paste, oil, and garlic. Add chicken and stir to coat. Let stand 30 minutes at room temperature or refrigerate up to 2 hours. Add scallions during last 10 minutes of marinating.

2. Prepare a medium-hot fire in a barbecue grill or preheat the broiler. Lightly oil grill rack or coat with nonstick vegetable spray. Thread chicken and scallions onto 8 to 10 small metal or soaked bamboo skewers.

3. Grill, turning, until chicken is white throughout but still juicy, 6 to 8 minutes.

---

50 SESAME CHICKEN FINGERS WITH APRICOT MUSTARD SAUCE

Prep: 5 minutes   Stand: 15 minutes   Cook: 10 to 11 minutes
Serves: 8

⅔ **cup apricot jam**
2 **tablespoons Dijon mustard**
2 **tablespoons lemon juice**
½ **cup unseasoned dry bread crumbs**
¼ **cup sesame seeds**
¼ **teaspoon salt**
¼ **teaspoon freshly ground pepper**

1 **egg beaten with 2 tablespoons water**
1 **pound thinly sliced chicken breast cutlets**
3 **tablespoons vegetable oil**
1 **teaspoon Asian sesame oil**

1. In a small saucepan, heat together jam, mustard, and lemon juice over medium-low heat, stirring, until melted smooth, 2 to 3 minutes. Set dipping sauce aside.

2. In a shallow dish, combine bread crumbs, sesame seeds, salt, and pepper. Place egg in another shallow dish. Dip chicken first into egg, then into bread crumbs, dredging. Shake any excess back into bowl. Let stand 15 minutes at room temperature. Use a sharp knife to cut chicken crosswise into strips about ¾ inch wide.

3. In a large frying pan, heat vegetable oil and sesame oil over high heat. Add half of chicken and cook, turning once or twice, until white throughout, about 4 minutes. Repeat with remaining chicken.

4. Serve chicken fingers on a platter, with a bowl of apricot mustard sauce in center for dipping.

51 NEAPOLITAN CHICKEN FRITTATA BITES

Prep: 20 minutes   Cook: 27 to 32 minutes   Makes: about 50

¼ cup olive oil, preferably
    extra-virgin
4 cups medium leeks (white
    and pale green), thinly
    sliced
3 garlic cloves, crushed
    through a press
¼ teaspoon crushed hot red
    pepper
2 cups slivered cooked
    chicken (about 8 ounces)
1 (10-ounce) package frozen
    chopped spinach, thawed
    and squeezed dry

¼ cup finely chopped
    prosciutto (about 1 ounce)
¼ cup chopped fresh basil
12 eggs
¾ teaspoon salt
4 ounces shredded mozzarella
    cheese (about 1 cup)
3 tablespoons grated
    Parmesan cheese

1. Preheat oven to 375°F. Grease a 9x13-inch baking dish. In a large frying pan, heat olive oil. Add leeks and cook over medium-low heat, stirring often, until softened, about 5 minutes. Add garlic and hot pepper and cook 2 minutes. Stir in chicken, spinach, prosciutto, and basil. Spread mixture in baking dish.

2. In a large bowl, whisk together eggs and salt. Pour over chicken mixture in baking dish. In a small bowl, toss together cheeses and sprinkle over eggs.

3. Bake 20 to 25 minutes, until frittata is pale golden and puffed. Let stand at least 15 minutes before cutting into 1½-inch squares. Serve warm or at room temperature.

52 TACO CHICKEN
Prep: 10 minutes   Cook: 8 minutes   Serves: 8

6 ounces corn tortilla chips, regular, low-fat, or seasoned

1½ tablespoons taco seasoning mix or chili powder

1 pound thinly sliced chicken breasts

¼ cup corn oil

1½ cups bottled chunky salsa or taco sauce

1. Preheat oven to 500°F. In a food processor, grind tortilla chips into crumbs. Add taco seasoning and process just to blend. Spread crumbs on a shallow dish. Dip chicken into oil, then into crumbs to coat.

2. Place chicken on a baking sheet. Bake until crumbs are brown and chicken is white throughout, about 8 minutes.

3. Cut chicken crosswise into ¾-inch-wide strips. Serve warm with salsa for dipping.

53 ROSEMARY CHICKEN FOCACCIA
Prep: 15 minutes   Cook: 32 minutes   Serves: 8

If your market carries it, make the recipe even simpler by using a 10- to 12-ounce focaccia bread in place of the pizza dough. Bake at 450°F. for about 5 minutes just to melt the cheese and heat the chicken.

3 tablespoons olive oil, preferably extra-virgin

1 large onion, thinly sliced

1 large garlic clove, crushed through a press

1 teaspoon dried rosemary, crushed

¼ teaspoon crushed hot red pepper

1 (10-ounce) tube refrigerated pizza dough

1½ cups shredded cooked or smoked chicken (about 6 ounces)

¼ cup grated Romano cheese

1. Preheat oven to 425°F. In a large frying pan, heat 2 tablespoons of olive oil. Add onion and cook over medium-low heat, stirring often, until very soft, about 10 minutes. Add garlic and rosemary and cook 2 minutes. Remove from heat and let cool 5 minutes. In a small bowl, combine hot pepper flakes with remaining 1 tablespoon oil.

2. Unroll pizza dough and place on a lightly oiled baking sheet. With fingers, press dimples into dough. Brush with hot pepper oil. Sprinkle chicken over dough. Spoon cooked onions over chicken. Sprinkle cheese on top.

3. Bake about 20 minutes, until dough is crisp and golden brown and cheese is melted. Let cool slightly. Cut into 1x2-inch rectangles. Serve in a napkin-lined basket.

54 CHICKEN SATAYS WITH SPICY PEANUT DIPPING SAUCE

Prep: 15 minutes   Cook: 6 to 8 minutes   Makes: 16

If you want to serve this as a light main dish, arrange the cooked skewers of satay on a bed of shredded lettuce dressed in a tangy vinaigrette and serve with warmed pitas or Indian flatbreads. If you are using bamboo skewers, remember to soak them for at least 30 minutes in cold water before grilling.

¼ cup smooth peanut butter	2 garlic cloves, crushed
3 tablespoons lime juice	through a press
3 tablespoons soy sauce	1 pound skinless, boneless
1½ tablespoons finely chopped	chicken thighs or breasts,
fresh ginger	cut into 16 cubes
1 teaspoon hot sesame oil	16 scallions, trimmed to leave
¼ teaspoon crushed hot red	1 inch of greens
pepper	

1. Preheat broiler or prepare a medium-hot fire in a barbecue grill. In a shallow dish, whisk together peanut butter, lime juice, soy sauce, ginger, sesame oil, pepper flakes, and garlic. Add chicken and scallions and stir to coat.

2. Thread chicken and scallions onto 16 small metal or soaked bamboo skewers. Broil or grill, turning, until richly browned outside and cooked through, 6 to 8 minutes.

3. Serve directly from skewers.

55 SAKE WINGS

Prep: 10 minutes   Chill: 1 hour   Cook: 1 hour   Makes: about 30

Sake is a slightly sweet Japanese rice wine. If you can't get it, use dry sherry.

½ cup soy sauce	2 garlic cloves, minced
½ cup sake	½ teaspoon crushed hot red
¼ cup chicken broth	pepper
1 tablespoon sugar	2½ pounds chicken "wingettes"
6 thin slices of fresh ginger	(about 30)

1. In a large baking dish, combine soy sauce, sake, broth, sugar, ginger, garlic, and hot pepper. Add chicken and turn to coat. Cover and refrigerate 1 hour, turning occasionally.

2. Preheat oven to 400°F. Drain off marinade from chicken. Bake chicken in dish, uncovered, turning occasionally, until richly browned, about 1 hour.

3. Serve warm or at room temperature.

56 BROILED HOT WINGS

Prep: 5 minutes   Stand: 15 minutes   Cook: 10 to 12 minutes
Makes: about 20

These are a whole lot easier than the deep-fried version and just as finger-lickin' good. "Wingettes" are wings with the tips removed; they are available in most supermarkets.

3 tablespoons vegetable oil
1 tablespoon Worcestershire
   sauce
1 tablespoon Tabasco or other
   hot pepper sauce
1 teaspoon lemon juice

¾ teaspoon cayenne
1½ pounds chicken "wingettes"
1 cup bottled blue cheese
   dressing
Celery sticks

1. In a shallow dish, combine oil, Worcestershire, Tabasco, lemon juice, and cayenne. Add chicken and stir to coat well. Let stand 15 minutes at room temperature or refrigerate up to 3 hours.

2. Preheat broiler. Arrange chicken wings in a single layer on a large baking sheet. Broil, turning once, 10 to 12 minutes, until well browned and crisp.

3. Serve wings on a platter with blue cheese dressing as a dipping sauce and celery sticks.

57 SWEET-AND-SOUR COCKTAIL NUGGETS

Prep: 20 minutes   Cook: 10 to 13 minutes   Makes: about 30

1 cup apricot preserves
¼ cup white wine vinegar
1 teaspoon Tabasco or other
   hot pepper sauce
1 red bell pepper, cut into
   1-inch chunks
1 green bell pepper, cut into
   1-inch chunks

½ pound skinless, boneless
   chicken breasts, cut into
   1-inch cubes
2 tablespoons vegetable oil
   Salt and freshly ground
   pepper

1. Soak about 30 small bamboo skewers in cold water to cover for at least 30 minutes. Prepare a hot fire in a barbecue grill or preheat broiler. In a small saucepan set at edge of grill or on stovetop, heat preserves and vinegar until preserves are melted, 2 to 3 minutes. Stir in Tabasco.

2. Thread a red or green pepper chunk and a chicken cube on each soaked skewer. Brush chicken and vegetables with oil and season lightly with salt and pepper.

3. Grill, turning once or twice, until peppers are just softened and chicken is white throughout but still juicy, 8 to 10 minutes.

58 DEVILED CHICKEN LOLLIPOPS
Prep: 45 minutes   Cook: 37 minutes   Makes: about 30

If you buy "drumettes," they are ready to dip and bake. Otherwise, use wingettes, and prepare as directed in step 1.

2½ **pounds chicken drumettes
   or "wingettes" (about 30)**
¼ **cup Dijon mustard**
2 **tablespoons vegetable oil**
3 **tablespoons orange
   marmalade**

2 **cups fresh whole wheat
   bread crumbs (from
   about 4 slices of bread)**

1. If using drumettes, proceed to step 2. If using "wingettes," use a small sharp knife to cut toward bone around narrow end of wing to loosen meat. Gently use knife to scrape meat down toward wider end, turning meat inside out over end to form a "lollipop."

2. Preheat oven to 375°F. In a small saucepan, heat mustard, oil, and marmalade over low heat, stirring, until marmalade is melted, about 2 minutes. Pour into a shallow dish. Spread bread crumbs onto a plate. Dip chicken first into mustard mixture, then roll in bread crumbs to coat. Place in a single layer with a little space between pieces on baking sheets.

3. Bake until crispy and rich golden brown, about 35 minutes. Serve warm or at room temperature.

59 CASHEW CRUNCHERS
*Prep: 45 minutes   Stand: 1 hour   Cook: 35 minutes
Makes: about 30*

These are delicious conversation pieces and surprisingly easy to make with chicken "wingettes" that come with the tips already chopped off. In some parts of the country, you can buy "drumettes," which have already been shaped as directed below.

2½ **pounds chicken "wingettes"
   or drumettes (about 30)**
¼ **cup dry sherry**
3 **tablespoons peanut oil**
2 **tablespoons soy sauce**

2 **tablespoons honey**
1 **tablespoon finely chopped
   fresh ginger**
2 **cups finely chopped
   cashews**

1. If using "wingettes," use a small sharp knife to cut toward bone around narrow end of wing to loosen meat. Gently use knife to scrape meat down toward wider end, turning meat inside out over end to form a "lollipop."

2. In a shallow 2-quart dish, combine sherry, oil, soy sauce, honey, and ginger. Add chicken, stirring to coat well. Refrigerate at least 1 hour or up to 8 hours.

3. Preheat oven to 375°F. Roll chicken in about three-quarters of chopped nuts, then place in a single layer with a little space between pieces on baking sheets.

4. Bake until crispy and richly golden brown, about 35 minutes. Sprinkle with remaining chopped nuts. Serve warm or at room temperature.

60   CHICKEN LIVER PÂTÉ NIÇOISE

Prep: 20 minutes   Chill: 3 hours   Cook: 9 to 10 minutes
Makes: about 2 cups

This is inspired by my friend food writer Brooke Dojny's wonderful recipe. Serve with plain crackers or small toasts.

¾   **pound chicken livers**
3   **tablespoons dry sherry**
1   **tablespoon milk**
6   **tablespoons butter**
⅓   **cup chopped shallots**
3   **tablespoons Cognac or**
        brandy
½   **teaspoon freshly ground**
        pepper

¼   **teaspoon salt**
⅛   **teaspoon ground mace**
¼   **cup chopped black olives,**
        preferably niçoise
2   **tablespoons small capers,**
        drained

1. Trim livers and cut into quarters; place in a small bowl. Pour sherry and milk over livers. Refrigerate 1 hour. Drain and pat dry.

2. In a large frying pan, melt 2 tablespoons of butter over medium-high heat. Add livers and cook, stirring often, until just barely pink in center, 5 minutes. Add shallots to pan, reduce heat to medium-low, and cook, stirring, until shallots are softened, about 2 minutes. Scrape livers and shallots into a food processor.

3. Add Cognac to frying pan and boil, stirring up browned bits from bottom of pan, 1 minute. Add liquid to livers in processor. Cut remaining 4 tablespoons butter into small pieces and add to livers along with pepper, salt, and mace. Process until smooth, scraping down sides of bowl once or twice, about 1 minute. Add olives and capers to pâté and pulse just to incorporate, about 10 seconds.

4. Spoon pâté into a small bowl or crock. Cover and refrigerate at least 2 or up to 24 hours. Let return to room temperature before serving.

61   RUMAKI
Prep: 30 minutes   Stand: 30 minutes   Cook: 10 to 14 minutes
Makes: about 30

My version of rumaki broils the bacon-wrapped livers individually and then spears them on toothpicks. If you prefer, they can be threaded onto the ends of soaked small bamboo skewers and charcoal grilled.

¼ **cup dry sherry**
¼ **cup soy sauce**
1 **tablespoon vegetable oil**
2 **garlic cloves, crushed through a press**
2 **teaspoons grated fresh ginger**
1 **teaspoon molasses**

¾ **pound chicken livers, rinsed and dried**
1 **(5½-ounce) can water chestnuts, drained and halved**
4 **scallions, green parts only**
12 **to 15 slices of bacon (about ⅔ pound), halved**

1. In a small, shallow dish, combine sherry, soy sauce, oil, garlic, ginger, and molasses. Trim chicken livers and cut in half. Place in marinade, stirring to coat all over. Marinate 30 minutes at room temperature or up to 3 hours in refrigerator. Add water chestnuts during last 15 minutes of marinating time. Cut scallion greens into 2-inch lengths and slice each piece lengthwise in half.

2. Preheat broiler. Wrap a piece of bacon around a piece of liver, a water chestnut, and a scallion slice to make about 30 appetizers. Secure with toothpicks. Arrange in a single layer on a broiler pan.

3. Broil about 6 inches from heat 10 to 14 minutes, turning once, until bacon is crisp and livers are no longer pink.

62 CHICKEN DRUMETTES WITH ROMESCO SAUCE

Prep: 15 minutes   Stand: 20 minutes   Cook: 19 minutes
Makes: about 24

Drumettes are chicken wings that have been fashioned into a drumstick. This used to be a time-consuming process, but they can now be purchased in the chicken section of many supermarket meat cases. Sometimes they are called "mini-drumsticks." If you can't find them, use "wingettes." Romesco, a wonderful Spanish sauce, is also excellent spooned over broiled or grilled chicken as a main course.

3 tablespoons slivered almonds
1 thin slice of French bread (about ¼ inch thick)
1 garlic clove, crushed
1 (7-ounce) jar roasted red peppers with liquid
¼ cup olive oil

2 tablespoons red wine vinegar
¼ to ½ teaspoon cayenne, to taste
¼ teaspoon salt
2 pounds chicken drumettes or "wingettes"

1. In a small dry frying pan, toast almonds over medium heat, stirring constantly, until golden brown and fragrant, about 3 minutes. Remove from pan. In same pan, toast bread until golden, about 30 seconds per side.

2. Tear toasted bread into pieces and place in a food procesor along with almonds. With machine on, drop in garlic and process to finely chop. Drain peppers, reserving liquid. Add peppers to processor. In a small bowl, combine olive oil, vinegar, cayenne, and salt. Add 3 tablespoons of mixture to processor. Puree to make a coarse paste, about 30 seconds, scraping down sides of bowl once or twice. Sauce should have consistency of a thick mayonnaise. If it is too thick, thin by mixing in some of reserved pepper liquid. Let Romesco sauce stand at least 15 minutes at room temperature or refrigerate up to 2 days before using.

3. Prepare a medium-hot fire in a barbecue grill or preheat broiler. Rub drumettes with remaining oil and vinegar mixture. Let stand 20 minutes at room temperature.

4. Grill or broil chicken, turning once or twice, until browned and crisp, about 15 minutes. Serve chicken with Romesco sauce for dipping.

Chapter 4

Fresh and Fabulous Chicken Salads

The quintessential ladies' lunch is chicken salad in a lettuce cup. But that is indeed only the beginning. Chicken salad ideas are so many and so varied that it was a real dilemma to choose for this chapter.

Most chicken salads are made with cooked white meat of chicken, making salads undoubtedly the best way to use up leftover chicken. But I often poach chicken expressly for salad, a job made really easy these days with the availability of skinless, boneless chicken breasts.

As part of a healthy diet incorporating more grains and vegetables, warm chicken salads have finally hit their stride. Whether grilled, stir-fried, or sautéed, thin-sliced cutlets cook up in almost no time to make the basis for all sorts of delicious pasta, rice, or vegetable salads. They are especially wonderful on a warm summer day, but equally tasty as a quick supper at any time.

---

63 POACHED CHICKEN BREASTS
Prep: 5 minutes   Cook: 10 to 15 minutes   Serves: 4

This master recipe for poaching chicken breasts can become a credible soup if you use broth rather than water and add about 3 cups of almost any cooked vegetables before serving.

1 **pound skinless, boneless chicken breasts**
  About 4 cups chicken broth or water

½ **teaspoon salt**
¼ **teaspoon freshly ground pepper**

1. Place chicken breasts in a medium saucepan. Cover with chicken broth, salt, and pepper. Bring just to a simmer over medium-low heat. Partially cover pan and cook 10 to 15 minutes, until chicken is no longer pink in center.

2. Remove pan from heat and let chicken breasts cool in liquid if you have time, or pat dry and use immediately. To keep chicken moist and juicy, cover with cooking liquid and store in refrigerator. Use within a day or two.

64   CARIBBEAN CHICKEN SALAD
Prep: 20 minutes   Cook: none   Serves: 4

1   red bell pepper
1   green bell pepper
1   ripe mango
3   cups diced cooked chicken
     (about 12 ounces)
½   cup chopped red onion
1½   tablespoons white wine
     vinegar
1   tablespoon lime juice

1   teaspoon honey
1   teaspoon Dijon mustard
½   teaspoon curry powder
½   teaspoon salt
¼   teaspoon freshly ground
     pepper
6   tablespoons vegetable oil
2   tablespoons chopped
     cilantro (optional)

1. Halve peppers and discard ribs and seeds. Slice crosswise into thin rings. Peel and thinly slice mango. Spread peppers out on 4 plates. Scatter mango slices and chicken over peppers. Sprinkle red onion on top.

2. In a small bowl, whisk together vinegar, lime juice, honey, mustard, curry powder, salt, and pepper. Whisk in oil. Drizzle over salads. Serve chilled, garnished with cilantro if you like.

65   CHICKEN CAESAR SALAD
Prep: 10 minutes   Cook: 6 to 8 minutes   Serves: 4

This popular restaurant item is easy to make at home.

1   pound skinless, boneless
     chicken breasts
6   tablespoons olive oil,
     preferably extra-virgin
2   garlic cloves, crushed
     through a press
4   slices of French bread,
     cut ½ inch thick
2   tablespoons balsamic
     vinegar

1   teaspoon Worcestershire
     sauce
¼   teaspoon freshly ground
     pepper
1   (2-ounce) can flat anchovies,
     drained and chopped
1   head of romaine lettuce,
     torn into bite-sized pieces
¼   cup grated Romano or
     Parmesan cheese

1. Preheat broiler. Flatten chicken to an even thickness. In a small mixing bowl, combine olive oil and garlic. Brush about 2 tablespoons of garlic oil over both sides of both bread and chicken.

2. Broil chicken about 4 inches from heat, turning once, until white throughout, 6 to 8 minutes. Broil bread, turning once, until golden, about 1 minute. As soon as chicken is cool enough to handle, cut crosswise into strips.

3. Whisk vinegar, Worcestershire, pepper, and anchovies into remaining garlic oil. In a large mixing bowl, toss lettuce with about three-quarters of dressing. Add cheese and toss again. Arrange chicken on top of lettuce and drizzle on remaining dressing. Garnish each salad with a toasted bread crouton.

66 CHICKEN AND CUCUMBER SALAD WITH MINTED YOGURT DRESSING

Prep: 15 minutes   Cook: none   Chill: 1 hour   Serves: 4

Marinating cooked chicken in yogurt makes it ever so tender. As a time-saver, look for cut-up fresh pineapple in your supermarket's produce department or salad bar.

1 cup plain yogurt
½ cup chopped fresh mint
½ teaspoon salt
¼ teaspoon freshly ground pepper
2 cups cubed cooked chicken
1 medium cucumber, peeled, seeded, and thinly sliced

1 small red onion, coarsely chopped
1 cup diced pineapple, either fresh or canned
Mint sprigs, for garnish

1. In a medium bowl, combine yogurt, mint, salt, and pepper. Mix well. Add chicken and stir to blend. Cover and refrigerate 1 hour.

2. Add cucumber, red onion, and pineapple to chicken. Stir to combine. Garnish salad with mint sprigs.

67 SANTE FE LAYERED SALAD

Prep: 20 minutes   Cook: none   Chill: 30 minutes   Serves: 6

This is a contemporary version of an old favorite—the do-ahead layered salad.

3 cups cooked cubed chicken (about ¾ pound)
1 cup corn kernels, fresh or frozen
1 cup canned black beans, rinsed and drained
1 red bell pepper, diced
⅔ cup thinly sliced scallions

1 cup mayonnaise
2 fresh or canned jalapeño peppers, minced
1½ tablespoons lime juice
1 tablespoon Dijon mustard
¼ teaspoon salt
2 tablespoons chopped cilantro or parsley

1. In a 2-quart glass bowl, layer half of chicken. Make another layer of all of corn and then beans. Layer remaining chicken, then bell pepper and scallions.

2. In a small bowl, whisk together mayonnaise, minced jalapeño peppers, lime juice, mustard, and salt. Spread over top of salad to cover completely. Refrigrate at least 30 minutes or up to 8 hours.

3. Just before serving, sprinkle cilantro on top. To serve, scoop down to get some of each layer of salad.

68   CHICKEN SPINACH SALAD WITH BACON AND BUTTERMILK DRESSING

Prep: 20 minutes   Cook: none   Serves: 6

Buttermilk makes a tangy homespun dressing, but gives a rich flavor to this rather sophisticated salad. If you don't have buttermilk, substitute plain yogurt. Prewashed, ready-to-use spinach can save you a lot of time here.

8 cups washed and torn spinach leaves
¾ pound thinly sliced cooked chicken breast
1 head of Belgian endive, thinly sliced
1 small red onion, thinly sliced
2 cups sliced mushrooms (about 6 ounces)
2 small seedless oranges, sectioned, with sections cut in half

8 slices of cooked bacon, crumbled
2 tablespoons orange juice
2 tablespoons white wine vinegar
1 tablespoon Dijon mustard
¼ cup plus 2 tablespoons mayonnaise
¼ cup buttermilk or plain yogurt
1½ teaspoons grated orange zest
   Salt and freshly ground pepper

1. In a large bowl, toss together spinach, chicken, endive, red onion, mushrooms, orange sections, and crumbled bacon.

2. In a small bowl, whisk together orange juice, vinegar, mustard, mayonnaise, buttermilk, and orange zest. Season with salt and pepper to taste.

3. Pour dressing over salad and toss to mix. Serve at once.

69   CHEF'S FRUITED CHICKEN SALAD

Prep: 20 minutes   Cook: none   Serves: 4

1 head of green leaf lettuce
½ pound thinly sliced smoked or cooked chicken
2 large nectarines, sliced
¼ pound Swiss cheese, sliced and cut into thin strips
½ cup thinly sliced scallions
1 cup blueberries

¼ cup chopped fresh mint
⅓ cup vegetable oil
2 tablespoons blueberry or other fruit vinegar
1 teaspoon Dijon mustard
½ teaspoon salt
¼ teaspoon freshly ground pepper

1. Make a bed of lettuce leaves on a platter or 4 plates. Arrange chicken, nectarines, and cheese decoratively on lettuce. Scatter scallions, blueberries, and chopped mint on top.

2. In a small bowl, whisk together oil, vinegar, mustard, salt, and pepper. Drizzle over salad(s) and serve.

70   GRILLED CHICKEN AND LENTIL SALAD

Prep: 25 minutes   Stand: 30 minutes   Cook: 35 to 40 minutes
Serves: 4 to 6

Serve this either hot off the grill with warm lentils or mix a few hours ahead and let the flavors meld and deepen, then serve at cool room temperature. The chicken can also be broiled.

1 **pound skinless, boneless chicken breasts or thighs**
¼ **cup red wine vinegar**
2 **tablespoons orange juice**
1 **tablespoon Dijon mustard**
1 **teaspoon grated orange zest**
¾ **teaspoon ground cumin**
½ **teaspoon salt**
½ **teaspoon freshly ground pepper**
3 **garlic cloves, minced**

½ **cup olive oil, preferably extra-virgin**
1½ **cups dried lentils, rinsed and picked over**
1 **red onion, chopped**
1 **green bell pepper, thinly sliced**
1 **large carrot, thinly sliced into rounds**
½ **cup chopped parsley**

1. Pound chicken gently to flatten to an even thickness. Place in a shallow dish just large enough to hold it in a single layer.

2. In a small bowl, whisk together vinegar, orange juice, mustard, orange zest, cumin, salt, pepper, garlic, and olive oil. Pour about 3 tablespoons dressing over chicken, smearing to coat all sides. Marinate 30 minutes at room temperature or up to 2 hours in refrigerator.

3. Meanwhile, in a medium saucepan, combine lentils with 3 cups of lightly salted water. Cover and simmer over low heat until tender, about 25 minutes. Drain off any remaining liquid. In a mixing bowl, combine lentils, red onion, bell pepper, carrot, ¼ cup of parsley, and remaining dressing. Toss to mix well.

4. Prepare a medium-hot fire in a barbecue grill. Grill chicken, turning occasionally, until chicken is white throughout, 10 to 15 minutes.

5. Let stand a few minutes, then carve crosswise into slices. Spoon lentils onto a large platter. Arrange chicken slices on lentils. Garnish with remaining parsley.

71   GRILLED CHICKEN TACO SALAD
Prep and stand: 25 minutes   Cook: 10 minutes   Serves: 4 to 6

1 pound skinless, boneless
    chicken breasts or thighs
2 tablespoons olive oil,
    preferably extra-virgin
1 tablespoon lime juice
2 teaspoons chili powder
¼ teaspoon salt
¼ teaspoon freshly ground
    pepper

4 cups shredded iceberg
    lettuce
1 avocado, cubed
1 cup shredded Cheddar
    cheese
1 cup bottled chunky salsa
3 cups tortilla chips

1. Prepare a hot fire in a barbecue grill or preheat broiler. Use your hand to flatten chicken to an even thickness, then place in a shallow dish. Add olive oil, lime juice, chili powder, salt, and pepper. Turn to coat. Let stand 20 minutes.

2. Grill or broil chicken, turning once, until white throughout, about 10 minutes. Thinly slice chicken across grain.

3. On 4 to 6 serving plates, make beds of lettuce. Add grilled chicken and avocado. Sprinkle with cheese, then spoon salsa over salad. Surround with tortilla chips.

72   FRIED CHICKEN SALAD
Prep: 10 minutes   Cook: 6 to 8 minutes   Serves: 4

This is a fried chicken supper in a flash—coleslaw included. If you don't have buttermilk, add 1 teaspoon lemon juice to ½ cup milk and let stand 5 minutes to thicken and curdle.

1 pound skinless, boneless
    chicken breasts or thighs
⅓ cup flour
⅓ cup yellow cornmeal
½ teaspoon salt
½ teaspoon freshly ground
    pepper
½ cup buttermilk
½ cup plus 2 tablespoons corn
    oil

1 large shallot, finely chopped
2 teaspoons Dijon mustard
2 tablespoons red wine
    vinegar
3 cups thinly sliced green
    cabbage
2 cups thinly sliced red
    cabbage

1. Cut chicken into 1½-inch chunks. In a shallow dish, combine flour, cornmeal, salt, and pepper. Pour buttermilk into another shallow dish. Dip chicken first into buttermilk, then into flour mixture to coat completely.

2. Heat oil in a large frying pan. Add chicken and cook over medium heat, turning occasionally, until golden brown outside, with no trace of pink in center, 5 to 7 minutes. (If frying pan is not large enough to accommodate chicken easily, cook in 2 batches.) Drain on paper towels.

3. Add shallot to pan drippings and cook until softened, about 1 minute. Whisk in mustard and vinegar, scraping up browned bits from bottom of pan.

4. In a large bowl, toss warm dressing with green and red cabbage. Divide among 4 serving plates. Arrange chicken on lettuce.

---

73 LEMONY WARM CHICKEN AND ASPARAGUS SALAD
Prep: 15 minutes   Cook: 10 to 11 minutes   Serves: 4

20 slender asparagus spears (about 1 pound), trimmed
 1 pound skinless, boneless chicken cutlets
½ teaspoon salt
¼ teaspoon freshly ground pepper
⅓ cup plus 2 tablespoons olive oil
½ cup sliced almonds

 3 tablespoons chopped shallots
1½ tablespoons white wine vinegar, preferably tarragon vinegar
 1 tablespoon lemon juice
½ teaspoon grated lemon zest
 2 bunches of watercress, tough stems removed
 4 thin lemon slices, for garnish

1. Cut asparagus on diagonal into 2-inch pieces. In a large saucepan of boiling salted water, cook asparagus until just crisp-tender, 2 to 3 minutes. Drain and rinse under cold running water; drain well. Set aside in a mixing bowl.

2. Cut chicken into strips and season with salt and pepper. Heat 2 tablespoons of olive oil in a large frying pan and cook chicken over medium-high heat, stirring, until white throughout, about 4 minutes. Remove chicken with a slotted spoon and add to asparagus.

3. Add almonds to drippings in pan, reduce heat to medium, and cook, stirring, until golden, about 3 minutes. Add almonds to chicken and asparagus. Add shallots and remaining ⅓ cup oil to pan and cook until softened, about 1 minute. Remove pan from heat and stir in vinegar, lemon juice, and lemon zest. Season with additional salt and pepper to taste. Pour dressing over chicken mixture and toss gently.

4. Serve warm chicken salad on a bed of watercress. Garnish with lemon slices.

74 PACIFIC CHICKEN SALAD
Prep: 10 minutes   Cook: 30 seconds   Chill: 30 minutes   Serves: 4

3 ounces snow peas (about
   1 cup), trimmed
3 tablespoons rice wine
   vinegar
3 tablespoons soy sauce
1½ tablespoons dry sherry
3 tablespoons vegetable oil
1½ tablespoons Asian sesame
   oil

½ pound thinly sliced cooked
   chicken
3 cups shredded iceberg
   lettuce
⅔ cup thinly sliced radishes
1 cup radish or alfalfa sprouts

1. In a medium saucepan of boiling salted water, cook snow peas about 30 seconds, until bright green and still crunchy. Drain and rinse under cold running water; drain well.

2. In a small bowl, whisk together vinegar, soy sauce, sherry, vegetable oil, and sesame oil. Toss chicken with about half of the dressing and marinate in refrigerator 30 to 60 minutes.

3. At serving time, toss lettuce and radishes with remaining dressing. Divide among 4 plates and arrange chicken on top. Sprinkle sprouts over salads and serve.

75 SAVANNAH TEAROOM CHICKEN SALAD
Prep: 10 minutes   Cook: none   Marinate: 8 hours   Serves: 8

This comes from an old friend. The secret is the bottled Russian dressing used as a marinade.

4 cups cubed cooked chicken
   breast (about 1 pound)
¼ cup bottled Russian salad
   dressing
3 medium celery ribs, thinly
   sliced
1 cup seedless green grapes

1 cup seedless red grapes
1 cup broken pecans
1¼ cups mayonnaise
2 tablespoons lemon juice
   Salt and freshly ground
   pepper
1 head Bibb or Boston lettuce

1. In a mixing bowl, toss chicken with Russian dressing to coat. Cover and refrigerate 8 hours or overnight.

2. About 1 hour before serving, add celery, green and red grapes, pecans, mayonnaise, and lemon juice to chicken. Stir to mix well. Season with salt and pepper to taste. Cover and refrigerate until ready to serve.

3. To serve, separate lettuce into leaf "cups." Spoon chicken salad into cups.

76 TOMATOES STUFFED WITH TARRAGON CHICKEN SALAD

Prep: 30 minutes   Cook: none   Chill: 30 minutes   Serves: 4

This is a sophisticated yet simple presentation that makes a classy lunch or warm weather supper. When good tomatoes are not in season, spoon the chicken salad into lettuce cups or hollowed-out bell peppers.

4 large ripe tomatoes
  Salt and freshly ground
    pepper
 ½ cup mayonnaise
 1½ tablespoons lemon juice
 1½ teaspoons grated lemon zest
 1 tablespoon chopped fresh
    tarragon or 1 teaspoon
    dried
	2 cups diced cooked chicken
	    breast (about 8 ounces)
	 ½ cup thinly sliced celery
	 ½ cup thinly sliced scallions
	 1 small head of leaf lettuce
	    Tarragon sprigs, for garnish

1. Cut tomatoes crosswise in half. Use a small knife or grapefruit spoon to scoop out seeds and pulp to form a shell. Sprinkle with salt and pepper, then invert tomatoes onto paper towels to drain about 30 minutes. Pat dry.

2. Meanwhile, in a medium bowl, whisk together mayonnaise, lemon juice, lemon zest, tarragon, and salt and pepper to taste. Add chicken, celery, and scallions. Stir to coat with dressing. Cover and refrigerate at least 30 minutes or up to 3 hours to allow flavors to blend.

3. To serve, spoon salad into tomato halves. Place 2 halves on a bed of lettuce on each of 4 serving plates. Garnish with tarragon sprigs.

77 PESTO CHICKEN AND PASTA SALAD

Prep: 10 minutes   Cook: 7 to 9 minutes   Serves: 6

Refrigerated pesto is a terrific convenience product that allows you to make this luscious salad in 10 minutes flat.

1 pound fusilli or short
    corkscrew pasta
 3 cups diced cooked chicken
 1 small red bell pepper, thinly
    sliced
	1 small yellow bell pepper,
	    thinly sliced
	 ¼ cup sliced black olives
	 1 cup pesto sauce, purchased
	    or homemade

1. Cook pasta in a large pot of boiling salted water until just tender, 7 to 9 minutes. Drain and turn into a mixing bowl. Let cool slightly.

2. Add all remaining ingredients to pasta. Toss to mix and coat with pesto. Serve at room temperature.

78   COBB SALAD
Prep: 30 minutes   Cook: none   Serves: 6

This is a classic chicken salad that makes a very pretty presentation on a large platter at a buffet. The ingredients can be prepared ahead, but the salad should be assembled shortly before serving.

3   cups shredded sliced
        iceberg lettuce
3   cups shredded chicory
1   small bunch of watercress,
        tough stems removed
2   cups diced cooked chicken
        (about 6 ounces)
6   slices of cooked bacon,
        crumbled
2   hard-cooked eggs, chopped
2   medium tomatoes, seeded
        and diced

1   avocado, peeled and diced
3   tablespoons white wine
        vinegar
1½   teaspoons Dijon mustard
¼   teaspoon salt
½   cup olive oil, preferably
        extra-virgin
⅓   cup crumbled blue cheese
⅓   cup thinly sliced scallions

1. On a large platter, toss together lettuce, chicory, and watercress. Spread out to make a bed. Arrange chicken, bacon, eggs, tomatoes, and avocado in separate rows over lettuce.

2. In a small bowl, whisk together vinegar, mustard, and salt. Whisk in olive oil until blended. Stir in cheese. Spoon dressing over all of salad layers. Sprinkle scallions on top.

79   CHICKEN WALDORF SALAD
Prep: 30 minutes   Cook: 5 to 8 minutes   Serves: 6

If you can get smoked chicken, so much the better. But any cooked chicken—poached, roast, or rotisserie—will turn this American classic side salad into a delicious main course.

1   cup broken walnuts
3   cups diced smoked chicken
        or cooked chicken breast
1   large Red Delicious apple,
        diced
1   large Golden Delicious
        apple, diced
2   celery ribs, thinly sliced

2   tablespoons dried currants
        or raisins
1   cup mayonnaise
2   tablespoons orange juice
1   tablespoon lemon juice
2   teaspoons grated orange zest
        Salt and freshly ground
        pepper

1. Preheat oven to 350°F. Spread nuts in a small baking dish and toast in oven, stirring once or twice, until nuts are fragrant and lightly browned, 5 to 8 minutes.

2. In a large bowl, combine chicken, diced apples, celery, toasted walnuts, and currants. Toss to mix.

3. In a small bowl, whisk together mayonnaise, orange juice, lemon juice, and orange zest. Season dressing with salt and pepper to taste. Add dressing to chicken salad and toss to coat evenly.

---

80 GREEK CHICKEN AND ORZO SALAD
Prep: 20 minutes   Cook: 8 to 10 minutes   Serves: 6

Orzo, a rice-shaped pasta, makes a great salad. Other small pasta, such as tiny shells or even elbows, can be substituted.

½ cup olive oil, preferably
  extra-virgin
¼ cup chicken broth
3 tablespoons red wine
  vinegar
1 large garlic clove, minced
3 tablespoons chopped fresh
  mint or 1½ teaspoons
  dried
¾ teaspoon salt
½ teaspoon freshly ground
  pepper
1 cup orzo

3 cups diced cooked chicken
1 small red onion, thinly
  sliced
1 small yellow bell pepper,
  diced
1 small zucchini, thinly sliced
⅓ cup sliced black olives
1 small head of romaine
  lettuce
1 tomato, cut into 6 wedges
6 small fresh mint sprigs, for
  garnish

1. In a small bowl, whisk together olive oil, broth, vinegar, garlic, mint, salt, and pepper. Set dressing aside.

2. In a large pot of boiling salted water, cook orzo until just tender, 8 to 10 minutes. Drain and transfer to a large mixing bowl. Add chicken, red onion, bell pepper, zucchini, and olives to orzo. Add dressing and toss to coat well. Let salad stand at least 15 minutes before serving.

3. On a large platter or 6 individual plates, make a bed of romaine leaves. Spoon salad onto lettuce. Garnish with tomato wedges and mint sprigs.

81   LAGUNA BEACH LUNCH
Prep: 15 minutes   Cook: none   Serves: 4

This salad re-creates the sunny flavors of a memorable lunch I enjoyed on that lovely California beach. Use any combination of mixed greens that is appealing and fresh. Smoked chicken is available in many delis, but any cooked chicken will work as well.

8 cups torn mixed salad
     greens
½ pound thinly sliced smoked
     chicken or cooked
     chicken breast
4 fresh or canned apricots,
     quartered
1 ripe avocado, thinly sliced
¼ cup coarsely chopped
     macadamia nuts
7 tablespoons olive oil,
     preferably extra-virgin

3 tablespoons lime juice
2 tablespoons white wine
     vinegar
1 tablespoon honey
1 teaspoon grated lime zest
1 garlic clove, minced
½ teaspoon salt
½ teaspoon coarsely ground
     black pepper

1. On a large platter or 4 plates, make a bed of salad greens. Arrange chicken, apricots, and avocado slices decoratively on greens. Sprinkle nuts on top.

2. In a small bowl, whisk together olive oil, lime juice, vinegar, honey, lime zest, garlic, salt, and pepper. Drizzle about half of dressing over salads. Pass remainder separately.

82   CHICKEN AND ORANGE SALAD LOUIS
Prep: 20 minutes   Cook: none   Serves: 6

If you don't want to spoon the chicken into the avocado halves, simply slice the avocado and use it to garnish the salad on the bed of watercress.

⅓ cup mayonnaise
¼ cup bottled chili sauce
1 tablespoon dry white wine
2 teaspoons prepared white
     horseradish
¼ cup finely chopped green
     pepper
¼ cup finely chopped celery
¼ cup finely chopped onion
     Salt and freshly ground
     pepper

3 cups diced cooked chicken
     (about ¾ pound)
1 seedless orange, peeled and
     diced
2 large ripe avocados
1 teaspoon lemon juice
1 bunch of watercress, tough
     stems removed

1. In a large bowl, whisk together mayonnaise, chili sauce, wine, and horseradish. Stir in green pepper, celery, onion, and salt and pepper to taste. Add chicken and diced orange and stir to coat completely.

2. Peel avocados, cut in half, and rub with lemon juice. Spoon chicken salad into hollows of avocado halves. Arrange watercress on 6 plates, scoop portions of salad onto watercress, and serve.

---

83 SPICY SESAME NOODLE AND CHICKEN SALAD

Prep: 30 minutes   Chill: 1 hour   Cook: 9 to 10 minutes
Serves: 6 to 8

One of my favorite Chinese restaurant dishes is also easy to make at home.

⅔ cup chunky peanut butter
⅓ cup soy sauce
3 tablespoons rice wine vinegar
3 tablespoons Asian sesame oil
1 tablespoon dry sherry
1 tablespoon honey
4 garlic cloves, minced

¾ teaspoon crushed hot red pepper
cups diced cooked chicken (about ¾ pound)
12 ounces vermicelli or thin spaghetti
1 bunch of broccoli, cut into florets
1 cup chopped scallions

1. In a food processor, combine peanut butter, soy sauce, vinegar, oil, sherry, honey, garlic, hot pepper, and ½ cup hot water. Process until dressing is well blended. Place chicken in a large mixing bowl and pour on dressing. Toss to coat. Cover and refrigerate 1 hour.

2. In a large pot of boiling salted water, cook vermicelli 6 minutes. Add broccoli and cook until it is crisp-tender and pasta is cooked, 3 to 4 minutes longer. Drain and rinse under cold running water; drain well.

3. Add vermicelli and broccoli to chicken. Add half of scallions and toss to mix. Serve at room temperature, with remaining scallions sprinkled on top.

84 TARRAGON CHICKEN SALAD WITH BRIE TOASTS
Prep: 10 minutes   Cook: 2 minutes   Serves: 4

Many markets now sell mixed tender salad greens called *mesclun*, either in sealed packages or loose in bulk. If you can't find the packages, use a mix of torn spinach and leaf lettuce.

10 ounces mesclun or other mixed tender greens (about 12 cups)	½ teaspoon dried tarragon
½ cup thinly sliced red onion	½ teaspoon salt
7 tablespoons olive oil, preferably extra-virgin	¼ teaspoon freshly ground pepper
2 tablespoons white wine vinegar, preferably tarragon vinegar	½ pound thinly sliced cooked chicken breast
2 teaspoons Dijon mustard	8 thin diagonal slices of French bread
1 garlic clove, minced	4 ounces Brie cheese, cut into 8 slices

1. Preheat broiler. Place greens and red onion in a large bowl. In a small bowl, whisk together olive oil, vinegar, mustard, garlic, tarragon, salt, and pepper. Pour about three-quarters of dressing over greens and toss to coat. Divide among 4 plates. Arrange chicken on top.

2. Broil bread about 4 inches from heat about 1 minute, until one side is lightly toasted. Turn bread over and place cheese on top. Broil until the cheese melts, about 1 minute longer.

3. Set Brie toasts at side of each salad and serve at once.

85 CAJUN CHICKEN AND RICE SALAD
Prep: 15 minutes   Cook: 20 minutes   Serves: 6

1 cup converted white rice	½ cup chopped parsley
10 ounces thinly sliced cooked chicken	¼ cup red wine vinegar
1 cup diced smoked ham (about 4 ounces)	1½ teaspoons grainy mustard
½ pound seeded and diced fresh plum tomatoes (1½ cups)	1 teaspoon Tabasco or other hot sauce
	1 garlic clove, minced
1 cup coarsely chopped green bell pepper	½ teaspoon dried oregano
¾ cup thinly sliced celery	½ teaspoon salt
⅔ cup chopped red onion	¼ teaspoon cayenne
	7 tablespoons olive oil, preferably extra-virgin

1. In a small saucepan, bring 2 cups lightly salted water to a boil. Add rice, cover, reduce heat to low, and cook about 20 minutes, until liquid is absorbed and rice is tender. Remove from heat and let stand, covered, 5 minutes.

2. In a large mixing bowl, combine cooked rice, chicken, ham, tomatoes, bell pepper, celery, red onion, and half of parsley. Toss gently to mix.

3. In a small bowl, whisk together vinegar, mustard, hot sauce, garlic, oregano, salt, and cayenne until blended. Whisk in olive oil.

4. Pour dressing over salad and toss to mix well. Let stand 10 minutes to allow flavors to blend. Sprinkle remaining parsley on top before serving.

---

86   COLORFUL COUSCOUS CHICKEN SALAD
Prep: 20 minutes   Cook: 2 minutes   Serves: 4 to 6

You can eat the salad in the traditional Moroccan manner by using the lettuce as a scoop and wrapping it around the couscous to eat out of hand, or you can simply spoon it over a bed of romaine and use a knife and fork. Couscous is an almost instant-cooking pasta, which can be found in the rice section of the market.

1 cup packaged couscous	½ teaspoon salt
2 cups diced cooked chicken (about ½ pound)	¼ teaspoon freshly ground pepper
1 large red bell pepper, diced	3 tablespoons white wine vinegar
⅔ cup thinly sliced scallions	½ cup plus 2 tablespoons extra-virgin olive oil
½ cup diced carrots	
⅓ cup sliced black olives	¾ cup crumbled feta cheese (6 ounces)
¾ cup fresh mint sprigs	
2 garlic cloves	1 head of romaine lettuce
1 teaspoon Dijon mustard	

1. Bring 1¾ cups salted water to a boil in a medium saucepan. Add couscous, remove pan from heat, and let stand, covered, until liquid is absorbed, about 5 minutes. Transfer to a large bowl and fluff couscous with a fork. Add chicken, bell pepper, scallions, carrots, and olives. Toss to combine.

2. In a food processor, finely chop mint with garlic. With machine on, add mustard, salt, pepper, vinegar, and olive oil; process to blend well. Pour dressing over couscous and toss to mix. Add cheese and toss again.

3. Line a large platter with romaine leaves. Spoon salad into center. Serve at room temperature.

87 SALSA CHICKEN AND RICE SALAD

Prep: 20 minutes   Cook: 30 to 33 minutes   Serves: 4 to 6

This is good as a warm salad with freshly cooked chicken and rice, but it is also terrific as a cold summer salad with leftover chicken and rice.

1 pound skinless, boneless chicken breast halves
2 cups chicken broth
1 cup converted white rice
½ cup olive oil, preferably extra-virgin
3 tablespoons white wine vinegar
1 tablespoon grainy mustard
¾ teaspoon ground cumin
½ teaspoon salt
½ teaspoon freshly ground pepper

3 large plum tomatoes, seeded and chopped
1 small green bell pepper, chopped
⅓ cup chopped red onion
1 large fresh or canned jalapeño pepper, chopped
1 head of red leaf lettuce
¼ cup chopped cilantro

1. In a covered saucepan, poach chicken in broth over medium-low heat until white throughout, 12 to 15 minutes. Remove chicken with a slotted spoon and bring broth to a boil. Add rice, reduce heat to low, and cover pan. Simmer until all of liquid is absorbed and rice is tender, about 18 minutes. When chicken is cool enough to handle, cut into thin strips.

2. In a small bowl, whisk together olive oil, vinegar, mustard, cumin, salt, and pepper. Stir in tomatoes, bell pepper, red onion, and jalapeño pepper. In a large bowl, combine about two-thirds of vinaigrette with warm rice. Toss to mix.

3. To serve, spoon rice onto a bed of lettuce leaves. Arrange chicken strips on top. Spoon remaining vinaigrette over salad. Serve garnished with cilantro.

88   THAI NOODLE AND CHICKEN SALAD
Prep: 20 minutes   Cook: 6 minutes   Serves: 4

If you can't find rice noodles, use angel hair pasta or capellini.

2   tablespoons rice wine
   vinegar
2   tablespoons chicken broth
   or water
1½ tablespoons soy sauce
1   tablespoon finely chopped
   fresh ginger
1   large garlic clove, minced
⅓   cup plus 2 tablespoons
   peanut oil
   Salt and freshly ground
   pepper

8   ounces maifun rice sticks
8   ounces chicken breast fillets,
   thinly sliced
½   red bell pepper, thinly
   sliced
4   ounces snow peas, trimmed
   and cut diagonally in half
½   cup thinly sliced scallions
½   cup dry-roasted peanuts,
   chopped
⅓   cup chopped cilantro

1. In a small bowl, whisk together vinegar, broth, soy sauce, ginger, garlic, and ⅓ cup of peanut oil. Season to taste with salt and pepper. Set dressing aside.

2. Break rice sticks into 3-inch lengths and cook in a large pot of boiling salted water until softened, about 2 minutes. Drain in a colander and rinse under cold water; drain well.

3. In a wok or a large frying pan, heat remaining 2 tablespoons oil. Add chicken and stir-fry 1 minute. Add bell pepper and stir-fry 2 minutes. Add snow peas and scallions and stir-fry 1 minute. Stir in peanuts, rice noodles, and dressing. Toss well, then toss again with cilantro. Serve hot or at room temperature.

89   CHICKEN PASTA SALAD NIÇOISE

Prep: 30 minutes   Cook: 12 to 13 minutes   Serves: 6

Salade niçoise is traditionally made with tuna, but cooked chicken breast works just as well.

¾ **pound ziti or other short tubular pasta**
½ **pound green beans, cut diagonally in half**
½ **cup olive oil, preferably extra-virgin**
3 **tablespoons balsamic or red wine vinegar**
2 **teaspoons Dijon mustard**
1 **garlic clove, minced**
¼ **teaspoon crushed hot red pepper**

½ **teaspoon salt**
3 **cups diced cooked chicken**
1 **small red onion, chopped**
½ **cup sliced black olives**
¼ **cup chopped parsley**
3 **tablespoons chopped fresh basil or 1 teaspoon dried**
12 **cherry tomatoes, halved**
1 **(2-ounce) can anchovies rolled in capers**

1. In a large pot of boiling salted water, cook pasta 8 minutes. Add green beans and boil until beans are crisp-tender and pasta is tender but still firm, 4 to 5 minutes longer. Drain into a colander and rinse under cold running water; drain well.

2. Meanwhile, in a large bowl, whisk together olive oil, vinegar, mustard, garlic, hot pepper, and salt. Add pasta and green beans, chicken, red onion, olives, parsley, and basil. Toss to mix well.

3. Spoon salad into a shallow serving bowl. Garnish with tomatoes and anchovies.

Chapter 5

Chicken in the Middle

For years and years, sandwiches were equated with peanut butter and jelly in a lunch box. There were chicken sandwiches, of course, but they garnered little respect. They were usually nothing more than leftover chicken on white bread with mayonnaise and maybe some lettuce.

Welcome to the new world of sandwiches. The knowledge that eating more grains in tandem with the ability to buy far better breads has elevated sandwiches in general and chicken sandwiches in particular. These days we have grilled sandwiches, salad sandwiches, skillet sandwiches, overstuffed sandwiches, and even new ways to garnish the simple chicken sandwich on white bread.

The cardinal rule for chicken sandwiches is simple: Use good chicken—not dried-out remnants. This can either be chicken cooked expressly for the sandwich or well-cared-for leftovers.

Since many sandwiches begin with cooked chicken, this is as good a place as any to talk about how to store leftover chicken. Chicken with the skin on should be stored that way, even if you plan to discard the skin later, since the skin acts as a protector to help retain moisture. Skinless, boneless cooked chicken is very prone to drying out, especially if sliced or chopped. So wrap cooked chicken well in plastic or foil, and refrigerate as soon as it is cool to retain moisture. Refrigerate poached chicken in the poaching liquid, perhaps the best way to retain flavor and moisture. Use cooked chicken within a few days.

90   THE BEST CHICKEN SALAD SANDWICH
Prep: 10 minutes   Chill: 15 minutes   Cook: none   Serves: 6

The best chicken salad sandwich starts with perfectly poached chicken breasts, ultra-fresh garnishes, and very good bread. It's as simple as that.

¾ cup mayonnaise
1 tablespoon lemon juice
2 tablespoons chopped chives
1½ tablespoons chopped fresh tarragon or ½ teaspoon dried
1 teaspoon grated lemon zest
½ teaspoon salt
¼ teaspoon freshly ground pepper

2½ cups finely diced cooked chicken breast (about ¾ pound)
½ cup finely chopped celery
12 slices of thinly sliced whole wheat bread
1 bunch of watercress, trimmed

1. In a large bowl, stir together mayonnaise, lemon juice, chives, tarragon, lemon zest, salt, and pepper. Stir in chicken and celery. Refrigerate at least 15 minutes or up to 4 hours.

2. Assemble 6 sandwiches, filling each pair of bread slices with a generous ⅓ cup chicken salad and some watercress sprigs.

91   CONTEMPORARY CLUB SANDWICH
Prep: 10 minutes   Cook: 5 minutes   Serves: 4

¾ cup mayonnaise
3 tablespoons minced chives
½ teaspoon dried tarragon
8 slices of turkey bacon
2 tomatoes, very thinly sliced
12 very thin slices of whole wheat bread, lightly toasted

½ pound thinly sliced cooked chicken breast
1 bunch of watercress, tough stems removed
8 pitted olives

1. In a small bowl, mix together mayonnaise, chives, and tarragon. In a large skillet, cook bacon over medium heat, turning, until crisp, about 5 minutes. Drain on paper towels.

2. Spread herbed mayonnaise over one side of each toast slice. Layer bacon and tomatoes between 2 slices of bread and top with third bread slice. Arrange chicken and watercress to make 4 triple-decker sandwiches.

3. Cut each sandwich diagonally into quarters. Skewer each quarter together with a toothpick stuck into an olive and then through sandwich.

92 MEDITERRANEAN CHICKEN AND GRILLED VEGETABLE POCKETS

Prep: 15 minutes   Stand: 20 minutes   Cook: 15 minutes   Serves: 4

Other vegetables can be subsituted here, but this combination is a Mediterranean classic. Spinkling the chicken with mint before grilling adds depth and character to the sandwich.

3 tablespoons olive oil, preferably extra-virgin
1 garlic clove, minced
½ teaspoon salt
½ teaspoon freshly ground pepper
5 tablespoons chopped fresh mint
1 cup plain yogurt
1 small eggplant (about 8 ounces), sliced lengthwise about ½ inch thick

2 medium zucchini (about 6 ounces each), sliced lengthwise about ½ inch thick
1 medium red onion, sliced about ½ inch thick
¾ pound thinly sliced chicken breast cutlets
8 small pita breads
1 medium tomato, chopped

1. Prepare a medium-hot barbecue fire or preheat a gas grill. In a small bowl, combine olive oil, garlic, salt, pepper, and 2 tablespoons chopped mint. In another small bowl, stir remaining 3 tablespoons mint into yogurt. Let garlic-mint oil and minted yogurt stand 20 minutes.

2. Brush eggplant, zucchini, and onion with about half of flavored oil. Grill vegetables, turning once or twice, until browned and tender, about 10 minutes. Let cool slightly, then coarsely dice vegetables. Brush chicken with remaining flavored oil. Grill chicken, turning once, until white throughout, about 5 minutes. Thinly slice chicken crosswise and combine with vegetables.

3. Wrap pita breads in foil and warm for a few minutes at edge of grill. Cut off about a third of the pita breads to form pockets. Fill with chicken and vegetables. Top with minted yogurt and chopped tomato.

93   CHICKEN REUBEN

Prep: 5 minutes   Cook: 2 to 3 minutes   Serves: 6

12 slices of seeded rye bread
¾ cup bottled Thousand
     Island salad dressing
1 pound thinly sliced cooked
     or smoked chicken breast

4 ounces thinly sliced Swiss
     cheese
3 cups drained canned or
     fresh sauerkraut

1. Preheat broiler. Lightly toast one side of each bread slice under broiler 1 to 2 minutes. Spread salad dressing over untoasted sides of bread.

2. Arrange chicken on spread side of 6 of bread slices. Top with cheese. Broil until cheese is melted, about 1 minute.

3. Add sauerkraut, then top with remaining bread slices, spread side down. Cut in half on diagonal and serve immediately.

94   CHICKEN AND PEPPER SUB

Prep: 20 minutes   Cook: 20 minutes   Serves: 4 to 6

Depending upon where you live, this might be a hoagie or a grinder or a sub or a hero. No matter, because your family will love it whatever you call it.

1 pound skinless, boneless
     chicken breasts or thighs,
     thinly sliced crosswise
Salt and freshly ground
     pepper
¼ cup olive oil
1 large onion, thinly sliced
1 green bell pepper, thinly
     sliced
1 medium yellow bell pepper,
     thinly sliced

3 garlic cloves, crushed
     through a press
1 (14½-ounce) can Italian-style
     stewed tomatoes
¼ teaspoon crushed hot red
     pepper
2 tablespoons balsamic or red
     wine vinegar
4 to 6 crusty sub sandwich or
     hoagie rolls, each about
     7 inches long

1. Season chicken lightly with salt and pepper. In a large frying pan, heat 2 tablespoons of olive oil over medium-high heat. Add chicken and cook until golden, about 4 minutes. Remove with a slotted spoon.

2. Add remaining 2 tablespoons of oil to pan, reduce heat to medium-low, and cook onion, green and yellow bell peppers, and garlic, stirring often, until very soft, about 8 minutes. Add tomatoes and hot pepper and simmer, partially covered, 5 minutes. Add vinegar and chicken and simmer 3 minutes. Season with salt and pepper to taste.

3. To serve, split rolls lengthwise and spoon filling inside. Serve with lots of napkins.

95 HOT SWISS CHICKEN AND BROCCOLI SANDWICH

Prep: 10 minutes   Cook: 12 to 14 minutes   Serves: 4

This sophisticated, open-face knife-and-fork sandwich makes a lovely lunch or brunch dish as well as a light supper main course.

½ **pound broccoli spears**
1 **pound thinly sliced chicken breast cutlets**
¼ **teaspoon salt**
⅛ **teaspoon freshly ground pepper**
3 **tablespoons butter**

2 **tablespoons flour**
¼ **teaspoon grated nutmeg**
1 **cup milk**
1 **cup chicken broth**
1 **cup shredded Swiss cheese**
8 **slices of sourdough bread, toasted**

1. Cook broccoli in a medium saucepan of boiling salted water until crisp-tender, 3 to 4 minutes. Drain and rinse under cold running water; drain well.

2. Season chicken with salt and pepper. In a large frying pan, melt butter over medium-high heat. Add chicken and cook, turning, until white throughout, about 5 minutes. Remove from pan.

3. Stir flour into pan drippings and cook, stirring, 1 minute. Gradually stir in nutmeg, milk, and broth. Bring to a boil, stirring constantly, until smooth and lightly thickened, 3 to 4 minutes. Remove pan from heat and stir in cheese until melted.

4. To serve, arrange chicken on toasted sourdough bread. Spoon cheese sauce over chicken and top with broccoli.

96 THANKSGIVING SANDWICH

Prep: 5 minutes   Cook: none   Serves: 6

My good friend and writing compatriate Brooke Dojny taught me the very best way to make a sandwich on the day after Thanksgiving. I now make it with leftover chicken and stuffing any day I feel like it.

⅓ **cup mayonnaise**
1 **teaspoon grated orange zest**
12 **thin slices of whole wheat bread**
12 **slices of cooked chicken breast**

1 **cup cooked bread stuffing**
1 **cup cranberry sauce or cranberry relish, homemade or purchased**
6 **leaves of soft Boston or Bibb lettuce**

In a small bowl, stir together mayonnaise and orange zest. Spread one side of each slice of bread with flavored mayonnaise. Make 6 sandwiches with chicken, stuffing, cranberry sauce, and lettuce. Cut into quarters and skewer together with frilly toothpicks, if desired.

97   OPEN-FACE MONTEREY CHICKEN MELT
Prep: 5 minutes   Cook: 1 minute   Serves: 4

½ cup creamy blue cheese
    salad dressing
4 whole wheat English
    muffins, split and lightly
    toasted
1 sweet onion, thinly sliced
¾ pound thinly sliced cooked
    or smoked chicken breast

2 small avocados, peeled and
    thinly sliced
2 cups shredded Monterey
    Jack cheese (about
    8 ounces)
2 cups alfalfa or radish
    sprouts

1. Preheat broiler. Spread 1 tablespoon salad dressing over each cut side of English muffin; place on a baking sheet. Make 8 sandwiches by layering on onion, chicken, and avocados. Sprinkle cheese on top.

2. Broil about 4 inches from heat source until cheese is melted and tinged with brown, about 1 minute. Sprinkle sprouts over sandwiches and serve at once.

98   CHICKEN PAN BAGNA
Prep: 10 minutes   Cook: none   Chill: 2 hours   Serves: 4

Try to find really good olives for this simple version of a French Mediter-ranean classic. Since the sandwich must be made ahead, it is an excellent picnic dish. Just be sure to keep the sandwich chilled until serving time.

2 cups diced smoked or
    cooked chicken breast
    (about ½ pound)
1 cup sliced mixed black and
    green olives
1 red bell pepper, diced
⅔ cup thinly sliced scallions
½ cup mayonnaise
2 tablespoons balsamic or red
    wine vinegar

2 teaspoons chopped fresh
    thyme or ¾ teaspoon
    dried
¼ teaspoon salt
¼ teaspoon freshly ground
    pepper
1 (12-ounce) loaf of French
    bread

1. In a mixing bowl, combine chicken, olives, bell pepper, and scallions. In a small bowl, whisk together mayonnaise, vinegar, thyme, salt, and pepper. Add to chicken and mix well.

2. Split loaf of bread lengthwise and pull out some of the soft interior to make a shallow cavity. Spoon chicken salad down length of one half, replace top, and wrap tightly in aluminum foil. Place on a plate and weight down with another plate. Refrigerate about 2 hours.

3. To serve, cut sandwich crosswise into 2-inch slices.

99   CHICKEN AND ASPARAGUS SPECIAL
Prep: 5 minutes   Cook: 9 to 10 minutes   Serves: 4

This makes a light sandwich for lunch or brunch. Use pencil-thin asparagus for the prettiest presentation and a good-quality mustard for the best flavor.

16 thin asparagus stalks	¼ cup sliced almonds
1 pound thinly sliced chicken breast cutlets	⅓ cup dry white wine
	1 tablespoon grainy Dijon mustard
½ teaspoon salt	
¼ teaspoon freshly ground pepper	⅓ cup mayonnaise
	4 slices of white bread, toasted
3 tablespoons butter	

1. Snap off and discard woody asparagus stems. Cook asparagus in a large pot of boiling salted water until crisp-tender, about 2 minutes. Drain and rinse under cold running water; drain well.

2. Season chicken with salt and pepper. In a large frying pan, cook chicken in butter over medium-high heat heat, turning, until white throughout, about 5 minutes. Remove from pan.

3. Add almonds to drippings and cook until golden, 1 to 2 minutes. Remove with a slotted spoon. Add wine to pan and boil over medium-high heat, stirring to scrape up browned bits from bottom of pan, until reduced to 2 tablespoons, about 1 minute. Remove pan from heat and stir in mustard and mayonnaise until smooth.

4. Spread toasts with part of mustard sauce. Add chicken and cover with asparagus. Spoon remaining sauce over asparagus and sprinkle toasted almonds on top. Serve at once.

100   EXTRA CHEESE AND CHICKEN PIZZA
Prep: 10 minutes   Cook: 12 to 15 minutes   Serves: 2 to 3

1 (10-ounce) tube refrigerated pizza dough	1½ cups thinly sliced cooked or smoked chicken breast
1½ cups shredded mozzarella cheese (about 6 ounces)	¼ cup grated Parmesan cheese
	1½ teaspoons dried oregano
½ pound seeded and thinly sliced fresh plum tomatoes	

1. Preheat oven to 425°F. Unroll dough and use your hands or a rolling pin to shape into a rectangle about 9x13 inches on a lightly oiled baking sheet. Sprinkle with mozzarella cheese, then layer on tomatoes and chicken. Combine Parmesan cheese and oregano and sprinkle over pizza.

2. Bake until cheese is melted and bubbly and edges of pizza are well browned, 12 to 15 minutes. Cut into squares to serve.

101   CHICKEN AND CHEDDAR RAREBIT
Prep: 5 minutes   Cook: 12 to 13 minutes   Serves: 4

Old English pub food makes a fine chicken supper. If you have cooked chicken, simply layer it on the English muffins, then cover with the sauce.

1 **pound thinly sliced chicken breast cutlets**	1 **teaspoon Worcestershire sauce**
3 **tablespoons butter**	¾ **teaspoon cayenne**
3 **tablespoons flour**	4 **whole wheat English muffins, split and toasted**
1½ **teaspoons dry mustard**	**Paprika**
1⅓ **cups milk**	
1½ **cups beer or ale**	
3 **cups shredded Cheddar cheese (about 12 ounces)**	

1. In a large frying pan, cook chicken in butter over medium heat, turning, until white throughout, about 5 minutes. Remove chicken from pan.

2. Stir flour into pan drippings, reduce heat to medium, and cook, stirring, 2 minutes. Add mustard and cook 1 minute. Gradually whisk in milk and bring to a boil, stirring until bubbly, 2 to 3 minutes. Stir in beer and simmer 2 minutes. Remove pan from heat and stir in cheese until melted. Season sauce with Worcestershire and cayenne.

3. Arrange chicken on English muffin halves. Spoon sauce over and dust with paprika. Serve 2 half muffins per person.

102   GRILLED CHICKEN BRUSCHETTA
Prep: 10 minutes   Stand: 35 minutes   Cook: 12 to 15 minutes Serves: 4

Make this only when you can get really ripe, luscious tomatoes and fresh basil.

⅓ **cup olive oil**	⅓ **cup chopped sweet white onion**
3 **garlic cloves, minced**	⅓ **cup chopped fresh basil, plus leaves for garnish**
4 **skinless, boneless chicken breast halves**	½ **teaspoon salt**
1½ **tablespoons balsamic vinegar**	½ **teaspoon coarsely ground black pepper**
1 **pound ripe tomatoes, peeled, seeded, and chopped**	8 **slices of crusty Italian bread, cut ½ inch thick**

1. Prepare a medium-hot charcoal fire or preheat a gas grill. In a small bowl, combine olive oil and garlic. Let stand 15 minutes. Use your hand to flatten chicken to an even thickness. Coat with about 1 tablespoon of garlic oil and let stand 10 minutes.

2. In a mixing bowl, combine remaining garlic oil with vinegar, tomatoes, onion, chopped basil, salt, and pepper. Let tomato salad stand at least 10 minutes at room temperature.

3. Meanwhile, grill chicken, turning once, until browned outside and white in center, 12 to 15 minutes. About 2 minutes before chicken is done, lightly grill both sides of bread at edge of grill.

4. To serve, spoon a small portion of tomato salad on each grilled toast. Cut chicken crosswise into ½-inch-thick slices and arrange over tomatoes. Spoon remaining tomato salad on top and garnish with basil leaves.

---

103   CHICKEN, SPINACH, AND SUN-DRIED TOMATO CALZONES

Prep: 15 minutes   Cook: 15 minutes   Serves: 2 to 4

Calzones are simply pizza turnovers and can hold all sorts of fillings. This is a particularly delicious one that makes a delicious snack or simple main course for an informal supper.

1 **(10-ounce) package frozen chopped spinach, thawed**
1 **cup shredded cooked chicken**
½ **cup part-skim ricotta cheese**
¼ **cup grated Parmesan cheese**
2 **tablespoons chopped sun-dried tomatoes**

2 **teaspoons chopped fresh basil or ½ teaspoon dried**
1½ **teaspoons dried oregano**
¼ **teaspoon freshly ground pepper**
1½ **cups bottled marinara sauce**
1 **(10-ounce) tube refrigerated pizza dough**

1. Preheat oven to 425°F. Drain spinach in a sieve, pressing to extract as much liquid as possible. In a medium bowl, combine spinach, chicken, ricotta, Parmesan, sun-dried tomatoes, basil, oregano, pepper, and ½ cup of marinara sauce.

2. Unfold pizza dough onto a lightly greased baking sheet; use your hands to flatten to a rough 12-inch square. Use a sharp knife to cut into 4 squares. Spoon filling into center of each square. Fold dough over to form a triangle. Press edges together, then crimp with a fork to seal. Make 3 slashes in each calzone to allow steam to escape.

3. Bake until golden brown, about 15 minutes. Heat remaining marinara sauce and serve as a dip for warm calzones.

104   CHICKEN SOUVLAKI
Prep: 10 minutes   Marinate: 30 minutes   Cook: 5 minutes
Serves: 4

Souvlaki is traditionally made with lamb. Meaty chicken thighs provide a tasty, low-fat variation. Souvlaki is spooned atop pitas and folded up for eating, which takes a bit of practice to do without spilling the filling. Novices can open a pocket in the pitas and spoon the filling inside.

2 tablespoons olive oil, preferably extra-virgin
2 tablespoons lemon juice
1 garlic clove, minced
½ teaspoon dried oregano
½ teaspoon salt
½ teaspoon freshly ground pepper

1 pound skinless, boneless chicken thighs, cut into 1-inch cubes
¾ cup plain yogurt
3 tablespoons tahini (sesame seed paste)
4 pita breads
1 small cucumber, diced

1. In a shallow 2-quart dish, combine olive oil, lemon juice, garlic, oregano, and ¼ teaspoon each of salt and pepper. Add chicken and stir to coat with marinade. Let stand at room temperature 30 minutes, tossing occasionally.

2. In a small bowl, combine yogurt, tahini, and remaining ¼ teaspoon each salt and pepper. Blend well.

3. Prepare a medium-hot barbecue fire or preheat a gas grill. Thread chicken onto metal skewers and grill, turning once or twice, until white throughout, about 5 minutes. Meanwhile, wrap pita breads in foil and warm at edge of grill.

4. Spoon chicken, seasoned yogurt, and cucumbers on pitas and fold up to eat.

105   CHICKEN ON A BUN
Prep: 10 minutes   Chill: 1 hour   Cook: 10 minutes   Serves: 4 to 6

⅔ cup mayonnaise
¼ cup pickle relish
3 tablespoons flour
3 tablespoons yellow cornmeal
½ teaspoon salt
½ teaspoon freshly ground pepper
1 pound thinly sliced chicken breast cutlets

¼ cup oil
4 to 6 thin slices of Cheddar or American cheese (optional)
4 large or 6 average sesame-seeded sandwich buns, split and lightly toasted
2 cups shredded iceberg or romaine lettuce
4 to 6 slices of tomato

1. For the sauce, stir together mayonnaise and pickle relish. Refrigerate at least 1 hour or up to 3 days.

2. In a shallow dish, stir together flour, cornmeal, salt, and pepper. Dip chicken to coat both sides. Heat half of oil in a large frying pan over medium-high heat. Add half of coated chicken and cook, turning, until golden brown and crisp outside and white in center, about 5 minutes.

3. If using cheese, place over chicken during last 2 minutes of cooking to melt. Remove chicken from pan. Repeat with remaining oil and chicken.

4. Spread cut sides of buns liberally with sauce. Make sandwiches with chicken, lettuce, and tomato.

---

106 TUSCAN CHICKEN AND ARUGULA SANDWICH

Prep: 5 minutes   Cook: 9 minutes   Serves: 4

1 **pound thinly sliced chicken breast cutlets**
¾ **teaspoon coarsely ground pepper**
½ **teaspoon salt**
3 **tablespoons extra-virgin olive oil**
3 **tablespoons chopped shallots**
⅓ **cup dry white wine**

2 **teaspoons chopped fresh thyme or ½ teaspoon dried**
½ **cup mayonnaise**
2 **small bunches of arugula**
1 **tomato, seeded and sliced**
8 **slices of crusty Italian bread, cut diagonally ½ inch thick and lightly toasted**

1. Season chicken with ½ teaspoon of pepper and ¼ teaspoon of salt, patting in pepper so it adheres. Heat olive oil in a large frying pan. Add chicken and cook over medium-high heat, turning, until golden and cooked through, about 5 minutes. Remove chicken from pan.

2. Add shallots to drippings and cook 1 minute. Add wine and thyme and boil, stirring up browned bits in bottom of pan, until reduced to 2 tablespoons, about 3 minutes. In a small bowl, stir shallots and reduced wine into mayonnaise.

3. Spread flavored mayonnaise over toast slices. Layer arugula, tomato slices, and chicken onto 4 toasts. Cover with remaining toasts. Cut in half to serve.

107   PHILLY CHICKEN CHEESE "STEAKS"

Prep: 10 minutes   Cook: 15 minutes   Serves: 4

If you're from Philadelphia, don't write. I know cheese steaks are beef, but please try this chicken version. I bet you will like it!

3 tablespoons vegetable oil
1 large onion, very thinly
   sliced
1 garlic clove, crushed
   through a press
1 pound thinly sliced chicken
   breast cutlets
¼ teaspoon salt

¼ teaspoon freshly ground
   pepper
4 Italian sandwich rolls, each
   6 or 7 inches long
1 tablespoon butter, softened
1½ cups shredded mild
   Cheddar cheese (about
   6 ounces)

1. Preheat broiler. In a large frying pan, heat 2 tablespoons of oil over medium-low heat. Add onions and cook, stirring often, until very soft and pale gold, about 10 minutes. Add garlic and cook 1 minute. Remove from pan using a slotted spoon.

2. Season chicken with salt and pepper. Thinly slice crosswise. Add remaining 1 tablespoon oil to pan. Cook chicken over medium-high heat, turning, until white throughout, about 3 minutes. Return onions to pan. Cover and keep warm.

3. Split rolls lengthwise and spread with butter. Broil, cut sides up, about 30 seconds, until golden. Pile chicken and browned onion onto bottoms of rolls. Top with cheese and broil until cheese is melted and bubbly, 30 to 45 seconds. To serve, put tops on sandwiches and cut each sandwich in half crosswise.

108   CHICKEN AND BEAN QUESADILLAS

Prep: 10 minutes   Cook: 10 to 15 minutes   Serves: 4

Quesadillas are usually grilled or fried on a griddle. These are baked, which is much easier and saves on oil, too.

2 cups shredded cooked
   chicken (about ½ pound)
2½ cups shredded Monterey
   Jack cheese with chiles
   (about 10 ounces)
1½ teaspoons chili powder

1½ cups drained and rinsed
   canned black beans
⅓ cup finely chopped onion
¼ cup chopped cilantro
8 (7-inch) flour tortillas
1 cup bottled salsa

1. Preheat oven to 375°F. In a medium bowl, toss together chicken, cheese, chili powder, beans, onion, and cilantro.

2. Place 4 tortillas on an ungreased baking sheet. Divide filling among them, spreading to within ¾ inch of edge. Cover with remaining tortillas, pressing gently on edges.

3. Bake until cheese is melted and tortillas are golden brown, 10 to 15 minutes. Let cool slightly, then cut each quesadilla into quarters. Serve with salsa.

109 CREAMED CHICKEN AND MUSHROOMS ON WAFFLES

Prep: 10 minutes   Cook: 15 minutes   Serves: 4

Reminiscent of chicken a la king, this is also a fine recipe for leftover chicken. Simply heat it in the sauce. A mix of wild and domestic mushrooms makes the sandwich more interesting.

¾ **pound skinless, boneless chicken breast or thighs, cut into 1-inch pieces**
¼ **teaspoon salt**
¼ **teaspoon freshly ground pepper**
3 **tablespoons butter**
¾ **pound thinly sliced mushrooms, wild or domestic or a mix**

3 **tablespoons flour**
1 **teaspoon dried tarragon**
1 **cup milk**
1½ **cups chicken broth**
2 **teaspoons lemon juice**
2 **tablespoons dry sherry**
8 **homemade or heated frozen waffles**
½ **cup thinly sliced scallions**

1. Season chicken with salt and pepper. In a large frying pan, melt butter over medium-high heat. Add chicken and cook, stirring often, until white throughout, about 5 minutes. Remove with a slotted spoon.

2. Add mushrooms to pan, reduce heat to medium, and cook, stirring, until softened, about 4 minutes. Add flour and cook, stirring, 2 minutes. Stir in tarragon, milk, and broth. Bring to a boil, stirring, until thickened, about 3 minutes. Reduce heat to medium-low and return chicken to pan. Stir in lemon juice and sherry and simmer 1 minute. Season with additional salt and pepper to taste.

3. Spoon chicken and mushrooms and sauce over waffles. Serve hot, with scallions sprinkled on top.

110 CHICKEN AND MIXED VEGETABLE PASTIES

Prep: 10 minutes   Cook: 18 to 22 minutes   Serves: 4

Pasties are Cornish pastry turnovers with savory fillings, often carried in workers' lunch boxes. Pasties are just as good in American lunch boxes, especially if accompanied by a thermos of hot tomato soup.

1½ cups chopped or shredded cooked chicken
1 cup shredded sharp Cheddar cheese (about 4 ounces)
1 cup frozen peas and carrots, thawed
1 tablespoon chopped shallots
1 teaspoon dried thyme

¼ teaspoon salt
¼ teaspoon freshly ground pepper
Pastry for a double-crust 9-inch pie or 2 refrigerated pie crust rounds
1 egg beaten with 1 tablespoon water

1. Preheat oven to 400°F. In a medium bowl, combine chicken, cheese, peas and carrots, shallots, thyme, salt, and pepper.

2. Roll out pastry to make two 9-inch circles (or unfold refrigerated crusts) and cut each circle in half. Mound filling in center of pastry half-circles. Brush edges with egg glaze. Fold over to make 4 triangular pasties and press pastry firmly around filling. Seal edges together by crimping with tines of a fork. Cut 2 or 3 slashes in crust of each pasty to allow steam to escape. Brush tops with egg glaze.

3. Place pasties on an ungreased baking sheet and bake until golden brown, 18 to 22 minutes. Serve warm.

Chapter 6

Soup's On and Chicken's in It

If your grandmother taught you that chicken soup is good for what ails you, she was right. A steaming, fragrant golden broth makes you want to breathe deeply, and the anticipation of a ladleful of tender chicken chunks and perhaps a gentle hint of herbs will bolster even the most flagging appetite.

Almost every chicken soup has a chicken stock as its base, and the quality of the finished product is dependent upon the sum of its ingredients. Consequently, I really like to make my own stock, whether it's the quick version or the really grand Brown Chicken Stock on page 84.

But I'm also finding these days that canned broth is really quite good, especially the reduced-sodium versions. All of the recipes in this book work well with canned broth or homemade stock. Homemade stock should not be salted until you are ready to use it to be sure that the result will not be excessively salty. Since canned broths vary considerably in their saltiness (even the reduced-sodium types), most of the soup recipes here suggest that additional salt be added at the end to taste in order to avoid sodium overkill.

Soup serving portions also vary according to the richness of the soup, but don't be afraid to make a lot. It's just as easy, and most soups improve in flavor on reheating.

111   QUICK CHICKEN STOCK

Prep: 5 minutes   Cook: 1½ hours   Chill: 1 hour
Makes: about 2 quarts

Instead of throwing away all those extra chicken backs and necks, make this simple stock to use as the basis for a quick vegetable soup or to enrich a chicken gravy.

3 pounds chicken backs,
   necks, wing tips, or
   giblets (except liver)
1 large onion, quartered
1 celery rib with leaves,
   quartered

1 carrot, quartered
½ cup parsley sprigs
1 bay leaf, broken in half
10 whole black peppercorns
    Salt

1. Place chicken parts in a large soup pot. Add 3 quarts of water. Bring to a boil, skimming off foam as it rises to top. Add remaining ingredients except salt. Reduce heat and simmer, partially covered, for about 1½ hours.

2. Strain stock through a fine-mesh sieve. Season with salt to taste. Let cool, then refrigerate 1 to 2 hours. Lift off and discard solidified fat.

112   BROWN CHICKEN STOCK

Prep: 20 minutes   Cook: 2¾ hours   Chill: 1 hour
Makes: about 2 quarts

Browning the bones and the vegetables gives a deep, rich flavor to the stock.

3 pounds chicken backs and
   wing tips
1 large onion, thickly sliced
1 celery rib with leaves,
   quartered
1 large carrot, quartered
2 garlic cloves, peeled

½ cup parsley sprigs
1 teaspoon dried thyme
1 bay leaf, broken
10 whole black peppercorns
¼ pound chicken giblets
   without liver
   Salt

1. Preheat oven to 400°F. Place chicken parts in a single layer in a roasting pan. Roast 20 minutes. Add onion, celery, carrot, and garlic cloves. Roast another 20 minutes, until bones and vegetables are lightly browned. Remove chicken and vegetables to a large soup pot. Add 2 cups water to roasting pan and return to oven for 5 minutes. Scrape bottom of the pan to stir up browned bits. Pour contents of roasting pan into soup pot. Add another 2½ quarts water, parsley, thyme, bay leaf, peppercorns, and giblets. Bring to a boil over medium heat, skimming off foam as it rises.

2. Reduce heat, partially cover pan, and simmer about 2 hours, adding water if needed to keep bones and vegetables covered. Strain stock through a fine-mesh sieve. Season with salt to taste. Let cool, then refrigerate at least 1 hour. Lift off and discard solidified fat.

113 CHICKEN ALPHABET SOUP

Prep: 15 minutes   Cook: 27 to 28 minutes   Serves: 4

Kids love alphabet macaroni, but other fanciful shapes such as wagon wheels or bow ties can be substituted.

1 medium onion, chopped	1½ cups frozen mixed
2 garlic cloves, crushed	vegetables
through a press	⅓ cup alphabet macaroni
2 tablespoons olive oil	2 cups cooked chicken, cut
5 cups chicken broth	into bite-sized pieces
1 (14½-ounce) can stewed	¼ cup chopped parsley
tomatoes	Salt and freshly ground
2 teaspoons Italian seasoning	pepper

1. In a large saucepan, cook onion and garlic in olive oil over medium heat until softened, about 5 minutes. Stir in broth, tomatoes, and Italian seasoning. Bring to a boil, reduce heat to medium-low, and simmer, partially covered, 10 minutes.

2. Add vegetables and macaroni. Cook, partially covered, until pasta is nearly tender, about 10 minutes. Add chicken and parsley and simmer 2 to 3 minutes. Season with salt and pepper to taste.

114 ENGLISH PUB CHICKEN AND CHEDDAR SOUP

Prep: 15 minutes   Cook: 15 to 17 minutes   Serves: 4

1 tablespoon butter	1½ cups beer or ale
1 medium onion, chopped	1 cup shredded Cheddar
1 small red bell pepper,	cheese (about 4 ounces)
chopped	2 cups diced cooked chicken
1 small celery rib, chopped	(about ½ pound)
2 (10¾-ounce) cans Cheddar	2 teaspoons Worcestershire
cheese soup	sauce
1½ cups milk	

1. In a large saucepan, melt butter over medium heat. Add onion, bell pepper, and celery and cook, stirring occasionally, until softened, about 5 minutes.

2. Add soup, milk, and beer. Bring to a boil, stirring, over medium-high heat. Reduce heat to medium-low and simmer, uncovered, 8 to 10 minutes to reduce slightly.

3. Remove pan from heat and add cheese, stirring until melted. Stir in chicken and Worcestershire sauce. Heat gently until warm, about 2 minutes.

115   CHICKEN AND CORN CHOWDER

Prep: 15 minutes   Cook: 30 to 32 minutes   Serves: 4 to 6

This soup tastes like summer, but is especially good on a cold winter night. With the choice of fresh or frozen corn, you can make it any season of the year.

3 slices of bacon, cut into 1-inch pieces
1 medium onion, chopped
1 celery rib, chopped
1 small red bell pepper, chopped
1 pound all-purpose potatoes, cut into ½-inch dice
4 cups chicken broth
1 teaspoon dried thyme

3 cups cubed cooked chicken (about ¾ pound)
3 cups fresh or frozen corn kernels
2 cups half-and-half or light cream
½ teaspoon freshly ground pepper
Salt

1. In a large saucepan, fry bacon over medium heat, stirring occasionally, until crisp, about 5 minutes. Remove bacon with a slotted spoon and drain on paper towel.

2. Add onion, celery, and bell pepper to pan drippings. Cook, stirring, until tender, about 5 minutes. Add potatoes, broth, and thyme. Simmer, partially covered, 15 minutes, or until potatoes are just tender.

3. Add chicken, corn, and half-and-half. Simmer, uncovered, until soup is hot and corn is tender, 5 to 7 minutes. Season with pepper and salt to taste. Garnish with bacon.

116   BRUNSWICK SOUP

Prep: 10 minutes   Cook: 25 minutes   Serves: 4 to 6

A quick and easy soup with all the flavors of the old-fashioned stew by the same name.

1 large onion, chopped
2 tablespoons vegetable oil
1 pound skinless, boneless chicken thighs, cut into 1-inch cubes
8 cups chicken broth
1 (14½-ounce) can stewed tomatoes

1½ cups frozen baby lima beans
1 cup frozen sliced okra
⅔ cup converted white rice
2 teaspoons dried thyme
1 tablespoon Worcestershire sauce
½ teaspoon Tabasco or other hot sauce

1. In a large saucepan, cook onion in oil over medium heat until softened, about 5 minutes. Add chicken, broth, stewed tomatoes, lima beans, okra, rice, and thyme. Bring to a boil, reduce heat to medium-low, and cook, partially covered, until rice is tender, about 20 minutes.

2. Season with Worcestershire and Tabasco.

117   TEN-MINUTE CHICKEN NOODLE SOUP
Prep: 5 minutes   Cook: 5 minutes   Serves: 4

8 cups chicken broth	4 ounces uncooked fine egg
1½ teaspoons poultry seasoning	noodles (about 1 cup)
1 pound skinless, boneless	Salt and freshly ground
chicken breasts, cut into	pepper
1-inch pieces	
1 (10-ounce) package frozen	
mixed vegetables	
(1¾ cups)	

In a large saucepan, bring broth and poultry seasoning to a boil over high heat. Add chicken, frozen vegetables, and noodles. Reduce heat to medium-low, cover pan, and simmer until chicken is cooked through and noodles are tender, about 5 minutes. Season with salt and pepper to taste before serving.

118   GOLDEN BUTTERMILK CHICKEN SOUP
Prep: 15 minutes   Cook: 30 minutes   Serves: 4

3½ pounds butternut squash	1 tablespoon olive oil
(about 2 squash), peeled,	4½ cups chicken broth
seeded, and cut into	2 teaspoons grated fresh
1-inch pieces	ginger
3 leeks (white and tender	1½ teaspoons grated orange zest
green), well rinsed and	½ teaspoon dried sage
thickly sliced	2 cups chopped cooked
3 carrots, cut into 1-inch	chicken
chunks	2 cups buttermilk
1 large celery rib, cut into	Salt and freshly ground
1-inch chunks	pepper

1. In a food processor, coarsely chop squash in 2 batches. Set aside. Coarsely chop leeks, carrots, and celery together in food processor.

2. In a large saucepan or flameproof casserole, heat olive oil over medium heat. Add chopped leeks, carrots, and celery and toss to coat vegetables with oil. Add ½ cup of broth, ginger, orange zest, and sage. Cover pan, reduce heat to low, and cook 10 minutes, stirring occasionally. Add chopped squash and remaining 4 cups broth. Raise heat to medium-low and simmer, covered, until vegetables are soft, about 15 minutes.

3. Use a slotted spoon to remove and reserve 1 cup of cooked vegetables. In batches, puree remaining soup and vegetables until smooth. Return to pan along with reserved vegetables, chicken, and buttermilk. Cook over medium-low heat until hot, about 5 minutes. Do not let boil or buttermilk may curdle. Season with salt and pepper to taste and serve.

119 HOT AND SPICY CHICKEN SOUP
Prep: 10 minutes   Cook: 22 minutes   Serves: 4

This is a simple version of a very complex soup. Adjust the heat by toning down the use of the chili and sesame oils.

2 garlic cloves, crushed through a press
1 tablespoon minced fresh ginger
1 tablespoon vegetable oil
8 cups chicken broth
½ cup converted white rice
1 pound skinless, boneless chicken breasts or thighs, thinly sliced

4 ounces fresh shiitake or white mushrooms, sliced (2 cups)
⅔ cup thinly sliced scallions
1 tablespoon Asian sesame oil
1 tablespoon hot chili oil
1 teaspoon soy sauce
1 tablespoon fresh lemon juice

1. In a large saucepan, cook garlic and ginger in oil over medium-low heat, stirring constantly, 1 minute. Add broth and rice; bring to a boil over high heat. Reduce heat to medium-low and simmer, covered, 15 minutes.

2. Add chicken, mushrooms, half of scallions, sesame oil, chili oil, and soy sauce. Simmer, partially covered, until chicken is cooked through and rice is tender, about 6 minutes. Stir in lemon juice.

3. Serve hot, with remaining scallions sprinkled on top.

120 GREEK LEMON CHICKEN SOUP
Prep: 5 minutes   Cook: 15 to 21 minutes   Serves: 4 to 6

This is a classic Greek soup called avgolemono, which takes only minutes to make. Don't allow the soup to boil after you swirl in the eggs or it may curdle.

7 cups chicken broth
½ teaspoon freshly ground pepper
¼ cup orzo or converted white rice
3 eggs
¼ cup fresh lemon juice

1½ cups chopped cooked chicken
3 tablespoons chopped fresh dill or chives
Salt
4 to 6 paper-thin slices of lemon

1. In a nonreactive medium saucepan, bring broth and pepper to a boil. Add orzo or rice, cover, and cook until tender, 12 to 14 minutes for orzo, about 18 minutes for rice.

2. In a small bowl, whisk eggs with the lemon juice until blended. Slowly whisk in 1 cup of hot broth. Over low heat, whisk egg mixture back into broth. Cook over low heat, stirring, 2 minutes. Add chicken and heat 1 minute. Stir in dill and season with salt to taste. Garnish each portion with a lemon slice.

121 VELVET CREAM OF CHICKEN SOUP

Prep: 10 minutes   Cook: 19 to 20 minutes   Serves: 6

The saffron lends a rich golden hue to this simple soup. Turmeric, which is an alternative, gives the same color but a less distinctive flavor.

- 4 tablespoons butter
- ¼ cup flour
- ¼ teaspoon crushed saffron threads or ground turmeric
- 8 cups chicken broth
- ¼ teaspoon ground mace or grated nutmeg
- ¼ teaspoon ground white pepper
- 2 cups half-and-half or light cream
- 4 cups cooked cubed chicken (about 1 pound)
- Salt
- 6 tablespoons chopped chives

1. In a large saucepan, melt butter over medium heat. Add flour and saffron and cook, stirring, 2 minutes. Slowly whisk in broth, mace, and white pepper. Cook, stirring frequently, until soup base comes to a boil and thickens, about 5 minutes.

2. Reduce heat to medium-low and stir in half-and-half. Simmer 10 minutes.

3. Add cubed chicken and season with salt to taste. Simmer 2 to 3 minutes, until chicken is heated through. Ladle into bowls and sprinkle 1 tablespoon chives over each portion.

122 CHINESE CHICKEN SOUP WITH WONTON NOODLES

Prep: 10 minutes   Cook: 7 minutes   Serves: 4

Instead of filled wontons, the wonton skins and other ingredients are added separately here to make a soup that is really quick and easy. Any brand or combination of frozen oriental vegetables will work nicely.

- 6 cups chicken broth, preferably reduced-sodium
- 2 tablespoons soy sauce
- 1 teaspoon Asian sesame oil
- 1 teaspoon grated fresh ginger
- 2 cups packaged fresh or frozen mixed oriental vegetables
- 6 wonton skins, cut into thin strips
- 1 cup thinly sliced cooked chicken
- ½ cup thinly sliced scallions

1. In a large saucepan, bring broth, soy sauce, sesame oil, ginger, and oriental vegetables to a boil over high heat. Reduce heat to medium-low and simmer, partially covered, until vegetables are just tender, about 5 minutes.

2. Add wonton skins and chicken. Cook 2 minutes. Stir in scallions and serve at once.

123   CHICKEN AND CHICK-PEA GAZPACHO

Prep: 10 minutes   Cook: none   Chill: 1 hour   Serves: 4 to 6

2 pounds fresh tomatoes, seeded and cut into 2-inch chunks
4 slices of French bread, torn into pieces
2 garlic cloves
¼ cup red wine vinegar
⅓ cup extra-virgin olive oil
4 cups tomato juice or vegetable juice cocktail
3 cups chicken broth
3 tablespoons chopped fresh basil
1 tablespoon Worcestershire sauce

½ teaspoon Tabasco, or more to taste
Salt
1 large green bell pepper, coarsely chopped
1 large sweet onion, coarsely chopped
1 cucumber, seeded and coarsely chopped
3 cups diced cooked chicken (about ¾ pound)
1 cup chick-peas (garbanzo beans), rinsed and drained

1. In a food processor, coarsely puree tomatoes, bread, and garlic. Add vinegar and olive oil and puree until smooth. Pour into a mixing bowl.

2. Stir tomato juice, broth, basil, Worcestershire, and Tabasco into tomato-bread puree. Season with salt to taste. Cover and refrigerate for at least 1 hour, until cold.

3. Stir in green pepper, onion, cucumber, chicken, and chick-peas. Serve immediately or chill up to 4 hours.

124   CHICKEN SOUP WITH MATZO BALLS

Prep: 10 minutes   Chill: 30 minutes   Cook: 35 to 45 minutes   Serves: 6

Chicken fat is traditional in matzo balls, but the vegetable oil used here is more contemporary, and cooking in broth instead of water adds good flavor.

3 eggs
3 tablespoons vegetable oil or rendered chicken fat
¾ cup matzo meal
1 teaspoon salt

½ teaspoon freshly ground pepper
5 quarts chicken broth
2 cups chopped cooked chicken (optional)

1. In a bowl, whisk together eggs and oil. Stir in matzo meal, salt, and pepper. Whisk in 3 tablespoons of broth. Cover and refrigerate 30 minutes.

2. In a 3- or 4-quart pot, bring 2 quarts of broth to a boil. Form dough into rough 1½-inch balls and drop into boiling broth. Reduce heat to medium-low, cover pot, and simmer until matzo balls are cooked through and no longer doughy in center, 30 to 40 minutes. Remove with a slotted spoon and use immediately or reserve for up to 4 hours.

3. To serve, heat remaining broth and drop in matzo balls and optional chicken. Simmer until heated through, about 5 minutes.

---

125 CHICKEN MINESTRONE
Prep: 15 minutes   Cook: 57 to 59 minutes   Serves: 6

Though this is usually a meatless soup, the addition of chicken makes it better and even more nutritious. Thrify Italians add the hard rind from the end of a wedge of Parmesan cheese to enrich the soup.

4 ounces Parmesan cheese, in 1 piece, preferably with rind
1 large onion, chopped
1 large celery rib, chopped
1 large carrot, chopped
2 garlic cloves, crushed through a press
3 tablespoons olive oil
1 (16-ounce) can tomatoes, with their juices
6 cups chicken broth
1½ pounds chicken thighs
1 tablespoon Italian seasoning

¼ teaspoon crushed hot red pepper
1 large potato (about 6 ounces), diced
½ cup ditali or other small tubular pasta
3 cups thinly sliced green cabbage, preferably savoy (about 6 ounces)
½ pound fresh green beans, cut into 1-inch pieces
1 (15-ounce) can undrained white cannellini beans
Salt and freshly ground pepper

1. Cut rind (if any) from cheese and reserve rind. Grate cheese.

2. In a large saucepan, cook onion, celery, carrot, and garlic in olive oil over medium heat, stirring frequently, until vegetables are softened, 5 to 7 minutes. Add tomatoes with their juices, broth, chicken, Italian seasoning, and hot pepper. Cover and simmer until chicken is cooked through, about 30 minutes.

3. Remove chicken and let stand until cool enough to handle. Pull meat from bones and tear into bite-sized pieces; discard skin and bones.

4. Add potato, cheese rind, and pasta to soup. Boil, uncovered, 10 minutes. Add cabbage, green beans, and cannellini beans. Simmer 10 minutes. Remove and discard cheese rind and return chicken to soup. Simmer 2 minutes to heat through. Stir in grated cheese. Season with salt and pepper to taste.

126   MEXICAN CHICKEN TORTILLA SOUP

Prep: 10 minutes   Cook: 14 to 16 minutes   Serves: 4

1 large onion, chopped
1½ tablespoons vegetable oil
1 garlic clove, chopped
2 (2-ounce) cans chopped green chiles
1 fresh jalapeño pepper, minced
1 teaspoon ground cumin
6 cups chicken broth
1 (14½-ounce) can Mexican-style stewed tomatoes

¾ pound skinless, boneless chicken breasts or thighs, sliced
3 tablespoons chopped cilantro
2 teaspoons lime juice
Salt and freshly ground pepper
4 ounces shredded Monterey Jack cheese (about 1 cup)
2 cups tortilla chips

1. In a large saucepan, cook onion in oil over medium heat until softened, 3 to 5 minutes. Add garlic, chiles, jalapeño pepper, and cumin. Cook, stirring, 1 minute. Add broth and tomatoes and bring to a boil. Add chicken, reduce heat to medium-low, and simmer, uncovered, 10 minutes.

2. Stir in cilantro and lime juice. Season with salt and pepper to taste. Serve in shallow bowls, sprinkled with cheese and tortilla chips.

127   GUACAMOLE SOUP WITH CHICKEN SALSA

Prep: 10 minutes   Cook: none   Chill: 2 hours   Serves: 6

If you like guacamole, you'll love this almost-instant, cooling summer soup. Serve with a basket of corn tortilla chips on the side.

4 ripe avocados, peeled and pitted
¼ cup lime juice
2 tablespoons lemon juice
4 cups chicken broth
3 cups half-and-half or light cream

½ teaspoon ground white pepper
¼ teaspoon ground cumin
Salt
1½ cups bottled chunky salsa
2 cups diced cooked chicken

1. In a food processor, puree avocado with lime juice and lemon juice. Add broth, half-and-half, white pepper, and cumin. Puree until smooth and creamy. Season with salt to taste. Cover and refrigerate until well chilled, about 2 hours.

2. Stir together salsa and chicken. Ladle cold soup into 6 shallow bowls. Top each with about ½ cup chicken salsa.

128   CHICKEN PASTA E FAGIOLE
Prep: 15 minutes   Cook: 63 to 66 minutes   Serves: 6

This thick, hearty Italian soup is made even better with the untraditional addition of chicken.

1 (3-pound) chicken, cut up	1 teaspoon dried rosemary
4 cups chicken broth	1 teaspoon dried marjoram
1 large onion, chopped	¼ teaspoon crushed hot red
2 medium carrots, peeled and	pepper
chopped	1 cup ditali or other small
2 celery ribs, chopped	tubular pasta (about 3
3 tablespoons olive oil	ounces)
2 garlic cloves, crushed	½ cup chopped parsley
through a press	¼ cup grated Parmesan cheese
1 (16-ounce) can tomatoes,	Salt and freshly ground
with their juices	pepper
2 (15-ounce) cans white	
cannellini beans, drained	

1. In a large saucepan, simmer chicken in broth, partially covered, 45 minutes. Remove chicken and let cool; remove meat from bones and discard bones. Reserve broth; skim off grease.

2. In a large saucepan, cook onion, carrots, and celery in olive oil over medium heat, stirring frequently, until softened, about 5 minutes. Add garlic and cook 1 minute. Add tomatoes with their juices, beans, rosemary, marjoram, hot pepper, reserved chicken broth, and 3 cups water.

3. Bring to a boil, reduce heat to medium-low, and add pasta. Simmer, partially covered, until pasta is tender, 12 to 15 minutes. Stir in parsley and cheese. Season with salt and pepper to taste.

129   QUICK CHICKEN TORTELLINI SOUP
Prep: 5 minutes   Cook: 13 to 14 minutes   Serves: 4

Frozen chicken tortellini are a great convenience food.

3 garlic cloves, chopped	10 ounces fresh spinach, thinly
2 tablespoons olive oil	sliced (about 6 cups)
8 cups chicken broth	¼ cup grated Parmesan cheese
1 teaspoon Italian seasoning	Freshly ground pepper
1 pound chicken tortellini	

1. In a large saucepan, cook garlic in olive oil over medium heat until fragrant, 1 to 2 minutes. Add chicken broth and Italian seasoning; bring to a boil over high heat. Add tortellini, reduce heat to medium, and simmer, partially covered, until pasta is tender but still firm, about 10 minutes.

2. Add spinach and simmer until wilted, about 2 minutes. Stir in cheese and season with pepper to taste. Serve at once.

130   SICILIAN CHICKEN SOUP WITH ESCAROLE AND PASTINA

Prep: 10 minutes   Cook: 52 minutes   Serves: 4

1 (3-pound) chicken, cut up
2 leeks (white part only), rinsed and cut into 1-inch lengths
2 carrots, quartered
1 celery rib, quartered
2 teaspoons dried oregano

4 cups chicken broth
⅔ cup pastina or tubettini
½ pound escarole, thinly sliced (about 5 cups)
   Salt and freshly ground pepper
¼ cup grated Parmesan cheese

1. In a large soup pot, simmer chicken (including back and neck), leeks, carrots, celery, oregano, broth, and 4 cups water for 45 minutes. Remove chicken and let cool; pull meat from bones, discarding bones. Strain broth; skim off grease.

2. In a large saucepan, bring broth to a boil. Add pastina and cook 5 minutes. Add chicken and escarole and simmer 2 minutes, or until escarole is wilted. Season with salt and pepper to taste. Sprinkle 1 tablespoon grated cheese over each portion.

131   CHICKEN VICHYSSOISE

Prep: 10 minutes   Cook: 20 minutes   Serves: 4

This classic French potato soup is usually served cold, but it is just as good hot on a chilly day. Cooked chicken adds texture and makes this a main course.

2 tablespoons butter
4 medium leeks (white part only), chopped
1½ pounds all-purpose potatoes, peeled and diced
6 cups chicken broth
1 cup half-and-half or light cream

3 cups diced cooked chicken (about ¾ pound)
½ teaspoon grated white pepper
⅛ teaspoon grated nutmeg
   Salt
¼ cup minced chives

1. In a large saucepan, melt butter over medium-low heat. Add leeks and cook, stirring frequently, until softened, about 5 minutes. Add potatoes and 3 cups of broth. Bring to a boil over high heat. Reduce heat to medium and simmer, partially covered, until potatoes are tender, about 15 minutes.

2. In batches, puree soup in a food processor until smooth. Return to saucepan and add remaining 3 cups broth, half-and-half, chicken, white pepper, and nutmeg. Season with salt to taste.

3. If serving hot, return soup to a simmer. If serving cold, refrigerate at least 2 hours, until well chilled. Sprinkle each serving with chives.

132   CHICKEN SOUP PRIMAVERA
Prep: 10 minutes   Cook: 5 minutes   Serves: 6

This is verdant soup to celebrate the first of the spring vegetables. It makes a lovely light first course.

8 cups chicken broth
1 teaspoon dried tarragon
½ teaspoon grated lemon zest
¼ pound baby carrots or
   3 slender carrots, cut
   into 1-inch lengths
¼ pound slender asparagus,
   cut into 1-inch diagonal
   pieces
3 ounces snow peas, strings
   removed

½ cup frozen baby green peas
12 ounces skinless, boneless
   chicken breasts, thinly
   sliced
½ cup thinly sliced scallions
1 tablespoon fresh lemon
   juice
Salt and freshly ground
   pepper

1. In a large saucepan, bring broth, tarragon, and lemon zest to a boil over high heat. Add carrots and cook 2 minutes. Add asparagus, snow peas, green peas, and chicken and simmer until chicken is tender and white, about 3 minutes.

2. Stir in scallions and lemon juice. Season with salt and pepper to taste and serve.

133   SHORT-CUT MULLIGATAWNY SOUP
Prep: 10 minutes   Cook: 25 minutes   Serves: 4

A classic Indian soup is here made so quickly and easily that you can serve it anytime.

3 tablespoons butter
1 medium onion, chopped
1 carrot, chopped
1 red bell pepper, chopped
1 celery rib, chopped
1 large tart apple, unpeeled,
   coarsely chopped
1 tablespoon curry powder
⅛ teaspoon ground cloves

4 cups chicken broth
½ cup quick-cooking brown
   rice
2 cups diced cooked chicken
1 (14½-ounce) can stewed
   tomatoes
Salt and freshly ground
   pepper

1. In a large saucepan, melt butter over medium heat. Add onion, carrot, bell pepper, and celery and cook until softened, about 5 minutes. Add apple, curry powder, cloves, and broth. Simmer, covered, 10 minutes.

2. Add brown rice, chicken, and stewed tomatoes. Simmer, uncovered, until rice is tender, about 10 minutes. Season with salt and pepper to taste.

134   COCK-A-LEEKIE
Prep: 30 minutes   Cook: 1 hour 10 minutes   Serves: 6

Prunes are traditional in this chicken and leek soup, and they add a pleasing hint of sweetness.

6 cups chicken broth	8 whole peppercorns
1 (3-pound) chicken, cut into 8 pieces	2 tablespoons butter
1 onion, quartered	6 medium leeks (white and tender green), rinsed and sliced
1 carrot, cut into 1-inch pieces	
1 celery rib, cut into 1-inch pieces	¾ cup quick-cooking barley
¼ cup parsley sprigs plus ¼ cup chopped parsley	6 pitted prunes
	Salt and freshly ground pepper
1 bay leaf, broken	

1. In a large soup pot, combine broth, 4 cups of water, chicken (including back and neck), onion, carrot, celery, parsley sprigs, bay leaf, and peppercorns. Bring to a boil over high heat, skimming off foam as it rises to surface. Reduce heat to medium-low, cover pan, and simmer until chicken is tender and cooked through, about 45 minutes.

2. Remove chicken from broth, let cool, and pull meat from bones, tearing it into bite-sized pieces. Strain broth, then skim off fat. (Or make a day ahead and refrigerate, then lift off solidified fat.)

3. In a large saucepan, melt butter over medium-low heat. Add leeks, cover, and cook, stirring occasionally, until softened, about 5 minutes. Add reserved broth and barley. Bring to a boil, reduce heat to medium-low, and cook, partially covered, 15 minutes. Add prunes and chicken and simmer, uncovered, 5 minutes. Season with salt and pepper to taste. Stir in chopped parsley just before serving.

135 WILD RICE AND MUSHROOM CHICKEN SOUP

Prep: 20 minutes   Cook: 1½ hours   Serves: 6

8 cups chicken broth
1 cup dry white wine
2½ pounds chicken thighs
1 medium onion, quartered
1 large celery rib, quartered
1 garlic clove, halved
10 whole peppercorns
4 whole cloves
1 large bay leaf, broken in half
1½ teaspoons dried thyme
1 cup wild rice
3 carrots, thinly sliced

6 ounces fresh shiitake mushrooms, stemmed, caps sliced
1 cup heavy cream or half-and-half
⅓ cup chopped parsley
3 tablespoons dry sherry or Madeira
1 tablespoon Worcestershire sauce
Salt and freshly ground pepper

1. In a large soup pot, combine broth, wine, chicken, onion, celery, garlic, peppercorns, cloves, bay leaf, thyme, and 2 cups water. Bring to a boil over high heat. Skim off any foam as it rises. Reduce heat to medium, cover pot, and simmer until chicken is tender, about 40 minutes.

2. Remove chicken from pot; let cool, then pull meat from bones and tear into bite-sized pieces. Strain broth; let cool, then skim off fat. (Or make ahead, refrigerate, and lift off solidified fat.)

3. In a large saucepan, bring defatted broth to a boil. Add wild rice, partially cover pan, reduce heat to medium-low, and simmer 30 minutes. Add carrots, mushrooms, chicken meat, and cream. Cover and simmer until carrots and rice are tender, about 20 minutes.

4. Stir in parsley, sherry, and Worcestershire. Season with salt and pepper to taste and serve.

136   QUICK CHICKEN AND BROWN RICE SOUP
Prep: 10 minutes   Cook: 20 minutes   Serves: 4 to 6

You can use leftover cooked chicken here, if you have it. Quick-cooking brown rice is a great new product to keep on hand for when time is short.

1 large onion, chopped
2 garlic cloves, chopped
1 tablespoon vegetable oil
1½ teaspoons dried savory
4 cups chicken broth
2 (14½-ounce) cans stewed tomatoes
1 cup quick-cooking brown rice

¾ pound skinless, boneless chicken thighs, cut into 1-inch pieces
2 cups frozen mixed vegetables
Salt and freshly ground pepper

1. In a large saucepan, cook onion and garlic in oil over medium heat until softened, about 5 minutes. Add savory, broth, stewed tomatoes, brown rice, and chicken. Bring to a boil, reduce heat, and simmer, partially covered, 10 minutes.

2. Add mixed vegetables and simmer 5 minutes. Season with salt and pepper to taste before serving.

137   CREAMY MINTED PEA AND CHICKEN SOUP
Prep: 15 minutes   Cook: 20 to 23 minutes   Serves: 4

Whether you serve it hot or cold, this is a fine way to highlight leftover chicken.

2 tablespoons butter
3 medium leeks (white part only), chopped (about 2 cups)
¾ pound all-purpose potatoes, peeled and diced
6 cups chicken broth
3 cups frozen peas
¼ cup chopped fresh mint or 2 teaspoons dried

1 cup half-and-half or light cream
3 cups cubed cooked chicken (about ¾ pound)
½ teaspoon Tabasco, or to taste
Salt and freshly ground pepper

1. In a large saucepan, melt butter over medium heat. Add leeks and cook, stirring occasionally, until softened, about 5 minutes. Add potatoes and 3 cups of broth. Bring to a boil, reduce heat to medium, and simmer, uncovered, 10 minutes.

2. Add peas and simmer until potatoes are tender, 5 to 8 minutes longer. Stir in mint.

3. In batches, puree soup in a food processor until smooth. Return to pan and add remaining 3 cups of broth, half-and-half, chicken, and Tabasco. Season with salt and pepper to taste. If serving hot, return to a simmer. If serving cold, refrigerate at least 2 hours until well chilled.

---

138   THAI CHICKEN AND LEMONGRASS SOUP
Prep: 10 minutes   Cook: 7 minutes   Serves: 6

Unsweetened coconut milk and lemongrass are both available in many supermarkets and in Asian food stores.

1   tablespoon vegetable oil, preferably peanut oil
½   pound thinly sliced skinless, boneless chicken breast, cut into ½-inch strips
1   garlic clove, minced
1   carrot, thinly sliced
¼   cup finely chopped lemongrass stalks or 1 tablespoon grated lemon zest
2   tablespoons minced fresh ginger
2   teaspoons minced fresh or canned jalapeño pepper

8   cups chicken broth
1   (14-ounce) can unsweetened coconut milk
2   ounces fresh shiitake mushrooms, stemmed and thinly sliced (1 cup), or 1 cup drained canned straw mushrooms
2   stalks of bok choy with leaves, thinly sliced on the diagonal (about 2 cups)
¼   pound soba noodles or capellini
½   cup thinly sliced scallions
2   tablespoons lime juice

In a large saucepan, heat oil over high heat. Add chicken and cook, stirring, 2 minutes. Add garlic and cook 30 seconds. Add carrot, lemongrass, ginger, jalapeño, broth, and coconut milk. Bring to a boil. Add mushrooms, bok choy, and noodles. Cook until pasta is tender, about 4 minutes. Stir in scallions and lime juice and serve at once.

Chapter 7

A Chicken in Every Pot

"A chicken in every pot" was an effective campaign slogan because everyone could relate to it. There are few things more warming, comforting, and secure than coming home to a house filled with the fragrance of a simmering chicken stew. Since braised and stewed chicken dishes are popular in every major cuisine, the feeling must be universal.

With a few exceptions, the process of stewing or braising is based on browning the chicken and perhaps some aromatic vegetables such as onions and garlic in a little oil or butter, adding a small amount of liquid and seasoning, then cooking the mixture covered on the stovetop or in the oven until all ingredients have blended to a flavorful finish.

Stews are very forgiving, which means they taste just as good if cooked longer than directed, often taste better reheated the next day, and allow for all sorts of ingredient substitutions. This also adds to the comforting nature of making a stew, especially for novice cooks. So, if you are just starting out, this might be a good place to begin.

139   HUNGARIAN CHICKEN STEW
Prep: 10 minutes   Cook: 48 to 53 minutes   Serves: 4 to 6

Serve this easy goulash variation with buttered wide noodles.

1 chicken (about 3 pounds),
    cut into 8 pieces
½ teaspoon salt
¼ teaspoon freshly ground
    pepper
2 tablespoons vegetable oil
1 large onion, thinly sliced
1 tablespoon Hungarian
    sweet paprika

2 cups chicken broth
¼ cup dry white wine
¼ cup tomato paste
½ teaspoon dried savory
½ teaspoon caraway seeds
1 cup drained sauerkraut
⅔ cup sour cream

1. Season chicken lightly with salt and pepper. In a large Dutch oven, heat oil over medium-high heat. Add chicken and cook, turning once or twice, until browned, about 8 minutes. Remove from pan.

2. Reduce heat to medium. Add onion and cook, stirring occasionally, until golden, about 7 minutes. Sprinkle paprika over onion and cook, stirring, 1 minute. Stir in broth, wine, tomato paste, savory, caraway seeds, and sauerkraut.

3. Return chicken to pan. Reduce heat to medium-low, cover, and simmer until chicken is tender and white to bone, 30 to 35 minutes.

4. Stir in sour cream. Cook, uncovered, about 2 minutes, to heat through, but do not let boil.

---

140   CIDER-BRAISED CHICKEN AND TURNIPS
Prep: 20 minutes   Cook: 1 hour 16 minutes   Serves: 4 to 6

¼ cup flour
½ teaspoon salt
½ teaspoon freshly ground
    pepper
1 chicken (about 3 pounds),
    cut into 8 pieces
3 tablespoons vegetable oil
1 large onion, chopped
1 carrot, chopped
1 celery rib, chopped
3 garlic cloves, crushed
    through a press

1½ teaspoons dried thyme
1 bay leaf
1½ cups apple cider
½ cup dry red wine
2 medium turnips, peeled and
    cubed
1 large tart green apple, cored
    and cubed
2 to 3 tablespoons red wine
    vinegar

1. Combine flour, salt, and pepper in a plastic bag. Add chicken a few pieces at a time and shake to coat lightly with flour. In a large Dutch oven, heat 2 tablespoons of oil over medium-high heat. Add chicken in 2 batches and cook, turning once or twice, until browned all over, about 8 minutes per batch. Remove chicken from pan.

2. Reduce heat to medium. Add onion, carrot, celery, and garlic. Cook, stirring often, until vegetables are softened, about 5 minutes. Add thyme, bay leaf, cider, and wine. Return chicken to pan, bring to a simmer, reduce heat to medium-low, and cook, covered, 30 minutes.

3. Meanwhile, heat remaining 1 tablespoon oil in a medium frying pan. Add turnips and apple and cook over medium-low heat, stirring often, until slightly glazed and nearly tender, about 10 minutes.

4. Add turnips, apple, and 2 tablespoons of vinegar to stew. Simmer, partially covered, 15 minutes. Remove and discard bay leaf. Taste and add additional vinegar if needed, depending upon sweetness of cider. Season with additional salt and pepper to taste before serving.

---

141   BOILED DINNER
Prep: 15 minutes   Cook: 1 hour 5 to 10 minutes   Serves: 6

¼ cup mayonnaise
¼ cup grainy Dijon mustard
10 whole peppercorns
4 whole cloves
6 sprigs parsley
1 bay leaf, broken in half
1 chicken (about 3 pounds), quartered
4 cups chicken broth
1 teaspoon dried thyme
2 cups baby carrots (about 6 ounces)

3 celery ribs, cut into 2-inch chunks
2 parsnips, peeled and cut into 1-inch chunks
½ pound small red potatoes
1½ cups frozen pearl onions
1 pound turkey or veal sausage, cut into 6 pieces
Salt and freshly ground pepper

1. In a small bowl, blend mayonnaise and mustard. Refrigerate until ready to use. Tie peppercorns, cloves, parsley, and bay leaf in a piece of cheesecloth.

2. Place chicken in a deep soup kettle. Add spice bag, broth, thyme, and enough water to cover chicken. Bring to a boil, skimming off any foam that rises to surface. Reduce heat to medium-low, cover, and simmer 30 minutes. Add carrots, celery, parsnips, potatoes, onions, and sausage. Cover and simmer until vegetables are tender, about 30 minutes longer.

3. Remove chicken, sausage, and vegetables from pot. Remove skin from chicken and when it is cool enough, pull meat from bones in large pieces; discard skin and bones. Arrange vegetables, sausage, and chicken pieces on a large, deep serving platter; cover with foil to keep warm.

4. Skim fat from broth, then boil to reduce by about one-fourth, 5 to 10 minutes. Strain broth and season with salt and pepper to taste. Ladle about 1 cup of broth over boiled dinner to moisten and warm. Serve chicken and vegetables in bowls with more of broth. Serve mustard sauce separately to stir into each serving.

142   COUNTRY CHICKEN STEW WITH CELERY SEED DUMPLINGS

Prep: 15 minutes   Cook: 45 minutes   Serves: 4 to 6

Celery seeds can turn bitter over time, so be sure your supply is no more than 6 months old.

4 cups chicken broth
1 chicken (about 3 pounds), cut into 8 pieces, skin removed
4 carrots, peeled and cut into 1-inch chunks
4 celery ribs with leaves, cut into ½-inch chunks
1 small onion, thinly sliced
1 bay leaf
1 teaspoon dried summer savory

Salt and freshly ground pepper
1¼ cups flour
2 tablespoons yellow cornmeal
1½ teaspoons baking powder
½ teaspoon celery seeds
3 tablespoons vegetable shortening
½ cup milk

1. In a large Dutch oven, combine broth and chicken. Simmer over medium heat, uncovered, 10 minutes, skimming off any foam that rises to surface. Add carrots, celery, onion, bay leaf, and savory. Simmer, partially covered, 15 minutes. Skim fat off surface of broth. Season with salt and pepper to taste.

2. In a large bowl, whisk together flour, cornmeal, baking powder, celery seeds, and ½ teaspoon salt. Cut shortening into small pieces and use your fingers to rub it in until mixture resembles coarse meal. Add milk and stir just until a sticky dough forms.

3. Dip a spoon into simmering stew, then spoon out generous tablespoons of dough and drop into stew to make about 12 dumplings. Cover pan and simmer over medium-low heat until dumplings are cooked through, about 20 minutes. Remove and discard bay leaf before serving.

143   CARIBBEAN CHICKEN STEW
Prep: 20 minutes   Cook: 46 minutes   Serves: 6

Curry powder, sweetened coconut cream, and hot peppers give this stew a distinctly Caribbean flavor. Look for cream of coconut in the beverage section of the grocery store.

1 chicken (about 3 pounds), cut into 8 pieces, skin removed	2 teaspoons curry powder
½ teaspoon salt	½ cup canned cream of coconut
¼ teaspoon freshly ground pepper	1 cup chicken broth
2 tablespoons vegetable oil	1 (14½-ounce) can stewed tomatoes
1 large onion, sliced	3 ears of fresh corn, shucked and cut into 3-inch lengths
1 large green bell pepper, cut in thin strips	¼ cup lime juice
2 garlic cloves, crushed through a press	3 tablespoons chopped cilantro
2 Scotch bonnet or jalapeño peppers, seeded and minced	

1. Season chicken lightly with salt and pepper. Heat oil in a Dutch oven and cook chicken over medium-high heat, turning once or twice, until browned, about 8 minutes. Remove from pan. Reduce heat to medium, add onion, bell pepper, and garlic, and cook until onion is softened, about 5 minutes. Add Scotch bonnet peppers, curry powder, cream of coconut, broth, and tomatoes.

2. Return chicken to pan, cover, and simmer 15 minutes. Add corn and simmer, covered, 15 minutes, until corn and chicken are tender and juices run clear when chicken is pricked. Stir in lime juice and cilantro and simmer, uncovered, 3 minutes longer.

144   CHICKEN MARENGO
Prep: 15 minutes   Cook: 44 minutes   Serves: 4

Invented by Napoleon's chef, who cooked it for the general after the battle of Marengo, this now has dozens of variations. Here is a basic one, still a simple and succulent dish to serve after a battle, or anytime at all.

1 chicken (about 3 pounds), cut into 8 pieces	1 (14½-ounce) can plum tomatoes, with their juices
¾ teaspoon salt	
¼ teaspoon freshly ground pepper	½ cup dry white wine
	2 tablespoons tomato paste
3½ tablespoons olive oil	½ pound sliced mushrooms
3 garlic cloves, crushed through a press	½ to 1 teaspoon Tabasco or other hot sauce, to taste
¾ teaspoon dried thyme	¼ cup chopped parsley

1. Season chicken with ½ teaspoon salt and ⅛ teaspoon pepper. In a large Dutch oven, heat 1½ tablespoons of olive oil and cook the chicken over medium-high heat, turning once or twice, until browned, about 8 minutes. Remove from pan. Add garlic and thyme and cook 30 seconds. Stir in tomatoes and juice, wine, and tomato paste. Return chicken to the pan. Reduce heat to medium-low, cover, and simmer 20 minutes.

2. Meanwhile, heat remaining 2 tablespoons olive oil in a large frying pan and cook mushrooms over medium heat, stirring often, until softened, about 5 minutes. Season with remaining ¼ teaspoon each salt and pepper.

3. After chicken has cooked 20 minutes, add mushrooms. Continue to cook until chicken is tender with no trace of pink near bone, about 15 minutes longer. Season with Tabasco and sprinkle with parsley.

145   CHICKEN CARBONNADES
Prep: 15 minutes   Cook: 48 to 54 minutes   Serves: 4

This tasty chicken version of a hearty Belgian specialty usually made with beef comes from the Perdue test kitchens.

2 pounds skinless, boneless chicken thighs	3 tablespoons flour
	1 tablespoon brown sugar
Salt and freshly ground pepper	2 cups beef broth
	1½ cups beer (12-ounce can)
4 slices of bacon, diced	2 tablespons red wine vinegar
3 tablespoons butter	1 tablespoon tomato paste
1 large Spanish onion, thinly sliced	¾ teaspoon dried thyme

1. Season chicken lightly with salt and pepper. In a large Dutch oven, cook bacon over medium heat until just crisp, about 5 minutes. Remove with a slotted spoon and drain on paper towel.

2. Add chicken to drippings in pan, raise heat to medium-high, and cook, turning once or twice, until browned all over, about 8 minutes. Remove chicken from pan. Discard pan drippings.

3. Add butter, onion, flour, and brown sugar to pan. Reduce heat to medium and cook, stirring often, until onion softens and flour turns a rich amber brown, 4 to 5 minutes. Add broth, beer, vinegar, tomato paste, and thyme. Bring to a boil, stirring up browned bits clinging to bottom of pan.

4. Return chicken and bacon to pan. Reduce heat to medium-low and simmer over medium-low heat, partially covered, 20 minutes. Uncover and simmer until sauce is lightly thickened, 10 to 15 minutes longer. Season with salt and pepper to taste before serving.

---

146   CHICKEN AND SAUSAGE RATATOUILLE
Prep: 30 minutes   Cook: 58 minutes   Serves: 6

½ **pound Italian sausage, cut into 6 pieces**
¾ **cup dry red wine or water**
1 **chicken (about 3 pounds), cut into 8 pieces**
½ **teaspoon salt**
¼ **teaspoon freshly ground pepper**
2 **tablespoons olive oil**
1 **large onion, thinly sliced**
3 **large garlic cloves, crushed through a press**
2 **small yellow crookneck squash (about ½ pound total), cut into ½-inch slices**

1 **small eggplant (about ¾ pound), cut into ¾-inch cubes**
1 **green bell pepper, sliced**
¾ **pound plum tomatoes, cut into wedges**
2 **teaspoons drained small capers**
¼ **cup chopped fresh basil**

1. In a large Dutch oven, bring sausage and wine just to a boil. Reduce heat to medium, cover pan, and simmer 5 minutes. Uncover and cook over medium heat, turning sausage frequently, until wine is evaporated and sausage is browned, about 5 minutes longer. Remove sausage from pan.

2. Season chicken with half of salt and pepper. Add olive oil to pan and cook chicken over medium-high heat, turning once or twice, until browned, about 8 minutes. Remove chicken to a plate as it browns.

3. Add onion and garlic to pan. Reduce heat to medium and cook, stirring often, until onion is softened, about 5 minutes. Return chicken and sausage to pan. Add squash and eggplant. Reduce heat to medium-low, cover, and simmer 20 minutes. Add tomatoes and simmer, covered, for 10 minutes. Stir in capers and basil and simmer, uncovered, 5 minutes. Season with remaining salt and pepper and serve.

147   CHICKEN AND MUSSEL CIOPPINO
Prep: 15 minutes   Cook: 25 minutes   Serves: 6

1 pound skinless, boneless
   chicken thighs, cut into
   1½-inch chunks
¼ teaspoon salt
¼ teaspoon freshly ground
   pepper
¼ cup olive oil
2 medium leeks (white and
   tender green), thinly
   sliced
1 small fennel bulb, chopped
1 small green bell pepper,
   chopped

3 garlic cloves, crushed
   through a press
1 teaspoon grated orange zest
1 teaspoon dried thyme
1 (14½-ounce) can stewed
   tomatoes
½ cup dry white wine
½ cup bottled clam juice
3 dozen small mussels,
   scrubbed and debearded

1. Season chicken with salt and pepper. In a large Dutch oven, heat olive oil over medium-high heat. Add chicken and cook, turning once or twice, until browned, about 5 minutes. Remove from pan.

2. Add leeks, fennel, bell pepper, and garlic to pot. Reduce heat to medium and cook, stirring, until leeks are tender, about 5 minutes. Add orange zest, thyme, stewed tomatoes, wine, clam juice, and chicken. Simmer, partially covered, 10 minutes.

3. Add mussels and cook, covered, until mussels open, about 5 minutes.

148   CHICKEN SAUERBRATEN
Prep: 20 minutes   Marinate: 8 to 12 hours   Cook: 58 minutes
Serves: 4 to 6

This is adapted from a recipe developed in the Perdue test kitchens—a wonderful variation on a classic German pot roast. Drumsticks, arguably the most flavorful of all chicken cuts, are the top choice here.

½ cup white wine vinegar or
   cider vinegar
3 medium onions, sliced
½ teaspoon salt
½ teaspoon freshly ground
   pepper
2½ pounds chicken drumsticks,
   skin removed
1 tablespoon vegetable oil

2 cups beef broth
2 tablespoons tomato paste
4 teaspoons lemon juice
4 teaspoons Worcestershire
   sauce
1 tablespoon brown sugar
1 (2-inch) strip lemon peel
6 gingersnaps, crumbled
   (about ½ cup)

1. In a shallow dish, combine vinegar, onions, salt, pepper, and ½ cup water. Add chicken and turn to coat evenly. Cover and refrigerate 8 to 12 hours, turning occasionally.

2. Remove chicken from marinade and pat dry. Reserve marinade. In a large Dutch oven, heat oil over medium-high heat. Cook chicken, turning to brown all over, about 8 minutes. Remove chicken from pan.

3. Add reserved marinade to pan along with broth, tomato paste, lemon juice, Worcestershire, brown sugar, lemon peel, and gingersnaps. Bring to a simmer and return chicken to pan. Reduce heat to medium-low, cover, and simmer, stirring occasionally, until chicken is tender, about 50 minutes.

---

149   CHICKEN, SHRIMP, AND OKRA GUMBO
Prep: 15 minutes   Cook: 29 minutes   Serves: 4

A good roux made by cooking flour in oil until nut-brown is the secret of a good gumbo. Since the clam juice is salty, you probably won't need any added salt.

3 tablespoons vegetable oil	1 cup bottled clam juice
3 tablespoons flour	1 (16-ounce) can tomatoes in
1 cup chopped scallions	juice
1 green bell pepper, chopped	1 teaspoon dried thyme
1 celery rib with leaves,	½ teaspoon cayenne
chopped	¾ pound skinless, boneless
2 garlic cloves, crushed	chicken thighs, cut into
through a press	1-inch chunks
½ pound fresh okra, trimmed	¾ pound peeled and deveined
and sliced, or 1 (10-ounce)	shrimp
package frozen sliced	¼ to ½ teaspoon Tabasco, or to
okra	taste
2 cups chicken broth	2 cups cooked white rice

1. Heat oil in a heavy 3- or 4-quart saucepan. Add flour and cook over medium-high heat, stirring constantly, until rich brown and nutty in fragrance, about 5 minutes. Remove pan from heat.

2. Immediately and carefully—oil may splatter—stir in scallions, green pepper, celery, garlic, and okra. Reduce heat to medium-low and cook, stirring, 1 minute. Add broth, clam juice, tomatoes with their juice, thyme, cayenne, and 1 cup water. Bring to a simmer, stirring and breaking up tomatoes. Add chicken and simmer, uncovered, 20 minutes, stirring occasionally.

3. Add shrimp and simmer until shrimp turn pink, about 3 minutes. Season with Tabasco to taste.

4. To serve, mound rice in shallow bowls. Ladle gumbo over and around rice.

150   BRUNSWICK STEW
Prep: 15 minutes   Cook: 54 to 56 minutes   Serves: 4 to 6

¼ cup flour
½ teaspoon salt
½ teaspoon freshly ground
   pepper
1½ teaspoons dried thyme
3 pounds chicken thighs
1 tablespoon vegetable oil
1 medium onion, thinly sliced
1 (14½-ounce) can stewed
   tomatoes

½ cup chicken broth
1 cup frozen baby lima beans
1 cup frozen sliced okra
1 cup fresh or frozen corn
   kernels
2 teaspoons Worcestershire
   sauce
1 teaspoon Tabasco or other
   hot sauce

1. Combine flour, salt, pepper, and half of thyme in a plastic bag. Add chicken a few pieces at a time and shake to coat lightly with flour. In a Dutch oven, heat oil over medium-high heat. Add chicken in 2 batches and cook, turning once or twice, until browned, about 8 minutes per batch. Remove from pan.

2. Add onion, reduce heat to medium, and cook, stirring occasionally, until softened, 3 to 5 minutes. Return chicken to pan and add tomatoes and broth. Cover and simmer 20 minutes.

3. Add lima beans and okra. Simmer, partially covered, 10 minutes. Add corn and simmer for 5 minutes. Stir in Worcestershire and Tabasco and serve.

151   CHICKEN AND SPRING VEGETABLE STEW
*Prep: 15 minutes   Stand: 20 minutes   Cook: 39 to 41 minutes
Serves: 4*

Leeks, morels, green peas, and asparagus are all culinary signs of spring. If you can't get morels, use any flavorful wild mushroom, such as shiitakes or porcini.

1 ounce dried morels or
   4 ounces fresh morels
4 chicken breast halves, skin
   removed
¼ teaspoon salt
¼ teaspoon freshly ground
   pepper
2 tablespoons butter
2 medium leeks (white and
   pale green), thinly sliced
½ teaspoon dried tarragon

¾ cup dry white wine
⅔ cup chicken broth
¾ cup heavy cream
½ cup small frozen peas
¼ pound slender asparagus,
   trimmed and cut
   diagonally into 1½-inch
   pieces
¼ cup chopped chervil or flat-
   leaf parsley

1. Soak dried morels in boiling water to cover for 20 minutes; drain. Rinse and dry fresh morels. Season chicken with salt and pepper.

2. Melt butter in a large Dutch oven over medium heat. Add chicken and cook, turning once or twice, until pale golden, about 6 minutes. Remove chicken from pan.

3. Reduce heat to medium-low. Add leeks and tarragon to pan, cover, and cook, stirring occasionally, until leeks are softened, about 8 minutes. Add wine and broth. Return chicken to pan. Cover and simmer 20 minutes.

4. Add cream, morels, peas, and asparagus. Simmer, uncovered, until asparagus and morels are just tender and chicken is white to bone, 5 to 7 minutes. Season with salt and pepper to taste. Sprinkle with chervil or parsley before serving.

---

152 STEWED CHICKEN NEVADA
Prep: 20 minutes   Cook: 53 to 58 minutes   Serves: 4 to 6

This recipe comes from a friend who lives in one of the several Basque communities in Nevada and Idaho.

1 **chicken (about 3 pounds), cut into 8 pieces**
½ **teaspoon salt**
¼ **teaspoon freshly ground pepper**
2 **tablespoons olive oil**
1 **large onion, chopped**
1 **celery rib, chopped**
1 **green bell pepper, chopped**
3 **garlic cloves, crushed through a press**
1 **pound waxy potatoes, peeled and cut into 1½-inch chunks**

1 **cup baby carrots**
¼ **pound smoked ham, cut into ½-inch dice**
1½ **cups chicken broth, preferably reduced-sodium**
1 **teaspoon dried thyme**
¼ **teaspoon crushed hot red pepper**
1 **(14½-ounce) can stewed tomatoes**

1. Season chicken with salt and pepper. In a large Dutch oven, heat olive oil and cook the chicken over medium-high heat, turning once or twice, until browned, about 8 minutes. Remove chicken from pan.

2. Add onion, celery, bell pepper, and garlic to pan. Reduce heat to medium and cook until vegetables are softened, about 5 minutes. Add potatoes, carrots, and ham and cook, stirring, until ham is lightly browned, about 5 minutes.

3. Stir in broth, thyme, and hot pepper. Return chicken to the pan. Cover and simmer until chicken is cooked through, 25 to 30 minutes. Add stewed tomatoes and simmer 10 minutes.

153   CHICKEN AND WINTER VEGETABLE RAGOUT

Prep: 15 minutes   Cook: 51 minutes   Serves: 6

Flouring chicken first helps it to brown nicely and also thickens the stew.

¼ **cup flour**	¾ **cup dry white wine**
¼ **teaspoon salt**	2 **teaspoons crumbled dried**
¼ **teaspoon freshly ground**	**leaf sage**
pepper	4 **slim carrots, peeled and cut**
1½ **pounds skinless, boneless**	**into 1-inch chunks**
chicken thighs	2 **small parsnips, peeled and**
2 **tablespoons vegetable oil**	**cut into 1-inch chunks**
1 **garlic clove, crushed**	1½ **cups frozen pearl onions**
through a press	1 **tablespoon Dijon mustard**
2 **cups chicken broth**	¼ **cup chopped parsley**

1. Combine flour, salt, and pepper in a plastic bag. Add chicken a few pieces at a time and shake to coat with flour. In a large frying pan, heat oil. Cook chicken in 2 batches over medium-high heat, stirring often, until lightly browned all over, about 8 minutes per batch.

2. Add garlic and cook 30 seconds. Add broth, wine, 1 teaspoon of the sage, carrots, and parnsips. Reduce heat to medium-low, partially cover pan, and simmer 25 minutes.

3. Add onions, mustard, and remaining 1 teaspoon of sage. Simmer, covered, until onions are tender, about 10 minutes. Sprinkle with parsley.

154   NEW MEXICAN CHICKEN WING AND GREEN CHILE STEW

Prep: 15 minutes   Cook: 1 hour   Serves: 4 to 6

Canned chiles makes this easy. Chicken wings can now be purchased with the tips already removed, which saves a lot of time.

4 **pounds chicken wingettes**	1 **cup chicken broth**
(wings with no tips)	1 **(14½-ounce) can stewed**
1 **teaspoon salt**	**tomatoes**
½ **teaspoon freshly ground**	1 **(4-ounce) can chopped mild**
pepper	**green chiles**
2 **tablespoons vegetable oil**	⅓ **cup sliced black olives**
1 **large onion, chopped**	1 **tablespoon chopped cilantro**
1 **tablespoon chili powder**	**or parsley**
1 **teaspoon ground cumin**	

1. Season chicken with salt and pepper. In a large frying pan, heat oil over medium-high heat. Add chicken in batches and cook, turning once or twice, until browned, about 10 minutes per batch. Remove chicken to a platter as it browns.

2. Add onion to pan, reduce heat to medium, and cook, stirring often, until softened, 3 to 5 minutes. Stir in chili powder and cumin and cook 1 minute. Add broth, tomatoes, and chopped chiles. Return chicken to pan.

3. Reduce heat to medium-low, cover, and simmer until chicken is very tender, about 30 minutes. Add olives and simmer, uncovered, 5 minutes longer to thicken sauce slightly. Stir in cilantro and serve.

155 GREEK CHICKEN AND ARTICHOKE STEW
Prep: 15 minutes   Cook: 48 minutes   Serves: 4 to 6

Frozen artichoke hearts are a boon to busy cooks. They are relatively inexpensive, always available, and require no preparation.

1 chicken (about 3 pounds), cut into 8 pieces
½ teaspoon salt
¼ teaspoon freshly ground pepper
1½ teaspoons dried marjoram
1 teaspoon dried thyme
2 tablespoons olive oil
1 medium onion, chopped
1 small fennel bulb, chopped
1 large garlic clove, minced

1 bay leaf
1 (14½-ounce) can diced tomatoes, with their liquid
½ cup dry white wine
½ cup chicken broth
1 (9-ounce) package frozen artichoke hearts, thawed
1 tablespoon ouzo, Pernod, or other anise liqueur (optional)

1. Season chicken with salt, pepper, ¾ teaspoon marjoram, and ½ teaspoon thyme. Heat olive oil in a Dutch oven. Add chicken and cook over medium-high heat, turning once or twice, until browned on all sides, about 8 minutes. Remove chicken to a plate.

2. Add onion, fennel, and garlic to pan. Reduce heat to medium and cook, stirring often, until onion and fennel are softened, about 5 minutes. Add bay leaf, tomatoes with their liquid, wine, broth, and remaining marjoram and thyme. Add chicken to pan along with any juices that have accumulated on plate.

3. Reduce heat to medium-low, cover, and simmer 30 minutes. Add artichokes and ouzo and simmer, covered, 5 minutes. Remove and discard bay leaf. Season with salt and pepper before serving.

156   BANGKOK CHICKEN STEW
Prep: 30 minutes   Cook: 20 minutes   Serves: 6

The Asian ingredients called for here are available in Asian markets and in many large supermarkets, too.

3   cups canned unsweetened coconut milk
2   cups chicken broth, preferably reduced-sodium
1½ tablespoons finely chopped lemongrass or 1½ teaspoons grated lemon zest
2   teaspoons finely chopped fresh ginger
6   skinless, boneless chicken breast halves
6   ounces fresh shiitake mushrooms, stemmed, caps sliced

6   scallions, cut into 1-inch diagonal slices
1   carrot, peeled and cut into thin julienne strips
¼   cup nam pla (Thai fish sauce)
1   to 2 fresh jalapeño peppers, minced
1   teaspoon honey
½   teaspoon hot chili oil
3   tablespoons slivered fresh basil leaves

1. In a large saucepan, bring coconut milk, broth, lemongrass, and ginger to a boil. Add chicken, cover pan, reduce heat to medium-low, and simmer 10 minutes.

2. Add mushrooms, scallions, carrot, nam pla, jalapeño pepper(s), honey, chili oil, and 2 tablespoons of basil. Simmer, uncovered, 10 minutes. Stir in remaining 1 tablespoon of basil and serve at once.

Chapter 8

Chicken's in the Oven

Baking and roasting are interchangeable terms. In chicken cookery, baking refers to cut-up parts and roasting to the whole bird. Both are done in a shallow pan in the oven, usually uncovered, to allow heat to circulate and crisp and brown the skin nicely. The dry oven heat actually caramelizes the exterior of the chicken to impart the characteristic rich, mellow flavor.

There is nothing quite like a golden brown, juicy roasted chicken. Over the years, I've learned a few tips for best results. I don't truss the bird in the classic manner, but I do tie the legs together with string to prevent the drumsticks from overcooking and drying out. Then I put the chicken on a shallow rack in a pan that is just a little larger than the bird, so that the drippings are concentrated and less likely to evaporate; the intense drippings produce wonderful gravy. I begin cooking the chicken at a high oven temperature to promote browning of the skin and to seal in juices, then reduce the heat for even and thorough cooking. Basting is of dubious value—I've not found basted chickens to be any moister than unbasted ones, and each time you open the oven door, the temperature drops at least 25 degrees. As for doneness, some roasting chickens have their own pop-up timers, but I like to double-check by inserting an instant-reading thermometer into the thigh away from a bone. Finally, I make the gravy right in the roasting pan set over the stove burner, which is a little awkward if the pan is large, but really makes the most of all those caramelized bits in the bottom of the pan that give gravy such great flavor.

There are a few tricks to chicken baking, too. Be sure to use a shallow pan large enough to allow at least 1 inch of space between the chicken parts placed in a single layer. Check for doneness, which means juices should run clear when pricked with a knife tip after the minimum cooking time in order to avoid overcooked, dry chicken. Breast pieces and wings will take less time than thighs and drumsticks.

157   FRESH HERB ROASTED CHICKEN
Prep: 10 minutes   Cook: 1½ hours   Serves: 4

Use any fresh herbs you have on hand or mix a few. I particularly like flat-leaf parsley with thyme, sage, chives, tarragon, or dill.

1 **whole frying chicken (about 3½ pounds)**	**Salt and freshly ground pepper**
1 **cup sprigs of fresh herbs, preferably a mix of 2 or 3 including flat-leaf parsley**	2 **teaspoons butter, softened**
	1 **cup chicken broth**
	¼ **cup dry white wine**

1. Preheat oven to 375°F. Use your fingers to loosen breast skin of chicken. Insert 4 to 6 whole herb sprigs under skin and spread to flatten them. Season chicken inside and out with salt and pepper. Fill chicken cavity with remaining fresh herbs. Tie legs together with kitchen string. Rub butter over skin. Place chicken, breast side up, on a rack in a roasting pan.

2. Roast until skin is a rich golden brown and an instant-reading thermometer inserted into thigh registers 180°, about 1½ hours. Remove chicken to a carving board.

3. Pour off fat from pan. Add broth and wine to pan and bring to a boil over medium heat, stirring up browned bits from bottom of pan. Boil until sauce is slightly reduced, about 5 minutes. Season with salt and pepper to taste.

4. Carve chicken and serve with pan sauce.

158   CHICKEN À L'ORANGE
Prep: 15 minutes   Cook: 2 to 2½ hours   Serves: 6

The classic sauce for duckling is also wonderful with roasted chicken.

1 **roasting chicken (5 to 6 pounds), giblets removed**	2 **lemons**
1 **tablespoon butter, softened**	½ **cup orange juice**
Salt and freshly ground pepper	¼ **cup dry white wine**
2 **oranges**	¼ **cup red currant jelly**
	2 **teaspoons Dijon mustard**
	2 **teaspoons cornstarch**
	1½ **tablespoons Cognac**

1. Preheat oven to 400°F. Rub chicken skin with 1½ teaspoons of butter. Season inside and out with salt and pepper. Cut 1 orange and 1 lemon into quarters and place in chicken cavity. Tie legs together with kitchen string. Place chicken, breast side up, on a rack in a shallow pan. Roast 30 minutes, reduce oven heat to 350°, and continue to roast until an instant-reading thermometer inserted into the thigh registers 180°, 1½ to 2 hours longer.

2. While chicken is roasting, grate 2 teaspoons zest from remaining orange and 1 teaspoon zest from remaining lemon. Peel and section orange. In a small nonreactive saucepan, combine orange juice, wine, jelly, mustard, and grated orange and lemon zest. Bring to a boil over medium heat. Dissolve cornstarch in Cognac and stir into sauce. Cook, stirring constantly, until lightly thickened, 1 to 2 minutes.

3. About 30 minutes before chicken is done, brush with some of sauce. Brush again after 15 minutes. Bring remaining sauce to a boil and whisk in remaining 1½ teaspoons butter until melted. Add orange sections and remove from heat.

4. Carve chicken and serve with sauce.

---

159   ROAST MEDITERRANEAN CHICKEN
Prep: 20 minutes   Cook: 2 hours 8 to 11 minutes   Serves: 6

Seasoned bulgur wheat pilaf mix is the basis for this simple yet slightly exotic stuffing. Look for it in the rice and grain section of your supermarket.

1 **(6-ounce) box seasoned bulgur wheat pilaf mix**	1 **roasting chicken (5 to 6 pounds)**
2½ **tablespoons olive oil**	**Salt and freshly ground pepper**
1 **medium onion, chopped**	2 **tablespoons flour**
1 **garlic clove, crushed through a press**	2 **cups chicken broth**
¼ **cup chopped fresh mint or 2 teaspoons dried**	

1. Prepare pilaf mix according to package directions. Preheat oven to 400°F. In a frying pan, heat 1½ tablespoons of olive oil. Add onion and cook over medium heat until softened, 3 to 5 minutes. Add garlic and cook 1 minute. Stir in half of mint. Toss with cooked pilaf.

2. Fill chicken cavity with pilaf. Brush skin with remaining 1 tablespoon oil. Season skin with salt and pepper and tie legs together with kitchen string. Place chicken, breast side up, on a rack in a shallow roasting pan. Roast 30 minutes. Reduce oven temperature to 350° and continue to roast until an instant-reading thermometer inserted into the thigh registers 180°, about 1½ hours longer.

3. Remove chicken from pan and pour off all but 2 tablespoons of drippings. Add flour to pan and cook over direct heat, stirring, for about 2 minutes, until lightly colored. Whisk in broth and remaining mint and cook, stirring, until thickened and bubbly, 2 to 3 minutes. Season with additional salt and pepper to taste.

4. Spoon stuffing into a serving bowl. Carve chicken and serve with stuffing and gravy.

160   ROAST CHICKEN WITH BREAD STUFFING

Prep: 45 minutes   Cook: 2 hours 41 minutes   Serves: 6 to 8

Nobody can roast a chicken like my grandma, but we all keep trying. Here is my latest effort to re-create her specialty.

5 tablespoons butter	½ teaspoon dried savory
2 medium onions, chopped	½ teaspoon salt
1 large celery rib with leaves, chopped	¼ teaspoon freshly ground pepper
1 chicken liver, finely chopped (optional)	5 cups day-old firm-textured white bread cubes
¼ cup chopped parsley	2¼ cups chicken broth
1 teaspoon dried thyme	1 large roasting chicken (6 or 7 pounds)
1 teaspoon dried sage	2 tablespoons flour
1 teaspoon dried marjoram	

1. Preheat oven to 400°F. In a large frying pan, melt 4 tablespoons of butter over medium heat. Add onions and celery and cook for 2 minutes. Add liver and cook 3 minutes longer. Stir in parsley, thyme, sage, marjoram, savory, salt, and pepper. Add bread cubes and ¼ cup of broth and toss to mix.

2. Fill chicken cavity with stuffing. Rub skin with remaining 1 tablespoon butter. Season generously with additional salt and pepper and tie legs together with kitchen string. Place chicken, breast side up, on a rack in a shallow roasting pan. Roast 30 minutes. Reduce oven temperature to 350° and roast until an instant-reading thermometer inserted in thigh registers 180°, about 2 hours longer.

3. Remove chicken from pan and pour off all but 2 tablespoons of drippings. Stir in flour and cook over medium heat, stirring, until golden, about 3 minutes. Whisk in remaining 2 cups broth. Boil, stirring, until thickened and bubbly, 2 to 3 minutes. Season with additional salt and pepper to taste.

4. Remove stuffing from chicken cavity and spoon into a serving bowl. Carve chicken and serve with stuffing and gravy.

161 CHRISTMAS ROAST CHICKEN

Prep: 20 minutes   Stand: 1 hour   Cook: 2 hours 44 to 47 minutes
Serves: 6 to 8

The Victorian-style stuffing used to stuff this bird can be assembled a day ahead. Packaged dried fruit "tidbits," found in the dried fruit section of the market, make it easy. Do not stuff the chicken until you are ready to roast it.

½ cup chopped dried fruit tidbits
6 tablespoons dry sherry
½ cup chopped walnuts, almonds, or pecans, or a mix
2½ tablespoons butter
1 medium onion, chopped
1 small celery rib, chopped
1 small tart apple, peeled, cored, and coarsely chopped
½ cup chopped unpeeled kumquats or seeded tangerines

¼ cup chopped parsley
¼ teaspoon pumpkin pie spice
1½ cups cubed day-old whole wheat bread
1 teaspoon salt
½ teaspoon freshly ground pepper
1 large roasting chicken (6 to 7 pounds)
1½ tablespoons flour
1¾ cups chicken broth

1. Preheat oven to 350°F. In a large mixing bowl, soak fruit tidbits in 3 table-spoons of sherry for 1 hour. Meanwhile, toast nuts on a baking sheet until golden and fragrant, 5 to 7 minutes.

2. In a large frying pan, melt 1½ tablespoons of butter over medium heat. Add onion and celery and cook, stirring often, until soft, about 5 minutes. Add to fruits in mixing bowl along with toasted nuts, apple, kumquats, parsley, pumpkin pie spice, and bread cubes. Toss to mix well. Season with ¼ teaspoon each salt and pepper.

3. Reduce oven temperature to 400°. Fill chicken cavity with stuffing. Rub skin with remaining 1 tablespoon butter; season with remaining salt and pepper and tie legs together with kitchen string. Place chicken, breast side up, on a rack in a shallow roasting pan. Roast 30 minutes. Reduce oven temperature to 350° and continue to roast until an instant-reading thermometer inserted into thigh registers 180°, about 2 hours longer.

4. Remove chicken to a carving board. Pour off all but 2 tablespoons drippings from pan. Add flour and cook over medium heat, stirring, 1 to 2 minutes. Whisk in broth and remaining 3 tablespoons sherry and bring to a boil, whisking, until gravy is thickened and smooth, about 3 minutes. Season with additional salt and pepper to taste.

5. Spoon stuffing into a bowl, carve chicken, and serve with gravy and stuffing.

162 GREEK ISLANDS ROASTED CHICKEN
Prep: 20 minutes   Cook: 2 hours 5 minutes   Serves: 6

The lemon and grape leaves used here are discarded after cooking, but they impart a delicate, haunting Mediterranean flavor to the roast chicken.

1 **roasting chicken (5 to 6 pounds)**	1 **teaspoon dried oregano**
1 **lemon, unpeeled and quartered**	1 **teaspoon salt**
4 **to 6 canned grape leaves, rinsed**	¾ **teaspoon freshly ground pepper**
1 **tablespoon butter**	2 **tablespoons flour**
	1¾ **cups chicken broth**
	¼ **cup lemon juice**

1. Preheat oven to 400°F. Rub outside of chicken with cut side of 1 lemon quarter. Wrap all 4 lemon quarters with grape leaves and use to fill chicken cavity. Rub chicken with butter and season with ½ teaspoon each oregano, salt, and pepper. Tie legs together with kitchen string. Place chicken, breast side up, on a rack in a shallow roasting pan. Roast 30 minutes. Reduce oven temperature to 350° and roast until an instant-reading thermometer inserted into thigh registers 180°, about 1½ hours longer.

2. Remove chicken to a carving board. Pour off all but 2 tablespoons drippings from pan. Add flour to drippings and cook over medium heat, stirring, 2 minutes. Whisk in broth, lemon juice, and remaining ½ teaspoon oregano. Bring to a boil, stirring, until gravy is thickened and smooth, 2 to 3 minutes. Season with remaining ½ teaspoon salt and ¼ teaspoon pepper.

3. Carve chicken, discarding lemons and grape leaves, and serve with gravy.

163 ROAST CHICKEN WITH MASHED POTATO AND SAUSAGE STUFFING
Prep: 10 minutes   Cook: 2½ hours   Serves: 6

3 **large russet potatoes (about 1¼ pounds), peeled and cut into chunks**	1 **teaspoon dried leaf sage**
⅓ **cup milk**	¾ **teaspoon salt**
½ **pound bulk sage-seasoned breakfast sausage meat**	⅜ **teaspoon freshly ground pepper**
1 **medium onion, chopped**	1 **roasting chicken (5 to 6 pounds)**
2 **cups coarse fresh bread crumbs (from about 3 slices of bread)**	1 **tablespoon butter, softened**
	2 **tablespoons flour**
	2 **cups chicken broth**

1. In a large pot of boiling salted water, cook potatoes until fork-tender, about 15 minutes. Drain and mash, using a potato masher or electric mixer. Mix in milk until smooth. Measure and reserve 2 cups mashed potatoes; save any extra for another use.

2. Preheat oven to 400°F. In a large frying pan, cook sausage and onion over medium heat, stirring often, until sausage is browned and onion is softened, about 7 minutes. Stir in mashed potatoes, bread crumbs, sage, ¼ teaspoon salt, and ⅛ teaspoon pepper.

3. Fill chicken cavity with stuffing. Rub skin with butter; season with remaining ½ teaspoon salt and ¼ teaspoon pepper and tie legs together with kitchen string. Place chicken, breast side up, on a rack in a shallow roasting pan. Roast 30 minutes, reduce oven heat to 350°, and continue to roast until an instant-reading thermometer inserted into thigh registers 180°, about 1½ hours longer.

4. Remove chicken to a carving board. Pour off all but 2 tablespoons of drippings. Add flour to pan and cook over medium heat, stirring, 2 minutes. Whisk in broth and bring to a boil, stirring, until gravy is thickened and smooth, 2 to 3 minutes. Season with additional salt and pepper to taste. Spoon stuffing into a serving bowl. Carve chicken and serve with gravy and stuffing.

164 THYME-ROASTED CLAY POT CHICKEN AND SPRING VEGETABLES

Prep: 15 minutes   Cook: 1 hour 35 to 40 minutes   Serves: 4

Clay cooking pots are relatively inexpensive and they produce an incomparably delicious, moist, and juicy roasted chicken. Follow the directions that come with the pot, especially the soaking method.

1 whole frying chicken (about 3½ pounds) Salt and freshly ground pepper	12 small spring onions, trimmed, or peeled pearl onions
4 fresh thyme sprigs plus 1 tablespoon chopped fresh thyme	12 baby carrots 16 tiny red potatoes (about 1 inch in diameter) or 8 larger ones, halved
¼ cup parsley sprigs	
2 large garlic cloves, peeled and halved	

1. Soak a 2-quart clay roaster and its lid in cold water to cover 15 minutes. Meanwhile, season chicken generously with salt and pepper. Fill chicken cavity with thyme and parsley sprigs and 2 pieces of garlic. Place chicken in pot, breast side up. Tuck vegetables around chicken and sprinkle them lightly with salt and pepper, then with chopped thyme.

2. Cover roaster with lid and set in center of a cold oven. Turn heat to 450°F. and roast, without opening pot, 1½ hours. Uncover and roast 5 to 10 minutes longer to crisp skin.

165   ROAST CHICKEN WITH KALE AND CORN BREAD STUFFING

Prep: 30 minutes   Cook: 2 hours 38 to 40 minutes   Serves: 6 to 8

You can make your own corn bread or buy it at a bakery. You can even use leftover corn muffins for the stuffing. Crumble and spread the corn bread onto a tray and let it dry out for 24 hours before using.

3 tablespoons butter
1 medium onion, chopped
1 medium celery rib, chopped
1 (10-ounce) package frozen chopped kale, thawed and well drained
4 cups crumbled day-old corn bread

1 teaspoon poultry seasoning
1 teaspoon salt
¾ teaspoon freshly ground pepper
1 large roasting chicken (6 to 7 pounds)
2 tablespoons flour
2 cups chicken broth

1. Preheat oven to 400°F. In a large frying pan, melt 2 tablespoons of butter over medium heat. Add onion and celery and cook, stirring often, until soft, about 5 minutes. Stir in kale, corn bread, poultry seasoning, and ½ teaspoon each salt and pepper.

2. Fill chicken cavity with stuffing. Rub skin with remaining 1 tablespoon butter; season with remaining ½ teaspoon salt and ¼ teaspoon pepper. Tie chicken legs together with kitchen string. Place chicken, breast side up, on a rack in a shallow roasting pan. Roast 30 minutes. Reduce oven temperature to 350° and continue to roast until an instant-reading thermometer inserted into thigh registers 180°, about 2 hours longer.

3. Remove chicken to a carving board. Pour off all but 2 tablespoons drippings from pan. Add flour to pan and cook over medium heat, stirring, 1 to 2 minutes. Whisk in broth and bring to a boil, whisking until gravy is thickened and smooth, 2 to 3 minutes. Season with additional salt and pepper to taste.

4. Spoon stuffing into a serving bowl. Carve chicken and serve with stuffing and gravy.

166 JAMBALAYA-STUFFED ROAST CHICKEN

Prep: 20 minutes   Cook: 2 hours 49 minutes   Serves: 6 to 8

Fried okra as a side dish and a pecan pie for dessert will turn this into a New Orleans–inspired feast.

3 tablespoons butter
½ cup chopped scallions
½ cup chopped celery
½ cup chopped red bell pepper
½ pound coarsely chopped chorizo or smoked kielbasa
½ teaspoon packaged Creole seasoning
½ teaspoon Tabasco or other hot pepper sauce

2½ cups cooked white rice
Salt and freshly ground pepper
1 large roasting chicken (6 to 7 pounds), giblets reserved
1 tablespoon flour
1 (14½-ounce) can stewed tomatoes

1. Preheat oven to 400°F. In a large frying pan, melt 2 tablespoons of butter over medium heat. Add scallions, celery, bell pepper, and sausage and cook, stirring often, until vegetables are softened, about 5 minutes. Stir in Creole seasoning, Tabasco, rice, and ½ teaspoon each salt and pepper.

2. Fill chicken cavity with rice stuffing. Rub skin with remaining 1 tablespoon butter; season with salt and pepper. Tie legs together with kitchen string. Place chicken, breast side up, on a rack in a shallow pan. Roast 30 minutes. Reduce oven temperature to 350° and continue to roast until an instant-reading thermometer inserted into thigh registers 180°, about 2 hours longer. Coarsely chop liver and add to roasting pan during last 45 minutes of cooking.

3. While chicken is roasting, simmer giblets in water to cover for 25 minutes. Drain and reserve 1 cup of broth. When chicken is done, transfer to a carving board. Pour off all but 3 tablespoons drippings from pan. Add flour to drippings and cook over medium-high heat, stirring, until lightly browned, about 3 minutes. Whisk in giblet broth and cook until bubbly and thickened, about 1 minute. Add stewed tomatoes and simmer 10 minutes. Season sauce with additional salt and pepper to taste.

4. Spoon stuffing into a serving bowl. Carve chicken and serve with stuffing and sauce.

167 OYSTERS ROCKEFELLER ROASTED CHICKEN

Prep: 30 minutes   Cook: 2 hours 41 to 45 minutes
Serves: 6 to 8

Ingredients from the famous New Orleans oyster dish make a fabulous and sophisticated stuffing for chicken.

8 slices of bacon
1 medium onion, chopped
1 small celery rib with leaves, chopped
1 small fennel bulb, chopped
1 (10-ounce) package frozen chopped spinach, thawed and squeezed dry
1 (6½- to 8-ounce) can whole oysters or ½ pint shucked fresh oysters, drained and chopped, liquor reserved

3 cups torn French bread (about 8 ounces)
   Salt and freshly ground pepper
1 large roasting chicken (6 to 7 pounds)
1 tablespoon butter, softened
2 tablespoons flour
2 cups chicken broth
2 tablespoons Pernod or other anise liqueur

1. Preheat oven to 400°F. In a large frying pan, cook bacon over medium heat until crisp, about 5 minutes. Drain bacon on paper towels and crumble. Pour off all but 3 tablespoons drippings from pan. Add onion, celery, and fennel. Cook, stirring, until just softened, 3 to 5 minutes. Stir in spinach, drained oysters, and crumbled bacon. Transfer to a large mixing bowl. Add bread and toss to mix well. Season with ¼ teaspoon each salt and pepper. If stuffing seems too dry, add a little of reserved oyster liquor.

2. Fill chicken cavity with stuffing. Rub skin with butter; season with salt and pepper. Tie legs together with kitchen string. Place chicken, breast side up, on a rack in a shallow roasting pan. Roast 30 minutes. Reduce oven temperature to 350° and continue to roast until an instant-reading thermometer inserted into thigh registers 180°, about 2 hours longer.

3. Remove chicken to a carving board. Pour off all but 2 tablespoons of drippings from pan. Add flour to remaining drippings and cook over medium heat, stirring, 1 to 2 minutes. Whisk in broth and Pernod and cook, whisking, until gravy is thickened and smooth, 2 to 3 minutes. Season with additional salt and pepper to taste.

4. Spoon stuffing into a serving bowl. Carve chicken and serve with stuffing and gravy.

168 ROASTED CHICKEN WITH RAISIN BREAD AND APPLE STUFFING

Prep: 20 minutes   Cook: 2 hours 37 to 40 minutes   Serves: 6 to 8

If you can get whole wheat raisin and nut bread, all the better, though any raisin bread will work here.

3 tablespoons butter
⅔ cup chopped onion
½ cup chopped celery
1 teaspoon crumbled dried leaf sage
6 slices of raisin bread, torn into small pieces (about 3 cups)
1 small tart apple, peeled and diced

1¾ cups chicken broth
Salt and freshly ground pepper
1 large roasting chicken (6 to 7 pounds)
2 tablespoons flour
½ cup cider or apple juice

1. Preheat oven to 400°F. In a large frying pan, melt 2 tablespoons of butter over medium heat. Add onion and celery and cook, stirring often, until softened, 3 to 5 minutes. Stir in sage, bread cubes, and apple. Add ¼ cup of chicken broth and toss to moisten lightly.

2. Fill chicken cavity with stuffing. Rub skin with remaining 1 tablespoon butter. Season with salt and pepper. Tie legs together with kitchen string. Place chicken, breast side up, on a rack in a shallow roasting pan. Roast 30 minutes. Reduce oven temperature to 350° and continue to roast until an instant-reading thermometer inserted into thigh registers 180°, about 2 hours longer.

3. Remove chicken to a carving board. Pour off all but 2 tablespoons drippings from pan. Add flour to drippings and cook over medium heat, stirring, 2 minutes. Whisk in cider and remaining 1½ cups broth. Bring to a boil, whisking, until thickened and bubbly, 2 to 3 minutes. Season with additional salt and pepper to taste.

4. Spoon stuffing into a serving bowl. Carve chicken and serve with stuffing and gravy.

169   SAGE-ROASTED CLAY POT CHICKEN AND WINTER VEGETABLES

Prep: 15 minutes   Cook: 1 hour 35 to 40 minutes   Serves: 4

Clay-roasting brings out the full flavors of both the chicken and the vegetables. Don't forget to soak the pot first and start in a cold oven to prevent cracking of the clay.

1 whole frying chicken (about 3½ pounds)	1 large onion, cut into 8 wedges
Salt and freshly ground pepper	1 large red potato (about 6 ounces), peeled and cut into 1½-inch chunks
6 fresh sage sprigs plus 1 tablespoon chopped fresh sage	1 sweet potato, peeled and cut into 1½-inch chunks
¼ cup parsley sprigs	12 brussels sprouts

1. Soak a 2-quart clay roaster and its lid in cold water to cover for 15 minutes. Meanwhile, season chicken generously with salt and pepper. Loosen breast skin and tuck 1 or 2 whole sage leaves under skin. Fill cavity with remaining whole sage and parsley sprigs. Place chicken in pot, breast side up. Tuck vegetables around chicken and sprinkle lightly with salt, pepper, and chopped sage.

2. Cover roaster and set in center of a cold oven. Turn heat to 450°F. and roast, without opening pot, 1½ hours. Uncover and roast 5 to 10 minutes longer to crisp skin.

170   ROAST CHICKEN WITH WILD RICE AND CHESTNUT STUFFING

Prep: 30 minutes   Cook: 2 hours 40 minutes   Serves: 6 to 8

Herb-seasoned long-grain and wild rice mix makes this extra-easy. Serve it for a harvest-time Sunday supper.

1 (6-ounce) box seasoned long-grain and wild rice mix	1 large roasting chicken (6 to 7 pounds)
3 tablespoons butter	Salt and freshly ground pepper
1 medium onion, chopped	2 tablespoons flour
½ pound mushrooms, sliced	1¾ cups chicken broth
1 cup drained canned chestnuts, quartered	¼ cup dry sherry or additional broth

1. Prepare rice mix according to package directions. Preheat oven to 400°F. In a large frying pan, melt 2 tablespoons of butter over medium heat. Add onions and cook 2 minutes. Add mushrooms and cook, stirring often, 3 minutes. Add cooked rice and chestnuts to pan and stir to mix.

2. Fill chicken cavity with rice stuffing. Rub skin with remaining 1 tablespoon butter. Season chicken with salt and pepper. Tie legs together with kitchen string. Place chicken, breast side up, on a rack in a shallow roasting pan. Roast 30 minutes. Reduce oven temperature to 350° and continue to roast until an instant-reading thermometer inserted into thigh registers 180°, about 2 hours longer.

3. Remove chicken to a carving board. Pour off all but 2 tablespoons of drippings from pan. Add flour to drippings and cook over medium heat, stirring, 2 minutes. Whisk in broth and sherry and bring to a boil, stirring, until gravy is thickened and smooth, about 3 minutes. Season with additional salt and pepper to taste.

4. Spoon stuffing into a serving bowl. Carve chicken and serve with stuffing and gravy.

---

171   CRISPY CORNY BAKED CHICKEN
Prep: 10 minutes   Cook: 25 to 45 minutes   Serves: 4

This is a particularly easy version of the back-of-the-box classic cornflake-coated chicken. Make the crumbs in a food processor from 4½ cups cereal or buy packaged cornflake crumbs. Using skinless chicken will lower the fat content considerably.

1¼ **cups cornflake cereal crumbs**	2½ **to 3 pounds assorted skinless chicken parts, such as drumsticks, thighs, and breasts, or 1 pound skinless, boneless chicken thighs or breasts**
¼ **cup flour**	
1 **teaspoon poultry seasoning**	
1 **teaspoon salt**	
½ **teaspoon freshly ground pepper**	
3 **tablespoons butter**	

1. Preheat oven to 425°F. In a paper bag, shake together cereal crumbs, flour, poultry seasoning, salt, and pepper. Place butter in a 10x15-inch jelly roll pan or a 9x13-inch baking dish and set in oven to melt. Roll chicken pieces in melted butter, then shake a few at a time in crumbs to coat.

2. Arrange chicken, skin side up, in a single layer, not touching, in jelly roll pan or baking dish. Place in oven and immediately reduce temperature to 375°. Bake without turning until chicken is browned and juices run clear when pricked, about 45 minutes for chicken on the bone and about 25 minutes for boneless chicken.

172   ROASTED CHICKEN BREAST
Prep: 10 minutes   Cook: 50 to 60 minutes   Serves: 3 to 4

Chicken producers are growing larger roaster birds with more white meat than ever before. You can even buy a whole chicken breast for roasting, which is perfect for small families who only like white meat. This is as quick and easy as it gets for a homemade roast chicken dinner.

1 **whole roasting chicken breast, about 2½ pounds**	2 **teaspoons butter, softened**
2 **cups prepared bread stuffing mix, any flavor**	**Salt and freshly ground pepper**

1. Preheat oven to 400°F. Place chicken in a small shallow roasting pan and spoon stuffing into space under breastbone. Rub skin with butter and season lightly with salt and pepper.

2. Roast chicken 15 minutes. Reduce oven temperature to 350° and continue to roast until chicken is white throughout but still juicy, 35 to 45 minutes longer.

173   PROSCIUTTO- AND RICOTTA-STUFFED CHICKEN BREASTS
Prep: 10 minutes   Cook: 35 minutes   Serves: 8

Although you could use bone-in chicken, it is much more elegant to serve this way. Either bone the chicken breasts yourself or ask the butcher to do it, leaving the skin intact.

⅔ **cup part-skim ricotta cheese**	1½ **teaspoons dried oregano**
¼ **cup grated Parmesan cheese**	½ **teaspoon freshly ground pepper**
3 **tablespoons chopped prosciutto**	8 **boneless chicken breast halves, with skin intact**
3 **tablespoons chopped chives**	2 **tablespoons olive oil**
2 **tablespoons chopped parsley**	

1. Preheat oven to 400°F. Lightly oil a shallow 2-quart baking dish. In a small bowl, combine ricotta, Parmesan, prosciutto, chives, parsley, oregano, and pepper. Blend well. Use your fingers to loosen skin from chicken breasts. Insert prosciutto-cheese filling under skin, then use your fingers to smooth skin around filling and chicken, tucking breasts under to form rounded dome shapes. Place breasts close together in baking dish. Drizzle with olive oil.

2. Bake, uncovered, 10 minutes. Reduce oven temperature to 375° and bake until chicken skin is golden and meat is white throughout, about 25 minutes longer. Baste once with pan juices during cooking.

3. Serve hot or at room temperature, cutting each breast half crosswise into 3 slices.

174   BAKED HERB-STUFFED CHICKEN ROLLS
Prep: 30 minutes   Cook: 30 minutes   Serves: 6

Any flavor of stuffing mix can be used for this version of roast chicken and stuffing.

1½ cups dry packaged herb-seasoned stuffing mix	6 skinless, boneless chicken breast halves
2½ tablespoons butter	¾ cup chicken broth

1. Prepare 1¼ cups of stuffing mix according to package directions. Reserve remaining ¼ cup dry stuffing mix.

2. Preheat oven to 400°F. Grease a shallow 2-quart baking dish with ½ table-spoon butter. Place chicken, 1 piece at a time, in a plastic bag or between 2 sheets of plastic wrap. Use a flat mallet to pound chicken to an even ½-inch thickness. Divide prepared stuffing into 6 portions and form each into a ball. Set a ball in center of each flattened chicken breast. Roll chicken around stuffing to enclose completely.

3. Place chicken, smooth side up, in baking dish. Sprinkle dry stuffing over chicken and dot with remaining butter. Pour broth around chicken.

4. Bake until chicken is white throughout and stuffing crumbs are browned, about 30 minutes. Serve with pan juices spooned over.

175   PEPPERY OVEN-FRIED CHICKEN
Prep: 10 minutes   Cook: 40 to 45 minutes   Serves: 6

3 tablespoons butter	1 teaspoon coarsely ground black pepper
2 tablespoons vegetable oil	¾ teaspoon salt
⅔ cup unseasoned dry bread crumbs	½ teaspoon cayenne
⅓ cup flour	4 pounds chicken parts

1. Preheat oven to 400°F. Place butter and oil in a large baking dish, at least 9x13 inches, and set in oven to melt butter.

2. In a plastic bag, combine bread crumbs, flour, black pepper, salt, and cayenne. Roll chicken in melted butter and oil, then shake a few pieces at a time in bread crumb mixture until coated. Place, skin side up, in baking dish.

3. Bake until browned and crisp and chicken juices run clear when pricked, 40 to 45 minutes.

176   CHICKEN CAROL
Prep: 15 minutes   Cook: 1 hour   Serves: 8

My friend Carol Pinard serves this to rave reviews.

2 tablespoons butter
1 package (about ½ ounce) dry
    Italian herb salad
    dressing mix
8 skinless, boneless chicken
    breast halves

1 (8-ounce) container
    whipped cream cheese
    with chives
2 cans undiluted cream of
    mushroom soup
1 cup dry white wine

1. Preheat oven to 350°F. Lightly butter a shallow 3-quart baking dish. In a large frying pan, melt butter with half of dry seasoning mix. Cook chicken, half at a time, over medium heat, turning once or twice, until golden, about 8 minutes per batch. Transfer chicken to prepared baking dish.

2. Stir cream cheese, soup, wine, and remaining dry salad dressing mix into drippings in frying pan. Stir to mix well. Pour over chicken. (Recipe can be prepared to this point up to 8 hours ahead and refrigerated. Return to room temperature for baking.)

3. Bake, uncovered, until chicken is white throughout and sauce is thickened and bubbly, about 45 minutes.

177   ROAST CHICKEN WITH THIRTY CLOVES OF GARLIC
Prep: 15 minutes   Cook: 1 hour 23 minutes   Serves: 4

When slow-cooked, the garlic is sweet and buttery. Spread the soft cloves on toasted French bread to accompany the chicken.

2 whole heads of garlic (about
    30 cloves)
1 chicken (about 3 pounds),
    cut into 8 pieces
½ teaspoon salt

¼ teaspoon freshly ground
    pepper
3 tablespoons olive oil
1 teaspoon rubbed sage
¼ cup dry red or white wine

1. Preheat oven to 350°F. Separate unpeeled garlic into cloves. Trim ends. Drop garlic cloves into a pot of boiling water for 10 seconds. Remove with a slotted spoon. Peels should slip off easily.

2. Season chicken with salt and pepper. In a large Dutch oven, heat olive oil over medium-high heat. Add chicken and cook, turning, until browned all over, about 8 minutes. Sprinkle with sage, toss garlic over and around chicken, and pour in wine. Cover tightly and bake until chicken and garlic are tender, about 1¼ hours.

178 PARMESAN POLENTA WITH CHICKEN MARINARA

Prep: 5 minutes   Cook: 47 to 50 minutes   Serves: 6

Polenta, an Italian form of cornmeal, is a delightful change from pasta. It can be served freshly cooked and soft or baked until firm, as it is here.

2 cups chicken broth
1 cup polenta or yellow cornmeal
1 cup cold water
3 tablespoons unsalted butter
¼ cup plus 2 tablespoons grated Parmesan cheese
½ teaspoon freshly ground pepper

¼ teaspoon salt
6 skinless, boneless chicken breast halves or thighs
4 cups prepared marinara sauce
½ cup dry red or white wine

1. In a heavy saucepan, bring broth to a boil over medium heat. In a mixing bowl, whisk polenta into cold water until smooth and free of lumps. Slowly whisk dissolved polenta into boiling broth. Reduce heat to medium-low and simmer, stirring almost constantly, until mixture is very thick and pulls away from side of pan, 12 to 15 minutes. Stir in butter, ¼ cup of cheese, pepper, and salt. Scrape polenta into a buttered 10-inch pie plate. Let cool to room temperature. Sprinkle remaining 2 tablespoons cheese over top.

2. Preheat oven to 350°F. Place chicken in a 2- or 2½-quart baking dish. Pour marinara sauce and wine over chicken. Cover with foil and bake until chicken is cooked through, about 35 minutes.

3. After chicken has been in oven about 15 minutes, place polenta in same oven on upper rack. Bake, uncovered, until lightly flecked with brown and heated through, about 20 minutes.

4. To serve, cut polenta into 6 wedges. Serve each wedge alongside chicken, with sauce spooned over both.

179 ORANGE-TARRAGON CHICKEN FOR A CROWD

Prep: 20 minutes   Cook: 43 to 50 minutes   Serves: 12

I once multiplied this recipe to serve 50 people, placing the chicken in large disposable pans and baking it in 2 ovens. Big bowls of rice pilaf with green peas and pimiento, along with a large tossed salad, rounded out a very easily accomplished meal.

12 **skinless, boneless chicken breast halves**	½ **cup orange juice**
1 **teaspoon salt**	½ **cup dry white wine**
½ **teaspoon freshly ground pepper**	½ **cup heavy cream**
1½ **teaspoons dried tarragon**	1 **tablespoon Pernod or other anise liqueur (optional)**
4 **tablespoons butter**	12 **thin orange slices, for garnish**
1 **medium onion, chopped**	
1 **tablespoon grated orange zest**	

1. Use your hands to flatten chicken breasts to a more even thickness. Season with salt, pepper, and 1 teaspoon of tarragon. In a large frying pan, melt 2 tablespoons of butter over medium-high heat. Add half of chicken and cook, turning once or twice, until golden, about 6 minutes. Remove to a 9x14-inch baking pan. Add remaining butter to pan and cook remaining chicken in same way. Add to baking pan.

2. Add onion to drippings in pan. Reduce heat to medium and cook, stirring often, until softened, 3 to 5 minutes. Add remaining ½ teaspoon tarragon, orange zest, orange juice, wine, and cream. Bring to a boil, stirring up browned bits clinging to bottom of pan. Cook 3 minutes. Stir in Pernod. Pour over chicken in pan. Cover tightly with foil. Bake immediately or refrigerate up to 24 hours, but return to room temperature to bake.

3. Preheat oven to 350°F. Bake chicken, covered, until white throughout, 25 to 30 minutes. Serve garnished with orange slices.

180   EASY HERBED-CHEESE CHICKEN
Prep: 5 minutes   Cook: 40 to 45 minutes   Serves: 4

There are lots of brands of herbed cheese spread available, even reduced-fat varieties.

1   **chicken (about 3 pounds),**
        cut into 8 pieces
1   **(4-ounce) package herbed**
        and spiced cheese spread

1   **tablespoon vegetable oil**
        Salt and freshly ground
        pepper

1. Preheat oven to 400°F. Use your fingers to loosen skin of chicken. Insert cheese under skin, using about 1 tablespoon for breasts and thighs and less for drumsticks and wings. Spread cheese over chicken as much as possible. Brush or rub skin with oil. Season lightly with salt and pepper.

2. Place chicken, skin side up, in a shallow baking pan and bake until skin is browned and crisp and juices run clear when pricked, 40 to 45 minutes.

181   LEMON-PEPPER BRAN FLAKE CHICKEN
Prep: 10 minutes   Cook: 15 minutes   Serves: 6

This is a quick and easy family supper that everyone will love. Make the crumbs by whirling bran flake cereal in the food processor or crushing in a plastic bag with a rolling pin.

6   **skinless, boneless chicken**
        breast halves
1½ **cups bran flake cereal**
        crumbs
1½ **tablespoons grated lemon**
        zest

1   **tablespoon cracked black**
        pepper
¼   **teaspoon salt**
4   **tablespoons butter, melted**
1   **lemon, cut into 6 wedges**

1. Preheat oven to 450°F. Use your hands to flatten chicken to an even thickness. In a shallow dish, combine bran flake crumbs, lemon zest, pepper, and salt. Dip chicken first into butter, then into crumbs to coat.

2. Place on a baking sheet. Bake until crumbs are golden brown and chicken is white throughout but still juicy, about 15 minutes.

3. Serve chicken garnished with lemon wedges to squeeze over.

Chapter 9

Chicken Pronto

Quick cooking is a way of life for all of us these days. But that is no reason to cut corners on taste and quality. Here is a collection of recipes that can be made from start to finish in 30 minutes or less.

Skinless, boneless chicken breasts and thighs are the answer to the harried cook's dilemma. Readily available in the market and relatively low in fat, they cook in practically no time at all. Just a few years ago, if you wanted skinless, boneless chicken, you had to do the job yourself—a task that required the skill of a surgeon. Thin slices to cook up in veal scaloppine look-alikes required partial freezing, then a sure hand with a sharp knife. Now, even the smallest supermarket carries boneless breasts and thighs, as well as thinly sliced cutlets.

In almost all of these recipes, breast and thigh meat are interchangeable. Wherever a choice is given, I list my preference as the first option. Sometimes I instruct you to use your hands to flatten the cut to a more even thickness for better and quicker cooking. Chicken cutlets are thinly sliced and cook in a few minutes—in fact, overcooking is the most serious problem here!

The versatility of skinless, boneless cuts is evident in this, the largest chapter in the book. The recipes range from home-style chicken and dumplings to sophisticated Chicken Amandine. There are also recipes for wonderful main courses that start with cooked chicken, either left from last night's roast or poached a few days ahead expressly for use later. Today, every good deli section offers rotisserie roasted chickens, which also lend themselves beautifully to these recipes. Whenever cooked chicken is called for, any of the above can be used.

Now get moving—you have 30 minutes until dinner!

182   CHICKEN BREASTS WITH APRICOT-CHERRY COMPOTE

Prep: 10 minutes   Cook: 16 minutes   Serves: 4

Tart dried cherries play well against the sweetness of dried apricots. Dried cranberries may be substituted for the cherries.

4 skinless, boneless chicken breast halves	⅓ cup chopped or thinly sliced dried apricots
¼ teaspoon salt	⅓ cup coarsely chopped dried tart cherries
⅛ teaspoon freshly ground pepper	¾ cup chicken broth
1 teaspoon dried leaf thyme	⅔ cup dry white wine
3 tablespoons butter	

1. Season chicken with salt, pepper, and ½ teaspoon of thyme. In a large frying pan, melt 1½ tablespoons of butter over medium heat. Add chicken and cook, turning once or twice, until golden and nearly cooked through, about 12 minutes.

2. Add apricots, cherries, and remaining thyme. Pour in broth and wine. Partially cover pan, reduce heat to medium-low, and simmer, stirring often, until fruit is nearly tender, about 3 minutes. Uncover and simmer 1 minute. Season sauce with additional salt and pepper to taste and serve.

183   BACON AND CHEDDAR CHICKEN BREASTS

Prep: 10 minutes   Cook: 18 to 19 minutes   Serves: 6

One of my most requested recipes, this is especially good with the addition of sliced tomato. If you serve it on a bed of shredded lettuce, it turns into a BLT on a plate.

6 slices of bacon, cut in half	1½ cups seasoned dry bread crumbs
6 skinless, boneless chicken breast halves	1 tomato, cut into 6 slices
1 egg beaten with 2 tablespoons water	1 cup shredded Cheddar cheese

1. In a large frying pan, cook bacon over medium heat until crisp, about 5 minutes. Drain on paper towels. Pour off all but 3 tablespoons of pan drippings.

2. Use your hands to flatten chicken to an even thickness. Dip chicken into egg, then into bread crumbs to coat.

3. In pan drippings, cook chicken over medium heat, turning once or twice, until coating is browned and chicken is just white throughout, about 12 minutes.

4. Top each chicken breast with a slice of tomato, crisscrosses of bacon, and cheese. Cover pan and continue to cook until cheese melts, 1 to 2 minutes.

184   BEER BATTER FRIED CHICKEN
Prep: 10 minutes   Cook: 12 to 15 minutes   Serves: 6

To keep the oil out, be careful not to break the golden batter "crust" when turning the chicken during frying.

1   cup flour
¾   cup beer
1   teaspoon salt
½   teaspoon freshly ground
      pepper

Vegetable oil, for frying
1½ pounds skinless, boneless
      chicken breast halves
      and/or thighs

1. In a medium bowl, whisk together flour, beer, salt, and pepper until smooth. In a deep 12-inch frying pan, heat ½ inch of oil to 375°F., or until a cube of bread fries golden in about 30 seconds.

2. Dip chicken, 1 piece at a time, into batter to coat completely. Let excess batter drip back into bowl. Carefully add to hot oil and fry, gently turning once with tongs or a slotted spoon, until rich golden brown on both sides, 12 to 15 minutes. Serve hot.

185   CHICKEN BAVARIAN WITH APPLE AND SAUERKRAUT
Prep: 10 minutes   Cook: 19 to 21 minutes   Serves: 4

Juniper berries are the essence of gin. They can be found in the spice section of supermarkets.

4   skinless, boneless chicken
      thighs
¼   teaspoon salt
⅛   teaspoon freshly ground
      pepper
2   tablespoons vegetable oil
1   large tart apple, such as
      Granny Smith, peeled
      and sliced about ¼ inch
      thick

1   small onion, sliced
1   cup drained sauerkraut
½   cup apple cider
1   bay leaf
4   crushed juniper berries or
      1½ tablespoons gin
¼   teaspoon caraway seeds

1. Use your hands to flatten chicken to an even thickness. Season with salt and pepper. In a large frying pan, heat oil over medium-high heat. Add chicken and cook, turning, until browned on all sides, 5 to 7 minutes. Remove from pan.

2. Add apple and onion to pan drippings. Reduce heat to medium and cook, stirring often, until just softened, about 4 minutes. Stir in sauerkraut, cider, bay leaf, juniper berries, and caraway seeds.

3. Return chicken to pan, pushing thighs down into sauerkraut. Cover and simmer over medium-low heat until chicken is tender with no trace of pink, about 10 minutes. Remove and discard bay leaf before serving.

186   CHICKEN AMANDINE
Prep: 5 minutes   Cook: 11 to 12 minutes   Serves: 4

1 **pound thinly sliced chicken breast fillets**	½ **cup sliced almonds**
¼ **teaspoon salt**	¼ **cup chopped shallots**
⅛ **teaspoon freshly ground pepper**	⅛ **teaspoon grated nutmeg**
2½ **tablespoons butter**	½ **cup dry white wine**
	½ **cup chicken broth**
	¼ **cup chopped parsley**

1. Season chicken with salt and pepper. In a large frying pan, melt 1½ tablespoons of butter over medium-high heat. Add chicken and cook, turning once or twice, until white throughout, about 6 minutes. Remove to a platter.

2. Add remaining 1 tablespoon butter, reduce heat to medium, and cook almonds and shallots, stirring constantly, until golden, 2 to 3 minutes. Use a slotted spoon to remove nuts and shallots and sprinkle over chicken.

3. Add nutmeg, wine, and broth to pan. Bring to a boil, scraping up browned bits clinging to the bottom. Boil, stirring occasionally, 3 minutes to reduce. Season with additional salt and pepper to taste. Spoon sauce over chicken. Sprinkle with parsley.

187   CHICKEN AND BISCUITS IN A FLASH
Prep: 5 minutes   Cook: 16 minutes   Serves: 4

1 **pound thinly sliced chicken breast cutlets**	3 **tablespoons butter**
¼ **teaspoon salt**	2 **tablespoons flour**
½ **teaspoon freshly ground pepper**	2½ **cups chicken broth**
1½ **teaspoons poultry seasoning**	4 **prepared or baked refrigerator biscuits, split**
	½ **cup thinly sliced scallions**

1. Season chicken with salt, pepper, and 1 teaspoon of poultry seasoning. In a large frying pan, melt 1½ tablespoons of butter over medium-high heat. Add half of the chicken and cook, turning once, until white throughout, about 5 minutes. Remove from pan and repeat with remaining butter and chicken.

2. Stir in flour and remaining ½ teaspoon poultry seasoning. Cook, stirring, 1 minute. Whisk in broth. Reduce heat to medium and cook, stirring constantly, until bubbly and thickened, about 3 minutes. Return chicken to pan and simmer 2 minutes.

3. To serve, place biscuits, cut sides up, on plates. Spoon chicken and gravy over biscuits. Sprinkle scallions on top.

188 BUTTERMILK CHICKEN FRIED CUTLETS

Prep: 10 minutes   Cook: 14 minutes   Serves: 4

1 pound thinly sliced chicken
   breast cutlets
1 cup buttermilk
¼ cup yellow cornmeal
¼ cup plus 2 teaspoons flour

½ teaspoon salt
1 teaspoon coarsely ground
   pepper
¼ cup vegetable oil
¾ cup chicken broth

1. Place chicken in a shallow dish and pour in ½ cup of buttermilk. Turn chicken to coat all pieces with buttermilk. In another shallow dish, combine cornmeal, ¼ cup of flour, salt, and pepper. Dredge chicken in cornmeal, patting coating onto chicken with your hands.

2. In a large frying pan, heat 2 tablespoons of oil over medium-high heat. Add half of chicken and cook, turning once, until white throughout, about 6 minutes total. Remove chicken from pan and repeat with remaining oil and chicken.

3. Add remaining 2 teaspoons flour and cook, stirring, 1 minute. Whisk broth and remaining ½ cup buttermilk into pan drippings, scraping up browned bits clinging to bottom. Simmer, stirring, 2 minutes. Season with additional salt and pepper to taste. Serve gravy ladled over chicken.

189 QUICK CASSOULET

Prep: 10 minutes   Cook: 18 minutes   Serves: 4 to 6

Canned beans and flavored stewed tomatoes, the secret ingredients in this easy recipe, should be staples in every kitchen.

1½ tablespoons olive oil
1 pound skinless, boneless
   chicken thighs, cut into
   1-inch chunks
½ pound garlicky kielbasa
   sausage, cut into ½-inch
   slices
1 onion, coarsely chopped
1 (16-ounce) can Great
   Northern white beans,
   drained

1 (14½-ounce) can Italian-
   seasoned stewed
   tomatoes
½ cup chicken broth
¼ cup chopped parsley
   Salt and freshly ground
   pepper

1. In a large flameproof casserole, heat olive oil over medium-high heat. Add chicken, sausage, and onion and cook, stirring often, until meats are lightly browned, about 8 minutes.

2. Add beans, tomatoes, and broth. Cover, reduce heat to medium-low, and simmer 10 minutes. Stir in parsley, season with salt and pepper to taste, and serve.

190   CHICKEN CHILE VERDE
Prep: 5 minutes   Cook: 8 minutes   Serves: 4

This very spicy dish is nicely tamed when spooned over steamed rice and served with warmed tortillas.

½ **pound thinly sliced chicken breast cutlets**
2 **tablespoons vegetable oil**
2 **tablespoons yellow cornmeal**
1½ **teaspoons ground cumin**
2 **cups chopped scallions (about 2 bunches)**

2 **cups chicken broth, preferably reduced-sodium**
1 **(4-ounce) can chopped mild green chiles**
½ **cup chopped fresh cilantro**

1. Cut chicken into thin strips. Heat oil in a medium frying pan over high heat. Add chicken and cook, stirring constantly, 1½ minutes, or until just golden.

2. Sprinkle with cornmeal and cumin, reduce heat to medium, and cook, stirring, 1 minute to toast lightly. Add scallions and cook, stirring, 30 seconds. Add broth and chiles and simmer, stirring often, until thickened, about 5 minutes. Stir in cilantro and serve.

191   GREEN CHILE CHICKEN WITH TORTILLAS
Prep: 10 minutes   Cook: 11 minutes   Serves: 4

2 **tablespoons vegetable oil**
1 **pound skinless, boneless chicken thighs or breasts, cut into 1-inch chunks**
2 **tablespoons yellow cornmeal**
2 **teaspoons chili powder**
1 **teaspoon ground cumin**
½ **cup chopped scallions**

2 **cups chicken broth**
1 **cup drained canned tomatillos**
1 **(2-ounce) can chopped green chiles**
½ **cup chopped cilantro**
8 **corn tortillas**
4 **cups shredded lettuce**

1. In a large frying pan, heat oil over medium-high heat. Add chicken chunks and cook, stirring, until golden, about 4 minutes. Sprinkle cornmeal, chili powder, and cumin over chicken and cook, stirring, 1 minute. Stir in broth, tomatillos, and chiles. Simmer, stirring often and mashing tomatillos, until sauce is slightly thickened, about 5 minutes. Stir in cilantro and simmer 30 seconds.

2. Warm tortillas in microwave-safe plastic wrap in a microwave oven for about 30 seconds on high. Spoon chicken with sauce into warm tortillas. Add lettuce. Roll up and eat by hand or with knife and fork.

192   CHICKEN DIANE
Prep: 5 minutes   Cook: 6 to 7 minutes   Serves: 2

This recipe, adapted from the steak classic of the same name, can easily be doubled, but the drama of the presentation lends itself well to a romantic dinner for two.

½ **pound thinly sliced chicken breast cutlets**	2 **teaspoons Dijon mustard**
⅛ **teaspoon salt**	1½ **teaspoons Worcestershire sauce**
½ **teaspoon coarsely ground black pepper**	3 **tablespoons Cognac or brandy**
1½ **tablespoons butter**	1 **tablespoon chopped parsley**
¼ **cup minced shallots**	

1. Season chicken with salt, then pat on pepper. In a large frying pan, melt butter over medium-high heat. Add chicken and cook, turning once or twice, until white throughout, about 5 minutes.

2. Add shallots and cook, stirring, until softened, 1 to 2 minutes. Stir in mustard and Worcestershire sauce. Remove frying pan from heat and pour Cognac over. Carefully ignite Cognac. Spoon flaming sauce over chicken until flames subside. Sprinkle with parsley and serve from frying pan.

193   QUICK COQ AU VIN
Prep: 10 minutes   Cook: 20 minutes   Serves: 4

4 **slices of thick-cut bacon, cut into 1-inch pieces**	1½ **cups frozen pearl onions, thawed**
¼ **cup flour**	⅔ **cup chicken broth, preferably reduced-sodium**
¼ **teaspoon freshly ground pepper**	1⅓ **cups dry red or white wine**
4 **skinless, boneless chicken breast halves**	
2 **cups sliced mushrooms (about 6 ounces)**	

1. In a large frying pan, cook bacon over medium heat until crisp, about 5 minutes. Remove with a slotted spoon and drain on paper towel. On a plate, combine flour and pepper. Use your hands to flatten chicken to an even thickness. Dip in flour to coat.

2. Cook chicken in bacon drippings over medium-high heat, turning once or twice, until browned on both sides, about 5 minutes total. Add mushrooms, reduce heat to medium, and cook, stirring, 2 minutes. Add onions and broth, stirring up browned bits clinging to bottom of pan. Reduce heat to medium-low, cover, and simmer 5 minutes.

3. Add wine and simmer, uncovered, until chicken is white throughout and sauce is lightly reduced, about 3 minutes.

194 SAUTÉED CHICKEN WITH CRANBERRY-PECAN COMPOTE

Prep: 10 minutes   Cook: 17 to 21 minutes   Serves: 4

4 skinless, boneless chicken
   breast halves
¼ teaspoon salt
⅛ teaspoon freshly ground
   pepper
1 teaspoon crumbled dried
   leaf sage
3 tablespoons butter
⅓ cup minced shallots

⅓ cup coarsely chopped
   pecans
¼ cup chopped fresh
   cranberries
1 teaspoon grated orange zest
⅓ cup dry white wine
⅓ cup chicken broth
4 thin orange slices

1. Use your hands to flatten chicken to an even thickness. Season chicken with salt, pepper, and ½ teaspoon of sage. In a large frying pan, melt 1½ tablespoons of butter over medium heat. Add chicken and cook, turning once or twice, until white throughout, 12 to 15 minutes. Remove from pan.

2. Melt remaining butter in pan. Add shallots and remaining sage and cook, stirring, until shallots soften, 1 to 2 minutes. Add pecans, cranberries, and orange zest and cook 1 minute. Stir in wine and broth and simmer 2 minutes. Return chicken to pan and cook about 1 minute to heat through.

3. Serve chicken and sauce garnished with orange slices.

195 CURRIED APPLE AND CHUTNEY CHICKEN

Prep: 10 minutes   Cook: 16 minutes   Serves: 4

Curry powder is a blend of several spices. For the freshest flavor, it should be replaced every six months or so. This dish is good served with rice and steamed broccoli.

¼ cup flour
1½ teaspoons curry powder
½ teaspoon salt
⅛ to ¼ teaspoon cayenne, to
   taste
1 pound thinly sliced chicken
   cutlets

4 tablespoons butter
1 tart apple, thinly sliced
½ cup cider, apple juice, or dry
   white wine
½ cup chicken broth
3 tablespoons chopped
   mango chutney

1. On a shallow dish, combine flour, curry powder, salt, and cayenne. Dip chicken into seasoned flour to coat lightly. In a large frying pan, melt 1½ tablespoons of butter. Add half of chicken and cook over medium-high heat, turning once, until white throughout, about 5 minutes. Remove from pan. Repeat with another 1½ tablespoons butter and remaining chicken. Remove second batch of chicken from pan.

2. Melt remaining 1 tablespoon butter in pan. Add apple slices, reduce heat to medium, and cook, stirring, until softened and lightly glazed, about 3 minutes. Add cider and broth, stirring up browned bits clinging to bottom of pan. Simmer until sauce is lightly reduced and thickened, about 2 minutes.

3. Stir in chutney. Return chicken to pan to heat through, about 1 minute. Serve at once.

---

196 SHORTCUT CHICKEN AND DUMPLINGS
Prep: 5 minutes   Cook: 19 minutes   Serves: 2 to 3

If you think chicken and dumplings are just for a big Sunday supper, try this shortcut recipe that's perfect for two people who have little time but want lots of great taste.

1½ **tablespoons flour**
1½ **teaspoons dried thyme**
½ **teaspoon dried marjoram**
¼ **teaspoon salt**
¼ **teaspoon freshly ground pepper**
½ **pound skinless, boneless chicken thighs or breasts, cut into 1-inch chunks**

1½ **tablespoons butter**
1 **(1-pound) bag frozen stew vegetables**
2 **cups chicken broth**
1 **(4½-ounce) tube refrigerated biscuit dough**

1. In a plastic or paper bag, shake together flour, 1 teaspoon thyme, ¼ teaspoon marjoram, salt, and pepper. Shake chicken in bag to coat with seasoned flour. Reserve excess flour.

2. Melt butter in a large frying pan with a lid. Cook chicken over medium-high heat, turning often, until browned, about 4 minutes. Stir in reserved seasoned flour and cook, stirring, 1 minute. Add vegetables and broth. Bring just to a boil.

3. Divide biscuits into 6 rounds and set on top of simmering liquid. Sprinkle with remaining ½ teaspoon thyme and ¼ teaspoon marjoram. Cover and simmer over low heat until dumplings are puffed and springy to touch, about 14 minutes. Serve chicken, dumplings, and broth in shallow soup bowls.

197   SPICED FRUITED CHICKEN
Prep: 10 minutes   Cook: 20 to 22 minutes   Serves: 4

- 4 skinless, boneless chicken breast halves
- ¼ teaspoon salt
- ⅛ teaspoon freshly ground pepper
- 2 tablespoons vegetable oil
- 1 medium onion, chopped
- 1 tablespoon minced fresh ginger
- 2 teaspoons chili powder
- ½ teaspoon ground cumin
- ½ teaspoon ground coriander
- ½ teaspoon ground mace
- ½ cup dry white wine
- ½ cup chicken broth
- 1 tablespoon lemon juice
- 1 tablespoon soy sauce
- 1 cup mixed chopped dried fruit tidbits (about 4 ounces)

1. Season chicken with salt and pepper. In a large frying pan, heat oil over medium heat. Add chicken and cook, turning once or twice, until browned, about 6 minutes. Remove from pan.

2. Add onion to the pan drippings and cook, stirring often, until softened, 3 to 5 minutes. Stir in chili powder, cumin, coriander, and mace. Cook, stirring, 1 minute. Add wine, broth, lemon juice, soy sauce, and fruit.

3. Return chicken to pan. Bring sauce to a simmer, reduce heat to medium-low, cover, and cook until chicken is white throughout, about 10 minutes.

198   HURRY-UP HASH
Prep: 10 minutes   Cook: 20 minutes   Serves: 4

- 5 cups frozen hash brown potatoes (about ½ pound), thawed
- 3 cups cubed cooked chicken (about ¾ pound)
- ¼ cup milk
- 1 teaspoon Worcestershire sauce
- 1 large onion, chopped
- 1 large green bell pepper, chopped
- 1 teaspoon dried thyme
- ¾ teaspoon freshly ground pepper
- ¼ teaspoon salt
- 3 tablespoons vegetable oil
- 4 fried or poached eggs (optional)
- Ketchup

1. In a large bowl, stir together potatoes, chicken, milk, Worcestershire, onion, bell pepper, thyme, pepper, and salt.

2. Heat oil in a large frying pan, preferably a 10-inch cast-iron skillet. Add hash and press with a spatula to flatten over bottom of pan. Cover and cook 5 minutes over medium-high heat. Use a spatula to stir up crusty bottom of the hash and cook in same way, stirring up 3 more times until hash is golden, a total of about 20 minutes.

3. Serve each portion of hash topped with an egg, if desired, and accompanied by ketchup.

199   LEMON AND THYME-CRUSTED CHICKEN CUTLETS

Prep: 10 minutes   Cook: 12 minutes   Serves: 4

If you use fresh herbs, the presentation here is elegant enough for company. While I suggest thyme, tarragon or dill will do as well here.

½ **cup milk**
1 **tablespoon lemon juice**
1 **pound thinly sliced chicken breast cutlets**
¼ **cup cornmeal**
¼ **cup flour**
1 **tablespoon chopped fresh thyme or 1 teaspoon dried**

½ **teaspoon salt**
½ **teaspoon freshly ground pepper**
¼ **cup olive oil**
Lemon wedges and fresh thyme sprigs, for garnish

1. In a shallow dish, combine milk and lemon juice. Add chicken, turning to coat completely. In another shallow dish, combine cornmeal, flour, thyme, salt, and pepper. Dredge chicken in cornmeal, patting coating onto chicken with your hands.

2. In a large frying pan, heat 2 tablespoons of olive oil over medium heat. Add half of chicken and cook, turning once, until golden brown and cooked through, about 6 minutes. Remove chicken from pan and repeat with remaining oil and chicken.

3. Serve chicken garnished with lemon wedges and thyme sprigs.

---

200   CHICKEN MARSALA

Prep: 10 minutes   Cook: 14 to 15 minutes   Serves: 4

¼ **cup flour**
½ **teaspoon salt**
¼ **teaspoon freshly ground pepper**
1 **pound thinly sliced chicken breast cutlets**

3 **tablespoons butter**
¼ **cup minced shallots**
1 **cup dry marsala**
2 **teaspoons lemon juice**
Chopped parsley, for garnish

1. In a shallow dish, combine flour, salt, and pepper. Dip chicken into seasoned flour to coat lightly.

2. In a large frying pan, melt 1½ tablespoons of butter over medium-high heat. Cook half of chicken, turning once, until white throughout, about 5 minutes. Remove to a plate. Repeat with remaining butter and chicken.

3. Add shallots to pan drippings. Cook until softened, 1 to 2 minutes. Add marsala and bring to a boil, scraping up browned bits from bottom of pan. Boil, stirring often, until slightly reduced, about 3 minutes. Stir in lemon juice. Season with additional salt and pepper to taste. Return chicken and any juices that have accumulated on plate to sauce to heat. Serve chicken and sauce garnished with parsley.

201   CHICKEN MILANO
Prep: 5 minutes   Cook: 11 to 13 minutes   Serves: 4

Milan is the fashion capital of Italy. This presentation is truly a designer dish with its brilliant red and green saucing. Keep the pesto and roasted peppers on hand for any last-minute entertaining occasion. The chicken can be served hot or at room temperature.

1 (7½-ounce) jar roasted red peppers, drained
2 large shallots
1 tablespoon balsamic vinegar
3 tablespoons olive oil, preferably extra-virgin
4 skinless, boneless chicken breast halves

¼ teaspoon salt
⅛ teaspoon freshly ground pepper
½ cup prepared pesto sauce
4 fresh basil sprigs (optional), for garnish

1. Cut 4 thin slices from roasted peppers and reserve for garnish. Place remainder in a food processor. With machine on, drop shallots through feed tube and process 15 seconds. Pour in vinegar and 1 tablespoon of olive oil. Puree until roasted pepper sauce is smooth, about 20 seconds.

2. Season chicken with salt and pepper. In a large frying pan, heat remaining 2 tablespoons oil. Add chicken and cook over medium-heat, turning once or twice, until white throughout, 10 to 12 minutes.

3. To serve, spoon about 2 tablespoons each of roasted pepper sauce and pesto alongside each other on serving plates. Use a knife to lightly swirl together and marbleize sauces. Place chicken atop sauces and garnish with reserved roasted pepper slices and basil, if desired.

202   QUICK CHICKEN FLORENTINE
Prep: 12 minutes   Cook: 18 minutes   Serves: 6

6 skinless, boneless chicken breast halves
1 (10-ounce) package chopped frozen spinach, thawed and squeezed dry
¾ cup seasoned dry bread crumbs
½ cup shredded mozzarella cheese

1 egg, beaten
2 tablespoons butter or vegetable oil
1 (10¾-ounce) can cream of mushroom soup
⅓ cup milk
¼ cup marsala

1. Place each chicken breast between pieces of plastic wrap. Working from center outward, lightly pound with a flat mallet or rolling pin to less than ¼-inch thickness. Remove plastic wrap.

2. In a medium bowl, toss together spinach, ¼ cup of bread crumbs, and cheese. Divide mixture among centers of flattened breasts. Roll up to enclose filling completely, pressing edges together to adhere. Dip rolls into egg, then roll in remaining crumbs to coat lightly.

3. In a large frying pan, melt butter over medium heat. Add chicken and cook, turning carefully to brown both sides, about 8 minutes. Remove rolls from pan.

4. Add soup, milk, and marsala to pan. Bring to a boil, stirring up browned bits on bottom. Return rolls to pan. Reduce heat to medium-low, cover, and simmer until chicken is white throughout, about 10 minutes.

---

203   QUICK CHICKEN GUMBO
Prep: 10 minutes   Cook: 17 minutes   Serves: 6

A real gumbo relies on a traditional roux and long simmering. This version combines browning the chicken with making the roux and cooks in practically no time at all.

3 **tablespoons flour**	4 **cups chicken broth**
1 **teaspoon dried thyme**	2 **(14½-ounce) cans stewed**
¼ **teaspoon salt**	**tomatoes**
¼ **teaspoon freshly ground**	1 **(10-ounce) package frozen**
pepper	**sliced okra, thawed**
1 **pound skinless, boneless**	½ **to 1 teaspoon Tabasco or**
chicken thighs or breasts,	**other hot pepper sauce**
cut into 1-inch cubes	3 **cups prepared instant white**
¼ **cup vegetable oil**	**rice**
¼ **pound smoked ham,**	
coarsely diced	

1. In a plastic bag, shake together flour, thyme, salt, and pepper. Add chicken a few pieces at a time and shake to coat. In a large saucepan, heat oil over high heat. Add chicken and cook, stirring, until richly browned, about 4 minutes.

2. Add ham and cook 1 minute. Stir in broth, tomatoes, and okra. Bring to a boil. Reduce heat to medium-low, cover, and simmer 12 minutes. Season with Tabasco to taste.

3. To serve, spoon rice into soup bowls. Ladle gumbo over rice.

204 MOLE IN A MINUTE
Prep: 5 minutes   Cook: 17 to 18 minutes   Serves: 6

Mole is a complex Mexican sauce with a lengthy list of ingredients and a long cooking time. Commercial chili powder and seasoned stewed tomatoes go a long way toward approximating the flavor in mere minutes.

1½ **pounds skinless, boneless chicken thighs**
¼ **teaspoon salt**
¼ **teaspoon freshly ground pepper**
2 **tablespoons chili powder**
3 **tablespoons vegetable oil**

½ **teaspoon ground cinnamon**
2 **(14½-ounce) cans Mexican or "chili-style" stewed tomatoes**
½ **ounce unsweetened baking chocolate, chopped**

1. Season chicken lightly with salt, pepper, and 1 tablespoon of chili powder. In a large frying pan or flameproof casserole, heat oil over medium heat. Add chicken and cook, turning once or twice, until browned, about 6 minutes. Stir in remaining chili powder and cinnamon; then add tomatoes and chocolate.

2. Cover pan, reduce heat to medium-low, and simmer until chicken is tender with no trace of pink, about 8 minutes. Remove chicken to a serving dish. Boil, uncovered, until sauce is slightly reduced and thickened, 3 to 4 minutes. Pour mole over chicken and serve.

205 CHICKEN WITH PEPPERED PEACHES
Prep: 10 minutes   Cook: 17 minutes   Serves: 4

4 **skinless, boneless chicken breast halves**
¼ **teaspoon salt**
1 **tablespoon chopped fresh mint**
1 **teaspoon coarsely ground black pepper**
2½ **tablespoons butter**

3 **medium shallots, thinly sliced**
2 **ripe, firm peaches, peeled and sliced**
½ **cup dry red or white wine**
2 **tablespoons peach brandy**
Mint sprigs, for garnish

1. Use your hands to flatten chicken breasts to an even thickness. Season with salt, 1 teaspoon of mint, and ½ teaspoon of pepper. In a frying pan, melt 1½ tablespoons of butter over medium heat. Add chicken and cook, turning once or twice, until golden outside and nearly cooked through, about 12 minutes. Remove from pan.

2. Melt remaining 1 tablespoon butter in pan. Add shallots and peaches and cook, stirring gently, until peaches are just softened, about 3 minutes. Season with remaining mint and pepper. Stir in wine and peach brandy. Return chicken to pan and simmer 2 minutes.

3. Serve chicken and sauce garnished with mint sprigs.

206 LOUISIANA SPICY PECAN CHICKEN
Prep: 10 minutes   Cook: 18 to 20 minutes   Serves: 4

4 skinless, boneless chicken breast halves or thighs	½ cup coarsely chopped pecans
¾ teaspoon dried thyme	¼ cup sliced scallions
½ teaspoon salt	¼ cup dry white wine
¼ teaspoon freshly ground pepper	¼ to ½ teaspoon Tabasco or other hot pepper sauce
3 tablespoons butter	

1. Season chicken with thyme, salt, and pepper. In a large frying pan, melt 2 tablespoons of butter over medium heat. Add chicken and cook, turning once or twice, until chicken is white throughout, 13 to 15 minutes. Remove chicken to a platter and cover with foil to keep warm.

2. Add remaining 1 tablespoon butter and pecans to pan and cook, stirring, until nuts are browned and fragrant, about 3 minutes. Stir in scallions and cook 30 seconds. Add wine and simmer 1 minute. Stir in Tabasco to taste.

3. Pour sauce over chicken and serve.

207 POACHED CHICKEN IN PARSLEY-DILL SAUCE
Prep: 15 minutes   Cook: 12 to 15 minutes   Stand: 10 minutes
Serves: 4

Serve this very pretty chicken main course with boiled baby carrots and sautéed red peppers for a colorful presentation. Use low-fat mayonnaise and nonfat yogurt, if you like.

1 pound skinless, boneless chicken breast halves	1 garlic clove, crushed through a press
¼ teaspoon salt	1 tablespoon Dijon mustard
⅛ teaspoon freshly ground pepper	½ cup chopped parsley
½ cup mayonnaise	2 tablespoons chopped fresh dill or 2 teaspoons dried
½ cup plain yogurt	

1. In a saucepan or frying pan large enough to hold chicken in a single layer, poach chicken in simmering lightly salted water to cover over medium-low heat until white throughout, 12 to 15 minutes. Drain and cool chicken on a plate in refrigerator for 10 minutes. Season with salt and pepper.

2. Meanwhile, stir together mayonnaise, yogurt, garlic, mustard, parsley, and dill. Let stand 10 minutes at room temperature.

3. To serve, spread a thin layer of sauce on serving plates. Cut chicken crosswise on a diagonal into ½-inch-thick slices. Arrange in fan shapes over sauce. Ladle on a ribbon of remaining sauce.

208 CHICKEN WITH SPICY PAPRIKA SAUCE
Prep: 10 minutes   Cook: 18 to 20 minutes   Serves: 3 to 4

6 skinless, boneless chicken thighs	2 tablespoons vegetable oil or butter
½ teaspoon salt	1 medium onion, thinly sliced
⅛ teaspoon freshly ground pepper	¼ teaspoon cayenne
1 tablespoon sweet Hungarian paprika	½ cup dry white wine
	½ cup heavy cream

1. Season chicken with salt, pepper, and 1 teaspoon of paprika. In a large frying pan, heat oil over medium heat. Add chicken and cook, turning once or twice, until lightly browned, about 5 minutes. Remove chicken to a plate.

2. Add onion to pan and cook, stirring often, until softened, 3 to 5 minutes. Sprinkle remaining 2 teaspoons paprika and cayenne over onion and stir to mix; then add wine. Bring to a boil, scraping up browned bits from bottom of pan.

3. Return chicken to pan along with any juices that have accumulated on plate. Reduce heat to medium-low, cover, and simmer until chicken is tender with no traces of pink, about 8 minutes. Stir in cream. Raise heat to medium-high and cook 2 minutes, uncovered, until sauce is slightly reduced. Season with additional salt and pepper to taste before serving.

209 CHICKEN SMOTHERED IN SHIITAKE MUSHROOMS
Prep: 10 minutes   Cook: 17 to 19 minutes   Serves: 4

Fresh shiitake mushrooms are readily available now, but if you can't get them, use regular fresh mushrooms and a few sliced dried mushrooms (any kind) that have been reconstituted by soaking in very hot water until softened.

1 pound skinless, boneless chicken thighs	⅓ cup chopped red onion
½ teaspoon ground coriander	2 garlic cloves, crushed through a press
¼ teaspoon salt	⅓ cup chicken broth
⅛ teaspoon freshly ground pepper	3 tablespoons dry sherry
3 tablespoons vegetable oil	2 teaspoons soy sauce
½ pound fresh shiitake mushrooms, stemmed, caps sliced	1 teaspoon hot chili oil

1. Season chicken with coriander, salt, and pepper. In a large frying pan, heat oil over medium-high heat. Add chicken and cook, turning once or twice, until nearly cooked through, 10 to 12 minutes. Remove from pan.

2. Add mushrooms, onion, and garlic to pan drippings. Cook over medium heat, stirring often, 3 minutes. Add broth, sherry, soy sauce, and chili oil.

3. Return chicken to pan. Partially cover, reduce heat to medium-low, and cook until chicken is cooked through with no trace of pink and mushrooms are tender, about 4 minutes.

---

210 CHICKEN AND BRANDIED PEARS
Prep: 10 minutes   Cook: 16 minutes   Serves: 4

Pears used for cooking should be slightly underripe—firm, yet yielding slightly to pressure.

4 **skinless, boneless chicken breast halves**	¼ **cup chopped shallots**
½ **teaspoon salt**	2 **pears, peeled and sliced ¼ inch thick**
¼ **teaspoon freshly ground pepper**	2 **tablespoons brandy**
1½ **teaspoons crumbled leaf sage**	⅓ **cup dry white wine**
2½ **tablespoons butter**	⅓ **cup chicken broth**
	½ **cup heavy cream**

1. Season chicken with salt, pepper, and half of sage. In a large frying pan, melt 2 tablespoons butter over medium-high heat. Add chicken and cook, turning once or twice, until lightly browned, about 5 minutes. Transfer to a plate. Add remaining ½ tablespoon of butter, shallots, pears, and remaining sage to drippings in pan. Cook, stirring, 2 minutes. Stir in brandy and cook 1 minute. Pour in wine and broth and bring to a boil, stirring up browned bits clinging to bottom of pan.

2. Return chicken to frying pan, reduce heat to medium-low, partially cover, and simmer until chicken is white throughout, about 6 minutes.

3. Remove chicken to a platter and cover with foil to keep warm. Add cream to sauce and boil 2 minutes to reduce slightly. Season generously with pepper and lightly with salt. Pour sauce over chicken and serve.

211 CHICKEN PARMESAN PRESTO
Prep: 10 minutes   Cook: 18 minutes   Serves: 4

4 skinless, boneless chicken
   breast halves
Salt and freshly ground
   pepper
2 tablespoons olive oil,
   preferably extra-virgin
2 garlic cloves, crushed
   through a press

3 cups bottled or canned
   marinara sauce,
   preferably with green
   peppers and mushrooms
¼ pound thinly sliced
   provolone cheese
2 tablespoons grated
   Parmesan cheese

1. Preheat oven to 400°F. Use your hands to flatten chicken to an even thickness. Season with salt and pepper. In a large frying pan, heat olive oil and cook chicken over medium heat, turning once or twice, until golden, about 5 minutes. Transfer to a shallow 2-quart baking dish.

2. Add garlic to pan drippings and cook until softened and fragrant, about 1 minute. Stir in marinara sauce. Ladle marinara sauce over chicken. Cover with provolone and sprinkle Parmesan cheese on top.

3. Bake, uncovered, until chicken is white throughout and cheese is melted and tinged with brown, about 12 minutes.

212 COLORFUL PEPPER CHICKEN
Prep: 10 minutes   Cook: 18 to 20 minutes   Serves: 4

4 skinless, boneless chicken
   breast halves
1 teaspoon dried oregano
¼ teaspoon salt
⅛ teaspoon freshly ground
   pepper
3 tablespoons olive oil,
   preferably extra-virgin
1 small red bell pepper, thinly
   sliced
1 small yellow bell pepper,
   thinly sliced

1 small green bell pepper,
   thinly sliced
1 medium onion, thinly sliced
2 garlic cloves, crushed
   through a press
½ cup dry white wine
1 tablespoon white wine
   vinegar
2 tablespoons chopped fresh
   basil or parsley

1. Season chicken with oregano, salt, and pepper. In a large frying pan, heat 2 tablespoons of oil over medium-high heat. Add chicken and cook, turning once or twice, until lightly browned, about 7 minutes. Remove from pan.

2. Add remaining 1 tablespoon oil to pan along with all 3 types of bell peppers, onion, and garlic. Cook, stirring often, 2 minutes. Add wine and return chicken to pan. Simmer, partially covered, until chicken is white throughout, 8 to 10 minutes. Stir in vinegar and basil. Simmer 1 minute and serve.

213 RAINBOW CHICKEN
Prep: 10 minutes   Cook: 8 to 10 minutes   Serves: 4

A colorful blend of vegetables showers this chicken. If you don't have a food processor, buy shredded peppers and carrots from the supermarket produce or salad section and shred the zucchini on a hand grater.

1 medium red bell pepper	¼ teaspoon freshly ground
1 medium carrot, peeled	pepper
1 medium zucchini	¼ cup olive oil
1 pound thinly sliced chicken	⅓ cup minced shallots
breast cutlets	¼ cup chopped fresh mint
½ teaspoon salt	½ cup dry white wine

1. Shred pepper, carrot, and zucchini in a food processor, using the coarse shredder or julienne disk, or on coarse holes of a hand grater. Set aside. Season chicken with half of salt and pepper.

2. In a large skillet, heat olive oil over medium-high heat. Add chicken and cook, turning, until golden on both sides and cooked through, 5 to 7 minutes. Remove to a small platter and cover with foil to keep warm.

3. Add shallots, shredded pepper, carrot, and zucchini, and mint to pan. Reduce heat to medium and cook, tossing, 1 minute. Add wine and simmer, stirring often, 2 minutes. Season with remaining salt and pepper. Spoon vegetables and sauce over chicken. Serve at once.

214 BAKED REUBEN CHICKEN
Prep: 5 minutes   Cook: 9 to 12 minutes   Serves: 4

3 slices of caraway rye bread	1 cup drained sauerkraut
4 skinless, boneless chicken	4 slices of Swiss cheese
breast halves	
⅔ cup bottled Thousand	
Island salad dressing	

1. Preheat oven to 500°F. In a food processor, grind bread to make about 1½ cups crumbs. Use your hands to flatten chicken to an even thickness. Dip chicken into salad dressing to coat completely, then dredge in bread crumbs to coat. Place in a single layer on a baking sheet.

2. Bake until coating is golden brown and chicken is white throughout, 8 to 10 minutes.

3. Preheat broiler. Divide sauerkraut on top of chicken breasts and top with cheese. Broil until cheese is melted, 1 to 2 minutes.

215   ALMOST-INSTANT SPANISH CHICKEN AND RICE

Prep: 10 minutes   Cook: 15 minutes   Serves: 4

⅛ teaspoon crushed saffron
   threads
1⅔ cups chicken broth
¾ pound skinless, boneless
   chicken breasts, cut into
   1-inch chunks
½ pound thinly sliced smoked
   sausage
2 tablespoons olive oil,
   preferably extra-virgin

1 (14½-ounce) can stewed
   tomatoes, preferably
   Creole-style
1 cup instant white rice
¼ cup chopped pimiento-
   stuffed olives
½ teaspoon Tabasco or other
   hot sauce

1. In a small saucepan, bring saffron and broth to a simmer, stirring to dissolve saffron. Meanwhile, in a large frying pan, cook chicken and sausage in olive oil over medium heat, stirring often, until chicken is white throughout, about 10 minutes. Add tomatoes and rice. Stir in simmering broth mixture.

2. Remove pan from heat, cover, and let stand until liquid is absorbed, about 5 minutes.

3. Stir in olives and Tabasco and serve.

216   CHICKEN PICCATA

Prep: 10 minutes   Cook: 14 minutes   Serves: 4

Thinly sliced chicken breast cutlets can be substituted for veal in almost any of the classic recipes. Here is a good example.

¼ cup flour
½ teaspoon salt
½ teaspoon freshly ground
   pepper
1 pound thinly sliced chicken
   breast cutlets
3 tablespoons olive oil
1 garlic clove, crushed
   through a press

½ cup dry white wine
½ cup chicken broth
1½ tablespoons lemon juice
¾ teaspoon grated lemon zest
4 thin lemon slices, for
   garnish
2 tablespoons chopped
   parsley

1. In a shallow dish, combine flour, salt, and pepper. Dip chicken into seasoned flour to coat lightly. In a large frying pan, heat half of olive oil over medium heat. Add half of chicken and cook, turning once or twice, until white throughout, about 5 minutes. Remove from pan. Repeat using remaining oil and chicken.

2. Cook garlic in pan drippings for 30 seconds. Add wine, broth, and lemon juice. Bring to a boil, stirring up browned bits from bottom of pan. Boil until lightly reduced, about 2 minutes. Stir in lemon zest. Return chicken to pan to reheat, about 1 minute.

3. Serve chicken and sauce garnished with lemon slices and with parsley sprinkled on top.

---

217 CHICKEN AU POIVRE
Prep: 10 minutes   Cook: 19 to 20 minutes   Serves: 4

Steak is traditional in this French classic, but I really prefer it made with chicken breasts.

4 skinless, boneless chicken breast halves
½ teaspoon salt
2 teaspoons cracked or coarsely ground black pepper
3 tablespoons butter
¼ cup thinly sliced shallots
½ pound mushrooms, thinly sliced, wild or cultivated or a combination

¾ teaspoon dried tarragon
2 tablespoons Cognac or brandy
½ cup dry white wine
2 tablespoons chopped parsley

1. Sprinkle chicken with salt, then use your hands to press in pepper. In a frying pan, melt 1½ tablespoons of butter over medium heat. Add chicken and cook, turning once or twice, until golden and white throughout, about 12 minutes. Remove from pan.

2. Melt remaining 1½ tablespoons butter in frying pan. Add shallots, mushrooms, and tarragon and cook over medium heat, stirring often, until mushrooms are softened, about 5 minutes.

3. Stir in Cognac and wine, scraping up browned bits from bottom of pan. Return chicken to pan and simmer 2 to 3 minutes to heat through. Serve at once, garnished with parsley.

218 POTPIE IN A PINCH
Prep: 5 minutes   Cook: 22 minutes   Serves: 6

Baking the crust separately is a restaurant trick that works at home, too.

1 refrigerated pie crust disk
(½ of a 15-ounce package)
2 tablespoons plus 1 teaspoon
flour
2 tablespoons butter
1 teaspoon poultry seasoning
1 cup milk
1 cup chicken broth
1 (10¾-ounce) can cream of
chicken soup

3 cups cubed cooked chicken
(about ¾ pound)
1 (10-ounce) package frozen
mixed vegetables,
thawed
1 cup frozen pearl onions,
thawed

1. Preheat oven to 450°F. Unfold pie crust and sprinkle 1 teaspoon of flour over pastry. Place crust, floured side down, on an ungreased baking sheet. Invert a 2-quart round casserole over crust and use a sharp knife to cut crust to same diameter as casserole dish. Use your fingers to crimp up edges of pastry crust, then use a knife or small cookie cutter to cut out small slashes or shapes in crust. Bake until golden, about 11 minutes.

2. Meanwhile, in a large saucepan, melt butter over medium heat. Add flour and poultry seasoning and cook over medium heat, stirring, 1 minute. Stir in milk, broth, and undiluted soup. Bring to a boil, stirring constantly. Add chicken, mixed vegetables, and onions. Reduce heat to medium-low and cook, stirring often, 10 minutes.

3. Spoon hot chicken mixture into casserole. Top with baked crust and serve.

219 CHICKEN IN RASPBERRY VINEGAR SAUCE
Prep: 5 minutes   Cook: 15 minutes   Serves: 4

Blueberries and blueberry vinegar are another option in this light summer dish.

1 pound thinly sliced chicken
breast cutlets
¼ teaspoon salt
¼ teaspoon freshly ground
pepper
½ teaspoon ground cardamom
2½ tablespoons butter

¼ cup minced shallots
1 cup chicken broth
3 tablespoons raspberry or
other fruit-flavored
vinegar
1 tablespoon honey
½ cup fresh raspberries

1. Season chicken with salt, pepper, and cardamom. In a large frying pan, melt 1 tablespoon of butter over medium-high heat. Add half of chicken and cook, turning once or twice, until white throughout, about 5 minutes. Remove from pan. Repeat, using another 1 tablespoon butter and chicken.

2. Add remaining ½ tablespoon butter and shallots to pan, reduce heat to medium, and cook, stirring until softened, about 1 minute. Add broth, raise heat to high, and bring to a boil, stirring up browned bits from bottom of pan. Boil 1 minute. Stir in vinegar and honey and boil 2 minutes longer to reduce sauce slightly. Season with additional salt and pepper to taste. Return chicken to pan and cook until heated through, about 1 minute.

3. Serve chicken with sauce spooned over it and raspberries sprinkled on top.

---

220 CHICKEN FRIED RICE
Prep: 15 minutes   Cook: 9 minutes   Serves: 4 to 6

To make this easy dish in a flash, use microwave-reheated leftover rice, or prepare instant or regular rice. Rotisserie or smoked chicken from the deli or leftover chicken—whether grilled, roasted, or poached—are interchangeable here.

2½ tablespoons vegetable oil	1 small yellow bell pepper, thinly sliced
2 eggs beaten with 1 tablespoon water (or ½ cup liquid egg substitute)	2 tablespoons minced fresh ginger
1½ cups thinly sliced scallions	2 tablespoons soy sauce
1 small red bell pepper, thinly sliced	6 cups hot cooked white rice
	3 cups diced cooked chicken (about ¾ pound)

1. Heat 1½ tablespoons of oil in a heavy 10-inch frying pan, preferably non-stick. Pour in half of beaten egg, tilting pan to coat bottom. Cook over medium heat until bottom is pale gold and flecked with brown, about 2 minutes. Loosen edges with a spatula, flip omelet over, and cook 1 minute on other side. Remove from pan. Repeat to make another omelet. Cut omelets into thin strips.

2. In same frying pan, heat remaining 1 tablespoon oil. Add scallions, red and yellow peppers, and ginger and cook over medium-high heat, stirring constantly, until just softened, about 3 minutes. Stir in soy sauce.

3. In a large mixing bowl, combine rice, chicken, omelet strips, and vegetables. Toss to mix well and serve.

221 CHICKEN SALTIMBOCCA
Prep: 10 minutes   Cook: 11 minutes   Serves: 4

Saltimbocca literally means "jump in the mouth" in Italian. It's so quick and easy that you must be ready to jump!

1 **pound thinly sliced chicken breast cutlets**	2 **tablespoons extra-virgin olive oil or butter**
2 **teaspoons chopped fresh sage or ¾ teaspoon crumbled dried sage**	2 **ounces thinly sliced prosciutto**
¼ **teaspoon salt**	3 **ounces thinly sliced mozzarella cheese**
¼ **teaspoon freshly ground pepper**	½ **cup dry white wine** **Fresh sage leaves (optional)**

1. Season chicken lightly with chopped sage, salt, and pepper. In a large frying pan, heat olive oil over medium-high heat. Add chicken in batches and cook until browned on one side, about 3 minutes per batch. Turn and layer on prosciutto and cheese. Reduce heat to medium-low, cover pan, and cook until cheese is melted and chicken is white throughout, about 2 minutes. Remove from pan.

2. Add wine to frying pan and cook, stirring up browned bits clinging to bottom. Boil until slightly reduced, about 1 minute.

3. Spoon sauce over chicken. Garnish with sage leaves, if desired.

222 CHICKEN SCHNITZEL WITH ANCHOVY BUTTER SAUCE
Prep: 15 minutes   Cook: 13 minutes   Serves: 4

Chicken effectively replaces veal in this classic Austrian recipe.

1¼ **cups fine fresh bread crumbs (from about 3 slices of bread)**	1 **pound thinly sliced chicken breast cutlets**
3 **tablespoons flour**	4 **tablespoons butter**
¼ **teaspoon salt**	3 **anchovy fillets**
¼ **teaspoon freshly ground pepper**	½ **cup dry white wine** **Lemon wedges and paprika, for garnish**
1 **egg**	

1. Spread bread crumbs onto a plate. In a shallow dish, combine flour, salt, and pepper. In another shallow dish, beat egg with 1 tablespoon water. Lightly coat chicken with seasoned flour, then dip in egg, and finally dip into bread crumbs, patting to adhere.

2. In a large frying pan, melt 2 tablespoons of butter. Add half of chicken and cook over medium-high heat, turning once, until white throughout, about 5 minutes. Remove from pan. Repeat with remaining 2 tablespoons butter and remaining chicken.

3. Add anchovies to pan drippings. Cook 1 minute, mashing anchovies with back of a spoon. Stir in wine, scraping up browned bits clinging to bottom. Simmer 2 minutes. Spoon sauce over chicken. Garnish with lemon wedges, dust with paprika, and serve.

223 CHICKEN SAN JUAN
Prep: 10 minutes   Cook: 20 to 21 minutes   Serves: 6

In Old San Juan, there are several restaurants that serve wonderful traditional Puerto Rican fare. This recipe is more a re-creation of a memory than it is a true rendition.

1 **pound skinless, boneless chicken thighs**
¼ **teaspoon salt**
⅛ **teaspoon freshly ground pepper**
1 **teaspoon ground cumin**
½ **teaspoon turmeric**
2 **tablespoons vegetable oil**
2 **garlic cloves, crushed through a press**
3 **ears of corn, cut crosswise into 2-inch lengths**

1 **sweet potato, peeled and cut into 1-inch chunks**
1¼ **cups chicken broth, preferably reduced-sodium**
2 **(14½-ounce) cans Mexican or "chili-style" stewed tomatoes**
1 **tablespoon chopped pickled jalapeño peppers**
½ **cup sliced black olives**

1. Season chicken with salt, pepper, cumin, and turmeric. In a large frying pan or flameproof casserole, heat oil over medium heat. Add chicken and cook, turning once or twice, until browned, about 6 minutes.

2. Add garlic and cook 30 seconds. Add corn, sweet potato, broth, tomatoes, and jalapeño peppers. Cover pan, reduce heat to medium-low, and simmer 8 minutes.

3. Add olives and simmer, uncovered, until stew is slightly thickened, chicken is white throughout, and vegetables are tender, 5 to 6 minutes.

224   ROSEMARY AND CITRUS CHICKEN
Prep: 5 minutes   Cook: 12 minutes   Serves: 4

1 pound thinly sliced chicken
   breast cutlets
¼ teaspoon salt
¼ teaspoon freshly ground
   pepper
1 teaspoon dried rosemary
3 tablespoons olive oil
¼ cup chopped red onion

¼ cup chicken broth
¼ cup dry white wine
¼ cup orange juice
2 tablespoons lemon juice
1 teaspoon grated orange zest
½ teaspoon grated lemon zest
   Orange and lemon slices,
   for garnish

1. Season chicken with salt, pepper, and half of rosemary. In a large frying pan, heat olive oil over medium-high heat. Add chicken and cook, turning once or twice, until white throughout, about 5 minutes. Remove from pan.

2. Add onion and cook, stirring often, until softened, about 3 minutes. Add broth, wine, orange juice, lemon juice, orange zest, lemon zest, and remaining ½ teaspoon rosemary. Bring to a boil, stirring up browned bits from bottom of the pan. Boil until sauce is reduced by about one-third, about 3 minutes. Return chicken to pan and heat through, about 1 minute.

3. Serve chicken and sauce garnished with orange and lemon slices.

225   SESAME NOODLE CHICKEN
Prep: 10 minutes   Cook: 6 minutes   Serves: 4

Cooked chicken is a fine addition to this spicy Chinese noodle classic.

2 tablespoons rice wine
   vinegar
2 tablespoons soy sauce
2 tablespoons smooth peanut
   butter
1 tablespoon minced fresh
   ginger
2 garlic cloves, minced
2 teaspoons honey
½ teaspoon crushed hot red
   pepper

3 tablespoons vegetable oil
1 tablespoon Asian sesame oil
¾ pound whole wheat
   vermicelli
¼ pound snow peas, trimmed
2 cups slivered cooked
   chicken (about 4 ounces)
1 cup thinly sliced scallions

1. By hand with a whisk or in a blender, combine vinegar, soy sauce, peanut butter, ginger, garlic, honey, and hot pepper. Mix well. Blend in vegetable and sesame oil until peanut sauce is smooth.

2. Break vermicelli in half. Cook pasta in a large pot of boiling salted water until tender but still firm, about 6 minutes. Add snow peas to pasta during last 30 seconds of cooking. Drain pasta and snow peas in a colander.

3. Toss pasta and snow peas with chicken, peanut sauce, and ½ cup scallions. Serve at room temperature, with remaining scallions sprinkled on top.

226 SKILLET CHICKEN WITH APPLE, THYME, AND CORN BREAD DRESSING

Prep: 10 minutes   Cook: 19 to 20 minutes   Serves: 4

I like dressing with a crusty edge, so the frying pan goes under the broiler at the end for a few minutes in this dish. An old-fashioned cast-iron skillet is a good choice.

4 skinless, boneless chicken thighs or breasts	1 medium onion, chopped
⅛ teaspoon salt	1 celery rib, chopped
⅛ teaspoon freshly ground pepper	1 tart apple, peeled and chopped
1½ teaspoons dried thyme	¾ cup chicken broth
3 tablespoons butter	1½ cups packaged corn bread stuffing mix

1. Preheat broiler. Use your hands to flatten chicken to an even thickness. Season with salt, pepper, and 1 teaspoon of thyme.

2. In a large frying pan with flameproof handle, melt 1 tablespoon of butter over medium heat. Add chicken and cook, turning once or twice, until white throughout, about 12 minutes. Remove to a plate.

3. Melt remaining butter in pan. Add onion, celery, and apple and cook over medium heat, stirring often, until softened, about 5 minutes. Stir in remaining ½ teaspoon thyme, broth, and stuffing mix. Cook, stirring, until liquid is absorbed, about 30 seconds.

4. Return chicken to pan along with any juices that have accumulated on plate. Spoon stuffing on top of chicken. Place pan under broiler about 4 inches from heat. Broil until stuffing is lightly browned and crisped, 1 to 2 minutes.

227   OPEN SESAME CHICKEN
Prep: 10 minutes   Cook: 13 minutes   Serves: 4

Sesame seeds give a flavorful crunch to the coating for pan-fried chicken.

¾ cup milk
1 teaspoon Tabasco or other hot pepper sauce
1 pound thinly sliced chicken cutlets
¼ cup cornmeal
¼ cup flour
3 tablespoons sesame seeds

2 tablespoons finely chopped parsley
½ teaspoon salt
½ teaspoon freshly ground pepper
¼ cup vegetable oil
½ cup dry white wine
Parsley sprigs, for garnish

1. In a shallow dish, combine milk and Tabasco. Add chicken; turn to coat completely. In another shallow dish, combine cornmeal, flour, sesame seeds, parsley, salt, and pepper. Dredge chicken in cornmeal coating, patting onto chicken with your hands.

2. In a large frying pan, heat 2 tablespoons oil over medium-high heat. Add half of chicken and cook, turning once, until white throughout, about 6 minutes. Remove chicken from pan and repeat with remaining oil and chicken.

3. Stir wine into pan drippings, scraping up browned bits clinging to bottom. Simmer, stirring, 1 minute. Season with additional salt and pepper. Spoon sauce over chicken. Garnish with parsley sprigs.

228   SPEEDY CHICKEN STEW
Prep: 5 minutes   Cook: 23 minutes   Serves: 4

Since all of the vegetables here except for the frozen pearl onions and peas are precut and can found on any supermarket salad bar, the preparation time is practically nil. Feel free to use other vegetables of your choice.

4 skinless, boneless chicken thighs
¼ teaspoon salt
⅛ teaspoon freshly ground pepper
1½ teaspoons poultry seasoning
2 tablespoons olive oil
1 cup baby carrots or sliced carrots

1 cup sliced celery
1 cup frozen pearl onions, thawed
1½ cups chicken broth
1 cup broccoli florets
½ cup frozen green peas

1. Season chicken with salt, pepper, and ½ teaspoon of poultry seasoning. Heat oil in a large frying pan over medium-high heat. Add chicken and cook, turning, until lightly browned, about 6 minutes.

2. Add carrots, celery, and onions, stirring to coat with oil. Add broth and remaining 1 teaspoon poultry seasoning. Bring to a boil, reduce heat to medium-low, cover, and simmer 10 minutes.

3. Add broccoli and simmer 3 minutes. Add peas and simmer 2 minutes. Uncover, raise heat to medium-high, and boil 2 minutes to reduce broth slightly. Season with additional salt and pepper to taste. Serve chicken, vegetables, and broth in shallow soup bowls.

229   CHICKEN WITH ZINFANDEL-PRUNE SAUCE

Prep: 10 minutes   Cook: 21 to 24 minutes   Serves: 4

12 pitted prunes
 1 cup zinfandel or other full-
      bodied red wine
½ teaspoon crumbled dried
      leaf sage
 4 skinless, boneless chicken
      breast halves

½ teaspoon salt
¼ teaspoon freshly ground
      pepper
 2 tablespoons butter
 2 tablespoons minced shallots
 2 teaspoons Dijon mustard
½ cup chicken broth

1. In a nonreactive medium saucepan, bring prunes, wine, and sage to a simmer. Cover and simmer over medium-low heat until prunes are plumped, 8 to 10 minutes. Drain, reserving cooking liquid.

2. Meanwhile, season chicken with salt and pepper. In a large frying pan, melt butter over medium heat. Add chicken and cook, turning once or twice, until golden and nearly cooked through, about 10 minutes. Remove from pan.

3. Add shallots to drippings in pan and cook, stirring, until softened, about 1 minute. Add mustard, broth, and reserved prune cooking liquid, stirring up browned bits in bottom of the pan. Return chicken to the pan and simmer, partially covered, until chicken is white throughout but still moist, 2 to 3 minutes. Serve chicken with sauce with prunes spooned over it.

230 STUFFING FRIED CHICKEN
Prep: 10 minutes   Cook: 15 to 20 minutes   Serves: 4

Serve with cranberry sauce and frozen mashed potatoes for a quick taste fix when Thanksgiving is still months away.

1½ **cups corn bread stuffing mix**
4 **skinless, boneless chicken breast halves**
1 **egg beaten with 1 teaspoon water**
3 **tablespooons butter**
½ **teaspoon crumbled dried leaf sage**

½ **cup chicken broth**
½ **cup half-and-half or light cream**
Salt and freshly ground pepper

1. In a food processor, crush stuffing mix to make crumbs. Use your hands to flatten chicken to an even thickness. Dip chicken into egg, then into stuffing crumbs.

2. In a frying pan, melt butter over medium heat. Add chicken and cook, turning carefully once or twice with a spatula, until crust is a rich golden brown and chicken is white throughout, 12 to 15 minutes. Remove to a platter and cover with foil to keep warm.

3. Add sage, broth, and half-and-half to pan drippings. Bring to a boil, stirring up browned bits clinging to bottom of pan. Boil, stirring often, until gravy is lightly thickened, 3 to 5 minutes. Season with salt and pepper to taste. Spoon gravy over chicken and serve.

231 POULET AU VINAIGRE
Prep 10 minutes   Cook: 15 to 20 minutes   Serves: 6

Good red wine vinegar is the secret to this simple recipe.

6 **skinless, boneless chicken breast halves**
¾ **teaspoon dried rosemary**
½ **teaspoon salt**
¼ **teaspoon freshly ground pepper**
2 **tablespoons olive oil, preferably extra-virgin**
4 **garlic cloves, crushed through a press**

1 **(14½-ounce) can diced tomatoes, drained**
1½ **cups chicken broth, preferably reduced-sodium**
⅓ **cup red wine vinegar**
1 **tablespoon butter, cut into small pieces**
3 **tablespoons chopped parsley**

1. Season chicken with rosemary, salt, and pepper. In a large frying pan, heat olive oil over medium-high heat. Add chicken and cook, turning once or twice, until lightly browned, 5 to 7 minutes. Remove from pan.

2. Add garlic to drippings in pan and cook 30 seconds. Add drained tomatoes, broth, and vinegar. Return chicken to pan and simmer, partially covered, until chicken is white throughout but still moist, 7 to 9 minutes.

3. Remove chicken to a platter and cover with foil to keep warm. Boil sauce over high heat until lightly reduced, 2 to 3 minutes. Remove from heat and swirl in butter.

4. Pour sauce over chicken, sprinkle with parsley, and serve.

---

232 SHORTCUT SHEPHERD'S PIE
Prep: 10 minutes   Cook: 20 minutes   Serves: 4

This is one good thing to do with leftover roast chicken and mashed potatoes. You can also start with deli rotisserie chicken and frozen mashed potatoes. High-temperature baking finishes this dish off quickly.

1 **medium onion, chopped**	3 **cups cubed cooked chicken**
1 **green bell pepper, chopped**	**(about ¾ pound)**
2 **garlic cloves, crushed**	4 **cups room-temperature**
through a press	**leftover mashed potatoes**
1 **tablespoon olive oil**	**or prepared frozen**
2 **(14½-ounce) cans Italian-**	**mashed potatoes**
style stewed tomatoes	¼ **cup grated Parmesan cheese**

1. Preheat oven to 500°F. In a large ovenproof frying pan, cook onion, bell pepper, and garlic in olive oil over medium-high heat until just softened, about 3 minutes.

2. Stir in tomatoes and simmer, uncovered, 7 minutes. Stir in chicken. Spread mashed potatoes over chicken mixture, spreading almost to edge of pan. Sprinkle cheese on top.

3. Bake until filling is bubbly hot and potatoes are tinged with gold and heated through, about 10 minutes.

Chapter 10

Chicken and Pasta Forever

Here are two of America's favorite foods, married in a variety of sauces and flavorings. Teamed together, they offer an unlimited wealth of delicious opportunities as well as the best of low-fat protein and complex carbohydrates.

Precisely because of the versatility of both chicken and pasta, the following recipes are starting points in which you can personalize a dish to fit your own taste and needs and what you have on hand. Just remember to stay within a category. For example, if a recipe calls for boneless chicken thighs, you can use boneless breasts just as easily. If bone-in skinless breasts are called for, bone-in skinless thighs or drumsticks will work just as well. The same applies to the pasta. If spaghetti is listed, vermicelli or linguine or any other long-strand pasta can be used. If rigatoni is the ingredient, penne or another short stubby pasta will work, too. In the case of both the chicken and the pasta, cooking times may need to be adjusted slightly in the variations, but the dish will work. I've chosen the chicken cuts and pasta shapes specified because I like them best in each dish, but on any given day (or depending upon what I have in the refrigerator or on the shelf), I might change my mind, too.

So, with chicken and pasta, the sky is the limit, Henny Penny.

233 MUSTARD CHICKEN PRIMAVERA
Prep: 10 minutes   Cook: 9 to 11 minutes   Serves: 4

To save time here, take advantage of the many cut-up vegetables available in the produce section or at the salad bar of supermarkets. Another vegetable, such as zucchini or broccoli, can be substituted for the asparagus.

¾ **pound bow tie pasta**
¾ **pound skinless, boneless chicken breast, cut into 1-inch chunks**
¼ **cup grainy Dijon mustard**
3 **tablespoons olive oil, preferably extra-virgin**
16 **slender asparagus spears, cut diagonally into 1½-inch pieces**

1 **cup slivered carrots**
1 **cup slivered red bell pepper**
¾ **cup thinly sliced scallions**
¾ **cup frozen baby green peas**
1 **cup heavy cream**
½ **cup chicken broth**
¼ **cup chopped fresh basil**
½ **teaspoon salt**
¼ **teaspoon freshly ground pepper**

1. In a large pot of boiling salted water, cook pasta until tender but still firm, 10 to 12 minutes. Drain in a colander.

2. Meanwhile, toss chicken with 2 tablespoons of mustard to coat lightly. In a large frying pan, cook chicken in olive oil over medium-high heat 3 minutes. Reduce heat to medium and add asparagus, carrots, and bell pepper. Cook, stirring, 2 minutes. Add scallions and cook 30 seconds. Add peas, cream, broth, basil, salt, pepper, and remaining 2 tablespoons mustard. Bring to a boil, reduce heat, and simmer until chicken is white throughout and vegetables are crisp-tender, 3 to 5 minutes.

3. Place hot cooked pasta in a large serving bowl. Pour sauce with chicken and vegetables over pasta. Toss to mix well. Serve in shallow bowls.

234 CHICKEN AND CHEESE CANNELLONI
Prep: 20 minutes   Cook: 40 to 42 minutes   Serves: 6

12 **cannelloni tubes (about 8 ounces)**
2 **cups chopped cooked chicken (about ½ pound)**
1½ **cups part-skim ricotta cheese**
⅓ **cup grated Parmesan or Romano cheese**
⅓ **cup chopped flat-leaf parsley**

1 **egg**
1 **garlic clove, minced**
¾ **teaspoon salt**
½ **teaspoon freshly ground pepper**
½ **teaspoon dried oregano**
½ **teaspoon grated nutmeg**
4 **cups marinara sauce**

1. In a large pot of boiling salted water, cook pasta until tender but still firm, 10 to 12 minutes. Drain in a colander, then dry on a kitchen towel until ready to use.

2. Meanwhile, in a mixing bowl, combine chicken, ricotta, Parmesan cheese, parsley, egg, garlic, salt, pepper, oregano, and nutmeg. Mix until well blended. Use a small spoon to insert filling into cannelloni tubes.

3. Spoon about 1 cup of marinara sauce over bottom of a 9 x 13-inch baking dish. Arrange filled cannelloni in dish in a single layer. Spoon remaining sauce over pasta. Cover with foil. (Recipe can be baked immediately or refrigerated up to 24 hours and returned to room temperature before baking.)

4. Preheat oven to 350°F. Bake cannelloni until sauce is bubbly and filling is hot, about 30 minutes.

235 BOW TIES WITH SUN-DRIED TOMATOES AND CHICKEN
Prep: 15 minutes   Stand: 30 minutes   Cook: 17 to 20 minutes
Serves: 6

Sun-dried tomatoes are a delicious way to liven up canned tomatoes for a winter pasta dish that smacks of summer. Use the sun-dried tomatoes that come in a package, not those packed in oil. They are salty enough; you probably won't need any added salt here.

2½ **cups chicken broth, preferably reduced-sodium**
1 **cup sun-dried tomato halves (about 2 ounces)**
1 **pound bow tie pasta**
1 **pound skinless, boneless chicken breasts**
½ **teaspoon freshly ground pepper**
¼ **cup olive oil, preferably extra-virgin**
1 **cup chopped scallions**
1 **(14½-ounce) can Italian-style stewed tomatoes**
Grated Parmesan cheese

1. Heat broth in a medium saucepan. Remove pan from heat and add sun-dried tomatoes. Let stand 30 minutes. Drain, reserving any liquid. Coarsely chop tomatoes. In a large pot of boiling salted water, cook pasta until tender but still firm, 10 to 12 minutes. Drain in a colander.

2. Meanwhile, use your hands to flatten chicken to a more even thickness. Season with pepper. In a large frying pan, heat 2 tablespoons of olive oil. Add chicken and cook over medium-high heat, turning once or twice, until white throughout, 10 to 12 minutes. Remove from pan and slice crosswise.

3. Add remaining 2 tablespoons oil to pan, reduce heat to medium, and cook scallions, stirring occasionally, until soft, 2 to 3 minutes. Add chopped sun-dried tomatoes to pan along with reserved liquid, stewed tomatoes, and chicken. Bring to a boil, reduce heat to medium-low, and simmer 5 minutes.

4. Toss sauce with pasta. Pass grated cheese separately.

236 CHICKEN SCAMPI WITH SPINACH FETTUCCINE

Prep: 15 minutes   Cook: 12 to 15 minutes   Serves: 4 to 6

Scampi sauce is a simple blend of garlic, wine, lemon, and herbs. It's just as good with chicken as it is with shrimp. Here it is served on spinach fettuccine for a sophisticated presentation.

1 pound spinach fettuccine	1 cup dry white wine
1 pound thinly sliced chicken breast cutlets	3 tablespoons chopped fresh basil or 1 teaspoon dried
¼ teaspoon salt	1 tablespoon chopped fresh thyme or ½ teaspoon dried
¼ teaspoon freshly ground pepper	
2 tablespoons butter	¼ to ½ teaspoon crushed hot red pepper
3 tablespoons olive oil, preferably extra-virgin	½ cup chopped flat-leaf parsley
¾ cup chopped scallions	
4 large garlic cloves, minced	
1½ cups chicken broth, preferably reduced-sodium	

1. Cook pasta in a large pot of boiling salted water until tender but still firm, 5 to 7 minutes. Drain in a colander.

2. Meanwhile, season chicken with salt and pepper. In a large frying pan, heat half each of butter and olive oil over medium-high heat. Add chicken and cook, turning once, until white throughout, about 5 minutes. Remove from pan.

3. Add remaining butter and oil to pan, reduce heat to medium, and add scallions and garlic. Cook, stirring often, until garlic is softened, 2 to 3 minutes. Add broth, wine, basil, thyme, and hot pepper. Bring to a boil and cook, stirring occasionally, until sauce is reduced by about one-fourth, 5 to 7 minutes. Return chicken to pan to reheat briefly, then remove chicken again.

4. Toss pasta and ¼ cup of parsley with sauce. Divide among plates. Arrange chicken on top and garnish with remaining parsley.

237 GRILLED CHICKEN AND CAPELLINI NESTS NIÇOISE

Prep: 30 minutes   Cook: 55 to 60 minutes   Serves: 6

Most of the work can be done in advance here, making this very pretty presentation perfect for summer entertaining. Dice the vegetables by cutting them roughly into ¼- to ½-inch cubes.

¼ cup plus 2½ tablespoons olive oil, preferably extra-virgin
1 large onion, chopped
2 garlic cloves, crushed through a press
2 small zucchini (about ½ pound total), diced
1 small eggplant (about ¾ pound), peeled and diced
1 medium green bell pepper, diced
¾ pound plum tomatoes, seeded and diced
1 cup dry white wine
½ cup chicken broth

½ cup halved and pitted niçoise olives
1 tablespoon drained small capers
1 tablespoon chopped fresh rosemary or 1 teaspoon dried
½ teaspoon crushed hot red pepper
6 skinless, boneless chicken breast halves
¾ teaspoon salt
½ teaspoon freshly ground pepper
1 pound capellini
¼ cup chopped fresh basil or parsley

1. In a large frying pan or flameproof casserole, heat ¼ cup olive oil. Add onion and cook over medium heat, stirring occasionally, until softened, 3 to 5 minutes. Add garlic, zucchini, eggplant, and bell pepper. Cover, reduce heat to medium-low, and cook, stirring occasionally, 20 minutes.

2. Add tomatoes, wine, and broth. Bring to a boil, reduce heat to low, and simmer, uncovered, 15 minutes. Add olives, capers, rosemary, and hot pepper and simmer 5 minutes longer. Keep warm until ready to use or make up to 1 day ahead and refrigerate. Reheat before serving.

3. Prepare a medium-hot fire in a barbecue grill. Brush chicken with 1½ teaspoons of olive oil. Season with ½ teaspoon salt and ¼ teaspoon pepper. Grill, turning once or twice, until browned outside and white throughout but still juicy, 12 to 15 minutes.

4. Meanwhile, cook pasta in a large pot of boiling salted water until tender but still firm, 4 to 5 minutes. Drain and place in a large bowl. Toss hot pasta with remaining 2 tablespoons olive oil, basil, and remaining ¼ teaspoon each salt and pepper.

5. Using about 1 cup of cooked pasta for each serving, place on dinner plates and swirl with a fork or your fingers to create a nest with a cavity slightly bigger than chicken breast. Spoon some sauce in and around nests, then set a grilled chicken breast half in each nest. Serve at once.

238 LEMON CHICKEN CAVATELLI WITH ARTICHOKE HEARTS

Prep: 10 minutes   Cook: 25 minutes   Serves: 4

4 bone-in chicken breast
   halves, skin removed
1 medium onion, chopped
2 tablespoons olive oil
2 cups chicken broth,
   preferably reduced-
   sodium
2 tablespoons lemon juice
1½ teaspoons grated lemon zest

¼ teaspoon crushed hot red
   pepper
1 (4-ounce) jar marinated
   artichoke hearts
¾ pound cavatelli
¼ cup grated Parmesan cheese
¼ cup chopped flat-leaf
   parsley

1. In a large frying pan, cook chicken and onion in olive oil over medium-high heat, turning, until chicken is browned and onion is golden, about 5 minutes. Add broth, lemon juice, lemon zest, and hot pepper. Drain marinade from artichoke hearts and add marinade to pan; reserve artichokes. Cook chicken, partially covered, until white to bone, about 20 minutes. Remove chicken from pan.

2. Meanwhile, in a large pot of boiling salted water, cook pasta until tender but still firm, about 10 minutes. Drain in a colander.

3. Toss pan sauce with pasta, artichokes, and cheese. Divide among 4 serving plates. Arrange chicken on top, garnish with parsley, and serve.

239 CHICKEN AND WILD MUSHROOM FETTUCCINE

Prep: 10 minutes   Cook: 20 minutes   Serves: 4

The woodsy taste of wild mushrooms is ideal for an autumn main course. Any wild mushroom, such as shiitake, portobello, or cremini or a combination, can be used. If you can afford a few morels, toss them in for an exquisite smoky flavor.

¾ pound skinless, boneless
   chicken thighs, cut into
   2-inch chunks
½ teaspoon salt
½ teaspoon freshly ground
   pepper
4 tablespoons butter
2 medium leeks (white part
   only), thinly sliced

¾ pound sliced fresh wild
   mushrooms
1 teaspoon dried tarragon
1 cup heavy cream
¼ cup Madeira or dry sherry
¾ pound fettuccine
¼ cup chopped parsley

1. Season chicken with ¼ teaspoon each salt and pepper. Heat 2 tablespoons of butter in a large frying pan over medium heat. Add chicken and cook, turning, until browned outside with no trace of pink inside, about 10 minutes. With tongs, remove chicken from pan.

2. Add remaining 2 tablespoons of butter to pan, reduce heat to medium-low, and add leeks, mushrooms, and tarragon. Cook, stirring occasionally, until mushrooms are tender and leeks are soft, about 7 minutes. Return chicken to pan and add cream and Madeira. Bring to a boil, reduce heat, and simmer, uncovered, 3 minutes to reduce sauce slightly. Season with remaining ¼ teaspoon each salt and pepper.

3. Meanwhile, in a large pot of boiling salted water, cook pasta until tender but still firm, 5 to 7 minutes. Drain in a colander.

4. Toss pasta with chicken and mushroom sauce. Divide among 4 dinner plates and sprinkle with parsley.

---

240   STRAW AND HAY CHICKEN
Prep: 10 minutes   Cook: 11 to 15 minutes   Serves: 6

Straw and hay pasta usually refers to a mix of egg (straw) and green spinach (hay) fettuccine in a creamy sauce. I've added white chicken and green spinach for even more "straw and hay."

½ **pound green fettuccine**
½ **pound white fettuccine**
¾ **pound skinless, boneless chicken breast, cut into thin strips**
¼ **teaspoon salt**
¼ **teaspoon freshly ground pepper**
¼ **cup olive oil, preferably extra-virgin**
1 **medium onion, chopped**
2 **garlic cloves, crushed through a press**

2 **ounces chopped prosciutto (about ⅓ cup)**
1 **(10-ounce) package frozen chopped spinach, thawed and squeezed dry**
¼ **teaspoon grated nutmeg**
1 **cup chicken broth**
1 **cup cream**
½ **cup dry white wine**
⅓ **cup grated Parmesan cheese**

1. In a large pot of boiling salted water, cook green and white fettuccine together until tender but still firm, 5 to 7 minutes. Drain in a colander.

2. Meanwhile, season chicken with salt and pepper. In a large frying pan, cook chicken in 2 tablespoons of olive oil over medium-high heat, stirring often, until white throughout, about 3 minutes. With a slotted spoon, remove chicken from pan.

3. Add remaining 2 tablespoons oil to pan, reduce heat to medium, and add onion. Cook, stirring occasionally, until softened, 3 to 5 minutes. Add garlic, prosciutto, spinach, and nutmeg. Cook, stirring often, 2 minutes. Add broth, cream, and wine. Bring to a boil over high heat, reduce heat to medium, and cook 3 to 5 minutes, until sauce thickens slightly. Season with additional salt and pepper to taste.

4. In a large serving bowl, toss sauce with pasta and chicken. Add cheese, toss again, and serve.

241 LINGUINE PUTTANESCA
Prep: 10 minutes   Cook: 16 minutes   Serves: 4 to 6

1   pound skinless, boneless
    chicken thighs, cut into
    1-inch chunks
¼   cup olive oil
3   garlic cloves, crushed
    through a press
2   anchovy fillets
2   (16-ounce) cans whole
    tomatoes, drained

½   cup sliced black olives
1   tablespoon drained small
    capers
1   teaspoon dried oregano
¼   to ½ teaspoon crushed hot
    red pepper
¾   pound linguine
⅓   cup chopped flat-leaf
    parsley

1. In a large frying pan, cook chicken in olive oil over medium-high heat 5 minutes, stirring often. Reduce heat to medium-low. Add garlic and anchovies and cook 1 minute, mashing anchovies with back of a spoon. Add tomatoes, olives, capers, oregano, and hot pepper. Simmer sauce, uncovered, 10 minutes.

2. Meanwhile, in a large pot of boiling salted water, cook linguine until tender but still firm, 8 to 10 minutes. Drain in a colander.

3. In a large serving bowl, toss pasta with sauce and parsley.

242 GRILLED CHICKEN WITH FUSILLI AND SALSA CRUDA
*Prep: 15 minutes   Stand: 30 minutes   Cook: 14 to 16 minutes
Serves: 4 to 6*

The pasta must be freshly cooked and hot to warm the salsa and partially melt the cheese here, but the recipe can be made with leftover grilled chicken, if you have some on hand.

1   pound fusilli
2   pounds fresh plum
    tomatoes, chopped
1   sweet red or white onion,
    chopped
2   garlic cloves, minced
2   fresh jalapeño peppers,
    minced
1   teaspoon salt
¼   cup olive oil, preferably
    extra-virgin

2   tablespoons red wine
    vinegar
4   ounces Monterey Jack
    cheese, cut into ½-inch
    dice
⅓   cup chopped cilantro
¾   pound thinly sliced chicken
    breast fillets (tenders)

1. In a large bowl, combine tomatoes, onion, garlic, peppers, salt, 3 tablespoons of olive oil, vinegar, cheese, and cilantro. Mix well. Let salsa stand 30 minutes at room temperature.

2. Meanwhile, in a large pot of boiling salted water, cook pasta until tender but still firm, 10 to 12 minutes. Drain in a colander.

3. Prepare a hot fire in a barbecue grill. Brush chicken with remaining 1 tablespoon oil and grill, turning once or twice, until white throughout and with deep brown marks outside, about 4 minutes.

4. Cut chicken into thin strips and place in a large serving bowl. Add pasta and salsa and toss to mix evenly. Serve warm or at room temperature.

---

243 DRUMSTICK GREMOLATA
Prep: 15 minutes   Cook: 40 to 42 minutes   Serves: 6

Gremolata is a blend of chopped parsley, garlic, and lemon zest. It is traditionally served with osso buco, but I find it freshens up all sorts of wintry dishes.

⅓ cup chopped parsley
1 tablespoon grated lemon zest
2 large garlic cloves, minced
2 pounds chicken drumsticks
¾ teaspoon salt
½ teaspoon freshly ground pepper
¼ cup olive oil
1 large onion, chopped
2 carrots, chopped

2 celery ribs, chopped
1 bay leaf, broken in half
1½ cups chicken broth, preferably reduced-sodium
¾ cup dry white wine
½ cup heavy cream
1 tablespoon fresh lemon juice
1 pound broad egg noodles

1. In a small bowl, mix together parsley, lemon zest, and garlic. Set gremolata aside.

2. Season chicken with ½ teaspoon salt and ¼ teaspoon pepper. In a large frying pan, cook chicken in 2 tablespoons of olive oil over medium-high heat, turning, until browned, 5 to 7 minutes. Remove from pan.

3. Heat remaining 2 tablespoons of oil in same pan. Add onion, carrots, and celery and cook, stirring occasionally, until softened, about 5 minutes. Return chicken to pan and add bay leaf and broth. Partially cover pan and simmer until chicken juices run clear when pricked with a knife tip, about 25 minutes.

4. Add wine and cream and simmer, uncovered, 5 minutes. Stir in lemon juice. Season with remaining ¼ teaspoon each salt and pepper. Remove and discard bay leaf.

5. Meanwhile, in a large pot of boiling salted water, cook noodles until tender but still firm, about 5 minutes. Drain in a colander.

6. Remove chicken from frying pan. Toss noodles with sauce. Make a bed of noodles with sauce. Arrange chicken on top. Sprinkle gremolata over all and serve at once.

244   CHILI CHEESE AND CHICKEN MACARONI
Prep: 10 minutes   Cook: 12 to 14 minutes   Serves: 4

10 ounces elbow macaroni	2 tablespoons flour
¾ pound skinless, boneless chicken breasts or thighs	2 cups milk
1½ tablespoons chili powder	2 cups shredded Cheddar cheese (8 ounces)
3 tablespoons butter	1 (4-ounce) can chopped green chiles
1 medium onion, chopped	

1. In a large pot of boiling salted water, cook macaroni until tender but still firm, about 8 minutes. Drain in a colander.

2. Meanwhile, sprinkle chicken with chili powder. In a large frying pan, melt 2 tablespoons of butter over medium heat. Add chicken and onion and cook, stirring occasionally, until chicken is lightly browned and onion is golden, about 7 minutes. With tongs, remove chicken from pan.

3. Melt remaining butter in pan. Stir in flour to make a paste. Cook, stirring, 1 to 2 minutes. Slowly whisk in milk. Bring to a boil, stirring until sauce thickens, 3 to 4 minutes. Remove from heat and stir in cheese until melted. Stir in chiles and chicken. Add sauce to macaroni, stir to blend, and serve.

245   MIDSUMMER NIGHT PASTA
Prep: 10 minutes   Cook: 10 minutes   Serves: 4

This is a dish that, as its name implies, calls for red, ripe summer tomatoes and garden-fresh basil. Smoked chicken is fabulous here, but leftover grilled chicken or rotisserie chicken from the deli will work, too.

2 pounds ripe tomatoes	6 tablespoons olive oil, preferably extra-virgin
1 pound rotini or other short pasta	2 tablespoons balsamic vinegar
2 cups cubed smoked or cooked chicken (about ½ pound)	¾ cup chopped fresh basil Salt and freshly ground pepper
3 ounces prosciutto, chopped	
3 large garlic cloves, minced	

1. Drop tomatoes into a large pot of boiling salted water for 30 seconds. Remove tomatoes with a slotted spoon. Add pasta to same boiling water and cook until tender but still firm, about 10 minutes. Drain in a colander.

2. Meanwhile, peel, seed, and chop tomatoes. Place chopped tomatoes and their juices in a large serving bowl. Add chicken, prosciutto, garlic, olive oil, vinegar, and basil. Mix well.

3. Add hot drained pasta to sauce and toss to mix. Season lightly with salt and generously with pepper. Serve warm or at room temperature.

246 CHICKEN AND RATATOUILLE LASAGNE

Prep: 20 minutes   Cook: 41 minutes   Serves: 6

Not your usual lasagne, this contemporary interpretation combines the country French vegetable stew ratatouille with Italian layered pasta.

1 **pound thinly sliced chicken breast cutlets**	1 **large garlic clove, crushed through a press**
1 **teaspoon dried marjoram**	1 **pound fresh plum tomatoes, sliced crosswise**
¾ **teaspoon salt**	
½ **teaspoon freshly ground pepper**	1 **tablespoon drained small capers**
6 **tablespoons olive oil, preferably extra-virgin**	¼ **cup chopped fresh basil or 1 teaspoon dried**
1 **large onion, thinly sliced**	½ **pound lasagna noodles, regular or precooked**
1 **small eggplant, thinly sliced**	
2 **small zucchini, thinly sliced**	¼ **cup grated Parmesan cheese**
1 **yellow bell pepper, thinly sliced**	

1. Season chicken with marjoram and ¼ teaspoon each salt and pepper. In a large frying pan, cook chicken in 2 tablespoons of olive oil over medium heat until tender and white throughout, about 5 minutes. Remove chicken from pan. Heat remaining ¼ cup oil in same pan. Add onion, eggplant, zucchini, bell pepper, and garlic and cook, stirring occasionally, until onion is softened, about 5 minutes. Cover pan and simmer 20 minutes. Add tomatoes, capers, and basil and simmer 10 minutes, covered. (If sauce seems too juicy, uncover during last 5 minutes of cooking to reduce.) Return chicken to sauce to reheat.

2. Meanwhile, cook pasta in a large pot of boiling salted water until tender but still firm, about 10 minutes. (If using precooked lasagna noodles, reconstitute according to package directions.) Carefully drain pasta in a colander, being careful that the noodles do not tear.

3. Preheat broiler. In an oiled 9x13-inch baking dish or in 6 individual ovenproof gratin dishes, make a layer of one-third of noodles, cutting to fit if using individual dishes. Add a layer of half of chicken and half of sauce. Make another layer using half of remaining lasagna noodles and all of remaining chicken and sauce. Cover with remaining lasagna noodles. Sprinkle with cheese over top.

4. Broil about 4 inches from heat, until cheese is melted and lightly browned, about 1 minute.

247 PENNE WITH CHICKEN, CANNELLINI, AND BROCCOLI RABE

Prep: 10 minutes   Cook: 10 minutes   Serves: 6

It's only recently that we Americans have truly begun to appreciate the versatility and goodness of beans. Italians have long known the secret.

1 **pound penne**	6 **garlic cloves, minced**
12 **ounces skinless, boneless**	1 **teaspoon dried rosemary**
chicken thighs, cut into	1½ **cups chicken broth**
1-inch chunks	1 **cup dry white wine**
¾ **teaspoon salt**	2 **(15-ounce) cans white**
½ **teaspoon freshly ground**	**cannellini beans, rinsed**
pepper	**and drained**
¼ **cup olive oil**	½ **cup grated Parmesan cheese**
1 **pound broccoli rabe, cut**	
into 1-inch pieces	

1. In a large pot of boiling salted water, cook pasta until tender but still firm, about 10 minutes. Drain in a colander.

2. Meanwhile, season chicken with ¼ teaspoon each salt and pepper. In a large frying pan, cook chicken in olive oil over medium-high heat, stirring often, to brown lightly, 3 minutes. Add broccoli rabe, garlic, and rosemary and cook, stirring, 2 minutes. Add broth, wine, and beans. Reduce heat to medium-low and simmer until sauce is slightly thickened and chicken is white throughout, 4 to 5 minutes.

3. Toss pasta with sauce, chicken, and broccoli rabe. Add cheese and salt and pepper to taste. Toss again and serve.

248 RIGATONI WITH BROCCOLI AND SWEET RED PEPPER

Prep: 15 minutes   Cook: 12 to 13 minutes   Serves: 4 to 6

1 **pound rigatoni**	3 **garlic cloves, crushed**
4 **cups broccoli florets (about**	**through a press**
10 ounces)	1 **teaspoon crumbled dried**
¾ **pound skinless, boneless**	**sage**
chicken breast, cut into	¾ **cup dry white wine**
1-inch chunks	¾ **cup chicken broth**
1 **large red bell pepper, diced**	½ **cup heavy cream**
1 **small onion, chopped**	**Salt and freshly ground**
¼ **cup olive oil, preferably**	**pepper**
extra-virgin	⅓ **cup grated Parmesan cheese**

1. Cook rigatoni in large pot of boiling salted water 10 minutes. Add broccoli and cook until pasta is tender but still firm and broccoli is crisp-tender, 2 to 3 minutes longer. Drain in a colander.

2. Meanwhile, in a large frying pan, cook chicken, bell pepper, and onion in olive oil over medium heat, stirring often, until vegetables are softened, about 5 minutes. Add garlic and sage and cook 30 seconds, stirring. Stir in wine, broth, and cream. Simmer 5 minutes. Season with salt and pepper to taste.

3. Toss pasta and broccoli with chicken and sauce. Add cheese, toss again, and serve.

---

249 STIR-FRIED CHICKEN SUKIYAKI
Prep: 10 minutes   Cook: 10 minutes   Serves: 4

Rice noodles, which are available in Asian markets and in many supermarkets, are softened simply by soaking in boiling water. Regular vermicelli, cooked as the package directs, can be substituted in this simplified version of Japanese sukiyaki.

8 **ounces rice noodles or regular vermicelli, broken in half**
3 **tablespoons vegetable oil**
1 **pound skinless, boneless chicken breasts, cut into ½-inch strips**
1 **medium red bell pepper, diced**
1 **cup thinly sliced scallions**
¼ **pound fresh shiitake mushrooms, stemmed, caps thinly sliced**

1½ **cups chicken broth, preferably reduced-sodium**
¼ **cup soy sauce**
2 **tablespooons mirin or dry sherry**
1 **tablespoon rice wine vinegar**
1 **tablespoon sugar**
¼ **cup chopped cilantro**

1. Put rice noodles in a medium bowl and add enough boiling water to cover. Cover bowl and let pasta soak until softened, about 10 minutes; drain. If using regular vermicelli, cook and drain according to package directions.

2. Meanwhile, in a large frying pan, heat 2 tablespoons of oil over high heat. Add chicken and cook, stirring constantly, until lightly browned, about 2 minutes. Remove with a slotted spoon.

3. Add remaining 1 tablespoon oil to pan, reduce heat to medium-high, and add bell pepper, scallions, and shiitake mushrooms. Cook, stirring constantly, 2 minutes. Return chicken to pan and add broth, soy sauce, mirin, vinegar, and sugar. Bring to a boil, reduce heat, and simmer 5 minutes.

4. Place rice noodles in a large serving bowl. Pour chicken and sauce over noodles. Add cilantro, toss, and serve.

250   CHICKEN RAVIOLI
Prep: 30 minutes   Cook: 6 to 10 minutes   Serves: 6 to 8

Fresh wonton skins can be purchased at any Asian market and in many supermarkets, where they are often frozen. These thin pasta sheets, about 3 inches square, are perfect for quick homemade ravioli.

2 cups chopped cooked
  chicken (about ½ pound)
1½ cups part-skim ricotta
  cheese
⅓ cup grated Parmesan
  cheese, plus additional
  for passing at table
⅓ cup chopped flat-leaf
  parsley
1 egg

1 teaspoon dried Italian
  seasoning
¾ teaspoon salt
¾ pound fresh wonton skins
  (50 to 60)
1 egg beaten with 1 teaspoon
  water
6 cups marinara sauce

1. In a mixing bowl, stir together chicken, ricotta, ⅓ cup grated Parmesan cheese, parsley, egg, Italian seasoning, and salt until well blended. For each wonton, place a wonton skin on a flat work surface and mound about 2 teaspoons of chicken filling in center. Brush edges of skin with egg glaze and fold over to make triangle, pressing edges to seal firmly. (Ravioli can be formed a few hours ahead and refrigerated between sheets of waxed paper.)

2. Bring a large pot of salted water to a boil. Add ravioli, in 2 batches if necessary to prevent crowding, and boil until ravioli are tender, 3 to 5 minutes. Remove with a slotted spoon and drain.

3. Meanwhile, heat marinara sauce; serve over ravioli. Pass additional Parmesan cheese at table.

251   WAGON WHEELS WITH PESTO CHICKEN
Prep: 5 minutes   Cook: 10 to 12 minutes   Serves: 4

Refrigerated pesto sauce is a great convenience product put to especially good use here. If you can't find wagon wheels, any other fanciful shape or even plain spaghetti can be used here.

¾ pound wagon wheel or
  other shaped pasta
¾ pound thinly sliced chicken
  breast cutlets
¼ teaspoon salt
⅛ teaspoon freshly ground
  pepper
2 tablespoons olive oil,
  preferably extra-virgin

1 cup dry white wine
1 cup chicken broth
1 cup prepared refrigerated
  pesto
½ cup chopped flat-leaf
  parsley

1. In a large pot of boiling salted water, cook pasta until tender but still firm, 10 to 12 minutes. Drain in a colander.

2. Meanwhile, season chicken with salt and pepper. In a large frying pan, cook chicken in olive oil over medium-high heat, turning once or twice, until tender and white throughout, about 5 minutes. Remove from pan.

3. Add wine and broth to drippings in pan. Bring to a boil, stirring up browned bits from bottom of pan. Boil until reduced by one-fourth, about 5 minutes. Stir in pesto.

4. In a large bowl, toss sauce with pasta. Add parsley and toss again. Spoon onto serving plates. Slice chicken crosswise and arrange on top of pasta. Serve at once.

---

252   MEDITERRANEAN CHICKEN ON ORZO
Prep: 10 minutes   Cook: 36 to 43 minutes   Serves: 4 to 6

This skillet chicken dish is also wonderful served over rice, but rice-shaped orzo pasta is a pleasing change of pace. Use really good olives, as they are a major flavor contributor.

1 **(3- to 3½-pound) chicken,**
   cut into 8 pieces
3 **tablespoons olive oil,**
   preferably extra-virgin
2 **cups frozen pearl onions,**
   thawed (about 10 ounces)
8 **ounces sliced mushrooms**
2 **garlic cloves, crushed**
   through a press
1 **cup chicken broth,**
   preferably reduced-
   sodium

1 **pound fresh plum tomatoes,**
   quartered
1 **teaspoon dried marjoram**
1 **teaspoon dried thyme**
1 **bay leaf**
½ **cup pitted brine-cured black**
   olives
1½ **cups orzo (8 ounces)**
¼ **cup chopped fresh mint**

1. In a large frying pan, cook chicken in 2 tablespoons of olive oil over medium-high heat, turning once or twice, until browned, 5 to 7 minutes. Remove from pan.

2. Add onions to drippings in pan, reduce heat to medium, and cook, stirring, until golden, 3 minutes. Add mushrooms and garlic and cook, stirring occasionally, 3 minutes. Add broth, tomatoes, marjoram, thyme, and bay leaf. Return chicken to pan. Cover and simmer until chicken is tender with no trace of pink near bone, 20 to 25 minutes. Add olives and simmer 5 minutes longer. Remove and discard bay leaf.

3. Meanwhile, in a large pot of boiling salted water, cook orzo until tender but still firm, about 5 minutes. Drain in a sieve. Toss orzo with remaining 1 tablespoon oil and mint.

4. Serve chicken, mushrooms, and sauce spooned over orzo.

253 ROTELLE WITH ARUGULA, BACON, AND CHICKEN

Prep: 15 minutes   Cook: 12 to 15 minutes   Serves: 6

This is one of those "little nothings" that you can whip up in a few minutes to make a very big impression on last-minute guests. Add a basket of breadsticks and a dessert of ripe peaches or pears with some crunchy biscotti, and you have a great supper.

1 pound rotelle or other corkscrew pasta
6 slices of bacon
¾ pound chicken breast fillets (tenders)
3 garlic cloves, crushed through a press
½ cup dry white wine

2 (14½-ounce) cans pasta-ready tomatoes
6 cups shredded arugula (2 to 3 bunches)
⅓ cup grated Parmesan cheese
¾ teaspoon coarsely ground pepper

1. In a large pot of boiling salted water, cook pasta until tender but still firm, 10 to 12 minutes. Drain in a colander.

2. Meanwhile, in a large frying pan, cook bacon over medium heat until crisp, about 5 minutes. Drain on paper towels. Add chicken to drippings in pan and cook over medium heat, turning once, until golden and white throughout, 3 to 5 minutes. Remove chicken and cut into thin strips.

3. Add garlic and cook, stirring, until softened, 1 to 2 minutes. Add wine and tomatoes and bring to a boil. Boil 3 minutes to reduce slightly. Stir in arugula.

4. Toss pasta with sauce and chicken. Add cheese and pepper and toss again.

254 PASTA PRONTO

Prep: 5 minutes   Cook: 12 minutes   Serves: 4

Extra garlic and parsley enliven this ultra-quick pasta dish.

1 pound ziti or other tubular pasta
¾ pound thinly sliced chicken breast cutlets
¼ teaspoon salt
⅛ teaspoon freshly ground pepper
2 tablespoons olive oil, preferably extra-virgin

4 garlic cloves, minced
2 (14½-ounce) cans diced tomatoes, with their juices
½ cup dry white wine
⅓ cup chopped flat-leaf parsley

1. Cook pasta in a large pot of boiling salted water until tender but still firm, about 12 minutes. Drain in a colander.

2. Meanwhile, cut chicken into thin strips and season with salt and pepper. In a large frying pan, heat olive oil over high heat. Add chicken and cook, stirring often, until golden, about 1 minute. Add garlic, reduce heat to medium, and cook, stirring, 1 minute. Stir in tomatoes and wine. Bring to a boil over high heat. Reduce heat to medium and cook 5 minutes.

3. Toss cooked pasta with sauce. Add parsley, toss again, and serve.

255 CHICKEN LIVER AND SAGE ONION FUSILLI

Prep: 15 minutes   Cook: 14 to 16 minutes   Serves: 6

Be sure the chicken livers are patted dry before cooking so that they will brown nicely.

¼ cup olive oil, preferably extra-virgin	¾ teaspoon salt
	¼ teaspoon ground allspice
1 large onion, very thinly sliced	1 cup chicken broth
	½ cup dry marsala wine
1 pound chicken livers, rinsed, patted dry, and coarsely diced	1 pound fusilli
	¼ cup chopped flat-leaf parsley
1 teaspoon dried sage	
1 teaspoon coarsely ground pepper	

1. In a large frying pan, heat 2 tablespoons of olive oil. Add onion and cook over medium heat, stirring often, until soft and golden, 8 to 10 minutes. Use a slotted spoon to remove onions from pan.

2. Season chicken livers with sage, pepper, salt, and allspice. Heat remaining 2 tablespoons oil in frying pan. Add livers to pan and cook over medium-high heat, stirring, until lightly browned but still rosy in center, about 3 minutes. Return onion to pan and add broth and marsala. Simmer, stirring, until livers are barely pink in center and sauce is slightly reduced, about 3 minutes.

3. Meanwhile, in a large pot of boiling salted water, cook pasta until tender but still firm, about 8 minutes. Drain in a colander.

4. In a large serving bowl, toss pasta with chicken liver sauce. Add parsley, toss again, and serve at once.

Chapter 11

Hot Off the Grill

Grilling chicken on the backyard barbecue is a truly American summer pastime. The trend started in earnest just after World War II, but it is really in the last decade or so that grilling out has become a real craze. Gas grills and versatile covered charcoal grills now come in a wide range of sizes and prices, and electric grills even make it possible for city apartment dwellers to barbecue on the back stoop.

Grilling and oven-broiling involve the same cooking techniques: relatively intense direct heat from under or over the food. In grilling, the fire can be controlled by adjustment of the coals or gas jets, or by moving the grill rack, while broiling heat can be changed by lowering or raising the oven rack. Recipes for grilling and broiling are usually interchangeable, though cooking times may vary somewhat. Because of grilling's popularity, recipe instructions in this chapter are given for the grill; if broiling, watch the food carefully to prevent burning and adjust the cooking time as needed.

Though not specifically noted in these recipes, soaked wood chips or other enhancers can be used to add even more flavor to foods grilled out of doors. Follow instructions in your grill manual.

Since grilling is a rather imprecise cooking method, be sure to test the chicken for doneness—the meat should no longer be pink and juices should run clear when pricked with a knife tip.

256 CAROLINA MOPPIN' BARBECUED CHICKEN

Prep: 10 minutes   Cook: 35 to 45 minutes   Serves: 4

In the Carolinas, barbecue sauce contains no tomato. The preference there is for a tangy acidic liquid that is brushed or "mopped" onto the chicken while it cooks.

½ cup ginger ale
¼ cup white wine vinegar
1½ tablespoons white wine
    Worcestershire sauce
1 tablespoon honey
2 garlic cloves, crushed
    through a press

½ teaspoon salt
¼ teaspoon crushed hot red
    pepper
1 (3-pound) chicken, cut into
    8 pieces

1. Prepare a medium-hot fire in a barbecue grill. In a small bowl, stir together ginger ale, vinegar, Worcestershire sauce, honey, garlic, salt, and hot pepper.

2. Grill chicken, skin side down, 10 minutes. Turn and grill 5 minutes longer. Brush with some of sauce and continue to grill, turning occasionally and brushing with more sauce, until chicken juices run clear when pricked with a knife tip, 20 to 30 minutes longer. (White meat will take less time than dark meat.) Stop basting about 5 minutes before chicken is done.

257 KANSAS CITY BARBECUE

Prep: 10 minutes   Cook: 45 to 50 minutes   Serves: 4

Many commercial barbecue sauces are based on recipes developed and marketed in Kansas City, a place aficionados consider one of a few stars in the barbecue crown. This sauce is a simple upgrade of a good commercial sauce.

1½ cups thick hickory smoke-
    flavored barbecue sauce
    (12-ounce bottle)
1 cup beer or ale

1 teaspoon Tabasco or other
    hot pepper sauce
2 (2½-pound) broiler/fryer
    chickens, halved

1. Prepare a medium-hot fire in a barbecue grill. In a small nonreactive saucepan, bring barbecue sauce and beer to a simmer. Reduce heat to medium-low and simmer 5 minutes. Stir in Tabasco.

2. Meanwhile, grill chicken, skin side down, 10 minutes. Turn and grill 10 minutes longer. Brush with some of sauce and continue to grill, turning occasionally and brushing with sauce until chicken juices run clear when pricked with a knife tip, 25 to 30 minutes longer. Stop basting about 5 minutes before chicken is done.

258 GARLIC-OREGANO GRILLED CHICKEN

Prep: 10 minutes   Stand: 1 hour   Cook: 20 minutes   Serves: 6

⅓ cup dry red wine
¼ cup olive oil
4 garlic cloves, chopped
1 tablespoon dried oregano
½ teaspoon salt

¼ teaspoon crushed hot red pepper
1½ pounds skinless, boneless chicken thighs

1. In a shallow 2-quart dish, combine wine, olive oil, garlic, oregano, salt, and hot pepper. Use your hands to flatten chicken to an even thickness and add to marinade; turn to coat both sides. Cover and refrigerate at least 1 hour and up to 6 hours.

2. Prepare a medium-hot fire in a barbecue grill. Remove chicken from marinade; reserve marinade. Grill chicken, turning once or twice and brushing often with marinade, until no longer pink but still juicy, about 20 minutes. Stop basting about 5 minutes before chicken is done.

259 GRILL-SMOKED SUMMER HERB CHICKEN

Prep: 10 minutes   Cook: 1 hour to 1 hour 20 minutes
Stand: 10 minutes   Serves: 4

If you have a rotisserie, cook the chicken on it. Otherwise, the covered grill-smoked method described below will do quite nicely. Do not attempt this in an oven broiler.

2 lemons
1 (3-pound) whole chicken, giblets removed
¼ cup chopped fresh herbs such as thyme, basil, rosemary, and/or chives

3 tablespoons olive oil
¾ teaspoon salt
½ teaspoon freshly ground pepper

1. Prepare a medium fire in a covered grill; push hot coals to one side. Or preheat a gas grill for an indirect fire. Cut 1 lemon in quarters and stuff into chicken cavity. Use your fingers to loosen skin of chicken breast and thighs from meat. Carefully insert herbs under skin, taking care not to break skin. Rub skin with 1 tablespoon of olive oil and season with salt and pepper. Do not truss chicken.

2. Set chicken, breast side down, on grill rack away from coals. Lower hood and grill 20 minutes. Carefully turn breast side up and continue to grill, covered, until thigh juices run clear when pricked with tip of a knife, 40 to 60 minutes longer. (An instant-reading thermometer should register 180°F.) Squeeze juice from remaining lemon and mix with remaining oil to brush over chicken during last 15 minutes of cooking.

3. Let chicken stand 10 minutes before carving.

260   ALL-AMERICAN BARBECUED CHICKEN
Prep: 30 minutes   Cook: 35 to 45 minutes   Serves: 4

The key to avoiding burned barbecue chicken is to wait until the chicken is about half done before brushing it with the sauce.

1 small onion, finely chopped	1 tablespoon Dijon mustard
1 cup chili sauce	1 teaspoon Tabasco or other
½ cup ketchup	hot pepper sauce
3 tablespoons molasses	3 pounds chicken parts
2 tablespoons Worcestershire	(breasts, thighs, and/or
sauce	drumsticks)
1 tablespoon cider vinegar	

1. In a nonreactive medium saucepan, combine onion, chili sauce, ketchup, molasses, Worcestershire, vinegar, mustard, and Tabasco. Mix well. Bring to a boil, reduce heat to medium-low, and simmer, partially covered, 20 minutes.

2. Meanwhile, prepare a medium-hot fire in a barbecue grill. Grill chicken, skin side down, 10 minutes. Turn skin side up and grill 5 minutes.

3. Brush chicken with some of sauce and grill, turning occasionally and brushing with more sauce, until chicken juices run clear when pricked with tip of a knife, 20 to 30 minutes longer. (Breast meat will take less time than thighs and drumsticks.) Stop basting about 5 minutes before chicken is done.

261   SPICY GRILLED THAI CHICKEN
Prep: 20 minutes   Marinate: 2 hours   Cook: 35 to 45 minutes
Serves: 4 to 6

1 (14-ounce) can unsweetened	1 tablespoon soy sauce
coconut milk	1 tablespoon curry powder
3 tablespoons fish sauce	3 garlic cloves, finely chopped
(nam pla)	½ to ¾ teaspoon crushed hot
3 tablespoons rice wine	red pepper, to taste
vinegar	1 (3½-pound) chicken, cut into
1 tablespoon lime juice	8 pieces

1. In a shallow 2-quart baking dish, combine coconut milk, fish sauce, vinegar, lime juice, soy sauce, curry powder, garlic, and hot pepper. Add chicken and turn to coat completely. Cover and refrigerate at least 2 or up to 8 hours.

2. Prepare a medium-hot fire in a barbecue grill. Remove chicken from marinade; reserve marinade. Grill chicken, skin side down, 10 minutes. Turn and grill, skin side up, 5 minutes. Brush with marinade and continue to grill, turning occasionally and brushing often with marinade, until chicken juices run clear when pricked with a knife tip, about 20 to 30 minutes longer. (Breasts will take less time than thighs or drumsticks.) Stop basting about 5 minutes before chicken is done.

262 MAPLE-MUSTARD DRUMSTICKS
Prep: 10 minutes   Cook: 37 to 42 minutes   Serves: 6

½ cup maple syrup
¼ cup bottled chili sauce
¼ cup cider vinegar
2 tablespoons prepared white
    horseradish

2 teaspoons dry mustard
2½ to 3 pounds chicken
    drumsticks

1. Prepare a medium-hot fire in a barbecue grill. Meanwhile, in a small non-reactive saucepan, combine maple syrup, chili sauce, vinegar, horseradish, and mustard. Cook over medium-low heat, stirring to dissolve mustard, until sauce is hot, about 2 minutes. Remove from heat.

2. Grill chicken, turning once, 15 minutes. Brush with some of sauce and continue to grill, turning and brushing occasionally with sauce, until chicken juices run clear when pricked with a knife tip, 20 to 25 minutes longer. Stop basting about 5 minutes before chicken is done.

263 CITRUS AND HONEY GRILLED CHICKEN BREASTS
Prep: 10 minutes   Stand: 30 minutes   Cook: 30 to 35 minutes Serves: 4

This is a lovely dish for company, especially when you garnish it with the very pretty, lightly grilled orange and lemon slices.

2 tablespoons vegetable oil
2 tablespoons orange juice
2 tablespoons lemon juice
1 tablespoon honey
1 teaspoon dried marjoram
1 teaspoon grated orange zest
½ teaspoon grated lemon zest
¼ teaspoon salt

¼ teaspoon freshly ground
    pepper
4 skinless, boneless chicken
    breast halves
4 orange slices, cut about
    ⅛ inch thick
4 lemon slices, cut about
    ⅛ inch thick

1. Prepare a medium-hot fire in a barbecue grill. In a small bowl, stir together oil, orange juice, lemon juice, honey, marjoram, orange zest, lemon zest, salt, and pepper. Brush some of glaze over chicken and let stand at room temperature 30 minutes.

2. Grill chicken, skin side down, 10 minutes. Turn and grill 5 minutes. Brush with glaze and continue to grill, turning and brushing occasionally, until chicken juices run clear when pricked with a knife tip, 15 to 20 minutes longer. Stop basting at least 5 minutes before chicken is done.

3. A few minutes before chicken is done, brush orange and lemon slices with some of the glaze and grill at edge of grill, turning once, until both sides are lightly tinged with brown, 1 to 2 minutes. Serve chicken garnished with grilled citrus slices.

264 GRILLED CHICKEN STUFFED WITH MINT PESTO

Prep: 20 minutes   Cook: 13 to 15 minutes   Serves: 6

The foods of the Mediterranean are lusty and delicious. This chicken is stuffed with a blend of Italian and Greek ingredients to make very pretty chicken rolls that can be served hot or at room temperature with equal success.

1¼ cups fresh mint leaves
3 tablespoons pine nuts
2 garlic cloves
½ teaspoon salt
½ teaspoon freshly ground pepper
⅓ cup plus 1 tablespoon olive oil, preferably extra-virgin

¼ cup grated Parmesan cheese
6 skinless, boneless chicken breast halves
Mint sprigs, for garnish

1. In a food processor, coarsely chop mint leaves, pine nuts, garlic, and ¼ teaspoon each of salt and pepper. With machine on, pour ⅓ cup of olive oil through feed tube and puree until smooth. Add cheese and process about 5 seconds to mix well. Use pesto immediately or refrigerate up to 24 hours.

2. Prepare a medium-hot fire in a barbecue grill. Pound chicken between pieces of waxed paper to an even ¼-inch thickness. Season with remaining salt and pepper. Spread pesto over chicken, then roll up to enclose pesto. Press gently to flatten rolls slightly and help chicken adhere to itself. Rub rolls with remaining 1 tablespoon oil.

3. Grill chicken, turning once or twice with a spatula, until white throughout, 13 to 15 minutes.

265 ORANGE MUSTARD GRILLED CHICKEN

Prep: 5 minutes   Stand: 30 minutes   Cook: 10 to 12 minutes
Serves: 4

The mustard marinade coats and protects the skinless chicken and forms an almost crunchy grilled "crust."

¼ cup Dijon mustard
2 tablespoons orange juice
1 tablespoon vegetable oil
1 teaspoon grated orange zest

¼ teaspoon freshly ground pepper
1 pound skinless, boneless chicken breast halves

1. In a shallow 2-quart dish, stir together mustard, orange juice, oil, orange zest, and pepper. Add chicken and turn to coat all over. Let stand 30 minutes at room temperature or refrigerate up to 2 hours.

2. Prepare a medium-hot fire in a barbecue grill. Grill chicken, turning once or twice with a spatula, until white throughout, 10 to 12 minutes.

266 GRILLED GINGER-APRICOT CHICKEN BREASTS
Prep: 10 minutes   Cook: 32 to 37 minutes   Serves: 6

⅓ cup apricot preserves
¼ cup lemon juice
1 tablespoon minced fresh
   ginger
2 teaspoons Dijon mustard

½ teaspoon salt
¼ teaspoon freshly ground
   pepper
6 bone-in chicken breast
   halves, skin on

1. Prepare a medium-hot fire in a barbecue grill. Meanwhile, in a small saucepan, warm preserves, lemon juice, ginger, mustard, salt, and pepper over medium heat, stirring, just until preserves melt, about 2 minutes.

2. Grill chicken, skin side down, 10 minutes. Turn and grill 5 minutes. Brush with some of glaze and continue to grill, turning occasionally and brushing with more glaze, until chicken juices run clear when pricked with a knife tip, 15 to 20 minutes longer. Stop basting about 5 minutes before chicken is done.

267 PEACHY KEEN CHICKEN BARBECUE
Prep: 10 minutes   Cook: 32 to 38 minutes   Serves: 4

If peaches aren't in season, grill pineapple slices instead and use pineapple preserves in the glaze.

½ cup peach preserves
2 tablespoons vegetable oil
1 tablespoon white wine
   vinegar
1 tablespoon soy sauce
1 teaspoon coarsely ground
   pepper

½ teaspoon salt
4 chicken breast halves,
   skin on
2 peaches, peeled and halved
8 scallions, trimmed to leave
   2 inches of green

1. Prepare a medium-hot fire in a barbecue grill. Meanwhile, in a small nonreactive saucepan, combine preserves, 1 tablespoon of oil, vinegar, soy sauce, pepper, and salt. Cook over medium heat, stirring, until preserves are melted, 2 to 3 minutes.

2. Grill chicken, skin side down, 10 minutes. Turn and grill 5 minutes. Brush with some of peach glaze and grill, turning and brushing with more glaze, until chicken juices run clear when pricked with a knife tip, 15 to 20 minutes longer.

3. About 5 minutes before chicken is done, stop adding glaze. Brush peaches and scallions with remaining oil. Grill, turning, until tinged with brown and softened, about 5 minutes. Serve peaches crisscrossed with scallions as an accompaniment to chicken.

268 LIME-CAYENNE GRILLED CHICKEN CUTLETS

Prep: 10 minutes   Cook: 5 to 7 minutes   Serves: 4

Here's a quick and easy barbecue that packs a real flavor wallop. I like to serve these cutlets as a sandwich inside crusty rolls spread with mayonnaise and topped with shredded lettuce.

3 tablespoons lime juice	½ teaspoon cayenne
3 tablespoons olive oil	¼ teaspoon salt
1 tablespoon honey	1 pound thinly sliced chicken
1 teaspoon grated lime zest	breast cutlets

1. Prepare a hot fire in a barbecue grill. In a small bowl, whisk together lime juice, olive oil, honey, lime zest, cayenne, and salt. Brush some of glaze over both sides of chicken.

2. Grill chicken, turning once or twice and brushing with any remaining glaze, until white throughout, 5 to 7 minutes.

269 SUMMER VEGETABLE AND CHICKEN KEBABS

*Prep: 10 minutes   Stand: 30 minutes   Cook: 10 to 12 minutes
Serves: 4*

Bottled red wine vinegar and oil salad dressing is the marinade secret here. Long, narrow Japanese eggplants are the perfect size for slicing and skewering, but a small regular eggplant cut into cubes can be substituted. Serve these colorful kebabs over rice as a quick and easy meal.

⅔ cup bottled red wine vinegar and oil salad dressing	1 long, narrow Japanese eggplant (about 6 ounces), cut into ½-inch rounds
¾ teaspoon dried oregano	
1 pound skinless, boneless chicken breasts, cut into 1½-inch chunks	1 small zucchini, cut into ½-inch rounds
	8 cherry tomatoes

1. In a shallow dish, stir together salad dressing and oregano. Add chicken to dish and stir to coat well. Let stand 30 minutes at room temperature or refrigerate up to 6 hours.

2. Prepare a medium-hot fire in a barbecue grill. Thread chicken, eggplant, zucchini, and tomatoes onto 4 long metal skewers, beginning and ending with tomatoes. Brush vegetables with some of marinade.

3. Grill, turning often, until chicken is white throughout and vegetables are softened and browned, 10 to 12 minutes.

270 CHICKEN FAJITAS

Prep: 15 minutes   Stand: 20 minutes   Cook: 9 to 11 minutes
Serves: 4

¼ cup fresh lime juice
2 tablespoons vegetable oil
1 tablespoon tequila
1 jalapeño pepper, seeded
   and minced
1 pound thinly sliced chicken
   breast cutlets
¼ teaspoon salt

8 scallions, trimmed to leave
   2 inches of green
1 large ripe avocado
8 (7- or 8-inch) flour tortillas
1 cup shredded Monterey
   Jack or Cheddar cheese
   (4 ounces)
1 cup bottled or fresh salsa

1. In a shallow 2-quart dish, combine 3 tablespoons of lime juice with oil, tequila, and jalapeño pepper. Season chicken lightly with salt and add to marinade; turn to coat well. Let stand 15 minutes at room temperature or refrigerate up to 1 hour. Add scallions to marinade and let stand 5 minutes longer. In a small bowl, mash avocado with remaining 1 tablespoon lime juice. Cover and refrigerate.

2. Prepare a hot fire in a barbecue grill. Grill chicken, turning once or twice, until white throughout, 5 to 7 minutes. Transfer to a cutting board. Grill scallions, turning, until browned all over, about 4 minutes. At same time, wrap tortillas in foil and heat at edge of grill until warm, about 4 minutes.

3. Cut chicken crosswise into thin strips. Toss chicken and grilled scallions with any juices from chicken. Spoon into warm tortillas and top with avocado, cheese, and salsa. Roll up and eat.

271 RANCH CHICKEN

Prep: 5 minutes   Stand: 30 minutes   Cook: 12 to 15 minutes
Serves: 4 to 6

6 skinless, boneless chicken
   breasts or thighs

1 cup creamy ranch salad
   dressing (8-ounce bottle)

1. Arrange chicken in a single layer in a shallow 2-quart baking dish. Pour dressing over chicken and turn to coat completely. Cover and let stand 30 minutes at room temperature or refrigerate up to 6 hours.

2. Prepare a medium-hot fire in a barbecue grill. Coat grill rack with a nonstick cooking spray. Remove chicken from marinade but do not pat dry. Grill, turning once or twice, until chicken is white throughout, 12 to 15 minutes.

272 SPICY GRILLED CHICKEN CUTLETS WITH PAPAYA SALSA

Prep: 15 minutes   Stand: 30 minutes   Cook: 5 to 7 minutes
Serves: 4

Chopped mango and fresh or canned pineapple can be used in place of the papaya in this tropical salsa.

1 **papaya, peeled and finely diced**	1½ **tablespoons lime juice**
1 **small red onion, chopped**	½ **teaspoon salt**
1 **small jalapeño pepper, seeded and minced**	1 **pound thinly sliced chicken breast cutlets**
2 **tablespoons chopped cilantro**	2 **tablespoons vegetable oil**
	1 **teaspoon dried thyme**
	½ **teaspoon cayenne**

1. In a small bowl, stir together papaya, red onion, jalapeño pepper, cilantro, lime juice, and ¼ teaspoon of salt. Refrigerate salsa at least 15 minutes or up to 4 hours.

2. Rub chicken all over with oil, then season with thyme, cayenne, and remaining ¼ teaspoon salt. Let stand at room temperature 15 minutes.

3. Prepare a hot fire in a barbecue grill. Grill chicken, turning once or twice, until white throughout, 5 to 7 minutes. Serve grilled chicken with salsa spooned on top.

273 INDONESIAN CHICKEN SATAYS

Prep: 20 minutes   Stand: 30 minutes   Cook: 10 to 12 minutes
Serves: 4

Metal skewers work just as well, but bamboo makes a prettier presentation in this simple version of an Indonesian classic.

⅓ **cup creamy peanut butter**	1 **pound skinless, boneless chicken breasts or thighs, cut into 1½-inch chunks**
3 **tablespoons lime juice**	
3 **tablespoons soy sauce**	
2 **tablespoons chopped fresh ginger**	4 **cups thinly sliced iceberg lettuce**
2 **large garlic cloves, minced**	¼ **cup thinly sliced scallions**
½ **teaspoon crushed hot red pepper**	2 **tablespoons chopped peanuts**

1. Prepare a medium-hot fire in a barbecue grill. Soak 8 to 12 bamboo skewers for at least 30 minutes in cold water. In a shallow dish, combine peanut butter, lime juice, soy sauce, ginger, garlic, and hot pepper. Stir to blend well. Add chicken to peanut butter mixture. Toss to coat completely. Let stand at room temperature 30 minutes.

2. Thread several pieces of chicken on ends of soaked bamboo skewers. Grill, turning, until chicken is browned outside and white throughout but still juicy, 10 to 12 minutes.

3. Serve skewered satays on a bed of shredded lettuce. Sprinkle scallions and peanuts on top.

---

274 GRILLED INDIAN CHICKEN AND VEGETABLE KEBABS

Prep: 20 minutes   Stand: 1 hour 10 minutes   Cook: 10 to 12 minutes
Serves: 4

1 pound skinless, boneless chicken breasts or thighs, cut into 1½-inch chunks
1½ cups plain yogurt
1½ tablespoons lime juice
1 tablespoon minced fresh ginger
2 garlic cloves, minced
1½ teaspoons ground cumin
½ teaspoon ground coriander
½ teaspoon salt
¼ teaspoon freshly ground pepper
1 red bell pepper, cut into 1½-inch chunks
8 scallions, trimmed to leave 2 inches of green
1 yellow crookneck squash, cut into ½-inch rounds

1. Place chicken in a shallow dish. In a small bowl, combine yogurt, lime juice, ginger, garlic, cumin, coriander, salt, and pepper. Mix well. Pour spiced yogurt over chicken and stir to coat completely. Cover and refrigerate at least 1 or up to 6 hours. Add bell pepper, scallions, and squash to marinade and stir to coat. Refrigerate 10 minutes longer.

2. Prepare a medium-hot fire in a barbecue grill. Thread chicken and vegetables onto 4 large metal skewers. Grill, turning often, until chicken is white throughout and vegetables are softened and browned, 10 to 12 minutes.

Chapter 12

The Whole Meal in a Pot

The idea of a whole meal in a pot has always had great appeal. In earlier times, perhaps it was simply because there may have been only one pot available. But even today, when we have all sorts of pots and pans, the one-dish meal, or casserole, remains exceedingly popular because it just plain tastes good to have all those flavors mingling together. Further, the casserole can usually be made conveniently ahead of time, and it is easily totable to church suppers or potluck parties. Lastly, it is still nice to have only one pot to wash.

To qualify here as as a one-dish chicken meal, the pot must also contain vegetables and a starch such as potato, rice, or pasta. These additions also heighten the nutritional value and generally reduce the cost of the dish, too. As a general rule, I like to brown the chicken in a little oil or butter before continuing with the recipe because this gives a richer flavor to the finished dish. You can leave the skin on the chicken or not for most cooking, but you may choose to lower the fat significantly by removing it. I have indicated my preferences in each recipe, but you have the option to do as you wish.

An added benefit to these meals in a pot is that almost all of them can easily be reheated on the stove top, in a conventional oven, or in a microwave. In fact, many are even better the second time around!

275   QUICK ARROZ CON POLLO
Prep: 15 minutes   Cook: 13 minutes   Serves: 6

Quick-cooking rice makes short work of this savory Spanish supper.

1 pound skinless, boneless
  chicken thighs, cut into
  1-inch chunks
½ teaspoon salt
¼ teaspoon freshly ground
  pepper
¼ teaspoon cayenne
½ pound kielbasa or other
  garlicky cooked sausage,
  cut into ½-inch slices

2 tablespoons olive oil
2 cups quick-cooking white
  rice
2 cups chicken broth
¼ teaspoon crushed saffron
  threads
1 (14½-ounce) can Mexican-
  style stewed tomatoes
1 cup frozen green peas

1. Season chicken with salt, pepper, and cayenne. In a large Dutch oven, cook chicken and sausage in olive oil over medium-high heat, turning, until browned all over, about 6 minutes.

2. Stir in rice, broth, saffron, tomatoes, and peas. Bring to a boil, reduce heat to low, and simmer until chicken is cooked through and liquid is absorbed, about 7 minutes.

276   HUNTER'S-STYLE CHICKEN AND RICE SUPPER
Prep: 20 minutes   Cook: 38 minutes   Serves: 6

6 skinless, boneless chicken
  thighs
1½ teaspoons dried oregano
½ teaspoon salt
½ teaspoon freshly ground
  pepper
3 tablespoons olive oil
1 large onion, chopped
½ pound mushrooms, sliced
2 garlic cloves, crushed
  through a press

1½ cups converted white rice
2 cups chicken broth
½ cup dry white wine
1 (14½-ounce) can Italian-style
  stewed tomatoes
1 teaspoon grated lemon zest
¼ cup chopped flat-leaf
  parsley

1. Season chicken with ½ teaspoon of oregano and ¼ teaspoon each salt and pepper. In a large Dutch oven, heat olive oil over medium-high heat. Add chicken and cook, turning, until brown on both sides, about 8 minutes. Remove chicken to a plate.

2. Add onion, mushrooms, and garlic to drippings in pan, reduce heat to medium, and cook, stirring, until onion is softened, about 5 minutes. Add rice and remaining oregano, salt, and pepper, stirring to coat with oil. Add broth and wine and bring to a boil. Reduce heat to low.

3. Return chicken to pan along with any juices that have accumulated on plate. Cover and cook 15 minutes. Add stewed tomatoes, lemon zest, and parsley, stirring them in gently. Continue to cook, covered, over low heat, until rice is tender and chicken juices run clear when pricked, about 10 minutes.

---

277   CHICKEN WITH WEST INDIES PEAS AND RICE

Prep: 20 minutes   Cook: 1 hour 3 to 20 minutes   Serves: 6 to 8

This is an excellent informal party dish. In West Indian cooking, the "peas" are actually beans—red, pink, or black, depending upon which island the cook is from.

4 pounds chicken parts, skin removed if desired	1½ teaspoons dried thyme
1 teaspoon salt	½ teaspoon ground allspice
½ teaspoon freshly ground pepper	¼ teaspoon crushed hot red pepper
3 tablespoons vegetable oil	1½ cups chicken broth, preferably reduced-sodium
1 large onion, chopped	
2 garlic cloves, crushed through a press	½ cup unsweetened coconut milk
1 or 2 Scotch bonnet or jalapeño peppers, minced	1 (16-ounce) can black, pink, or red beans, drained
1½ cups converted white rice	½ cup chopped scallions

1. Preheat oven to 350°F. Season chicken with salt and pepper. In a large Dutch oven, heat oil over medium heat. Add chicken in batches and cook, turning, until browned, about 7 minutes per batch. Remove chicken to a platter.

2. Add onion to drippings in pan, reduce heat to medium, and cook, stirring occasionally, until softened, 3 to 5 minutes. Add garlic and Scotch bonnet peppers and cook 1 minute. Add rice, thyme, allspice, and hot pepper. Stir to coat rice with oil. Stir in broth, coconut milk, and beans. Return chicken to pan along with any juices that have accumulated on platter.

3. Cover with foil and bake until liquid is absorbed, rice is tender, and chicken has no trace of pink near bone, 45 to 60 minutes. Stir in scallions and serve.

278   ISLAND CHICKEN AND RICE
Prep: 20 minutes   Cook: 47 to 56 minutes   Serves: 6

Spicy-sweet flavors abound throughout the Caribbean. This is an adaptation of a dish I enjoyed during a vacation to Puerto Rico.

4 pounds chicken parts
1 teaspoon salt
½ teaspoon freshly ground
    pepper
¼ teaspoon cayenne
2 tablespoons olive oil
1 large onion, chopped
3 garlic cloves, crushed
    through a press
1 tablespoon minced fresh
    ginger

1½ cups converted white rice
⅓ cup chopped cilantro
2½ cups chicken broth
½ cup canned unsweetened
    coconut milk
1 (2-ounce) can chopped green
    chiles
1 (14½-ounce) can stewed
    tomatoes

1. Season chicken with salt, pepper, and cayenne. In a large Dutch oven, heat olive oil over medium-high heat. Add chicken in 2 or 3 batches, turning, until browned, about 7 minutes per batch. Remove chicken from pan as it browns.

2. Add onion and garlic to drippings in pan. Reduce heat to medium and cook, stirring often, until onion is softened, 3 to 5 minutes. Add ginger, rice, and half of cilantro. Stir to coat rice with oil. Add broth, coconut milk, and chiles. Return chicken to pan.

3. Cover and simmer over low heat 20 minutes. Stir in tomatoes. Cover and cook until rice is tender and chicken has no trace of pink near bone, about 10 minutes longer. Stir in remaining cilantro and serve.

279   CHICKEN AND SAFFRON RISOTTO
Prep: 15 minutes   Cook: 31½ minutes   Serves: 4

½ pound slim asparagus, cut
    diagonally into 1-inch
    pieces
¼ pound snow peas, trimmed
    and cut diagonally in half
4½ cups chicken broth,
    preferably reduced-
    sodium
1½ cups dry white wine
¼ teaspoon crushed saffron
    threads

¾ pound skinless, boneless
    chicken breasts, cut into
    1-inch chunks
¾ teaspoon salt
¾ teaspoon freshly ground
    pepper
2 tablespoons olive oil
1½ cups Arborio rice
1 cup frozen green peas
⅔ cup thinly sliced scallions
½ cup grated Parmesan cheese

1. In a large saucepan of boiling salted water, cook asparagus 2 minutes. Add snow peas and boil 30 seconds. Drain into a colander and rinse vegetables under cold water. Drain well.

2. In a medium saucepan, bring broth, wine, and saffron to a simmer. Meanwhile, season chicken with ½ teaspoon each salt and pepper. In a large saucepan, heat olive oil over medium-high heat. Add chicken and cook, stirring, until golden, about 5 minutes. Stir in rice, reduce heat to medium-low, and cook, stirring, 2 minutes.

3. Add 5½ cups of saffron broth to the rice. Cook, stirring often, until rice is nearly tender, about 20 minutes.

4. Stir in green peas, scallions, asparagus, and snow peas along with remaining ½ cup liquid. Simmer 2 minutes. Stir in cheese. Season with additional salt and pepper to taste.

280 CHICKEN, TOMATO, AND ROASTED GARLIC RISOTTO

Prep: 10 minutes   Cook: 31 to 32 minutes   Serves: 4

Roasted garlic is so mellow that you can eat it spread on bread like butter. It is also fabulous in this risotto, an adaptation of a stellar recipe from Brooke Dojny.

1 whole head of garlic, unpeeled, separated into cloves	½ teaspoon salt
¼ cup olive oil	½ teaspoon freshly ground pepper
4½ cups chicken broth, preferably reduced-sodium	1½ cups Arborio rice
	½ cup grated Parmesan cheese
1½ cups dry white wine	3 cups seeded and chopped fresh tomatoes (about 1 pound)
1 pound skinless, boneless chicken breasts, cut into 1-inch chunks	1 cup fresh basil leaves, shredded

1. Preheat oven to 450°F. Place garlic cloves on a small sheet of foil, drizzle with 1 tablespoon of olive oil, and loosely wrap cloves in foil. Roast until garlic is soft, about 20 minutes.

2. Meanwhile, in a medium saucepan, bring broth and wine to a simmer. Season chicken with salt and pepper. Heat remaining 3 tablespoons oil in a large saucepan. Add chicken and cook over medium heat, stirring often, until golden, about 5 minutes. Add rice and cook, stirring, 1 to 2 minutes. Stir in 5½ cups of simmering broth to pan. Simmer over medium-low heat, uncovered, stirring often, until rice is nearly tender, about 20 minutes.

3. Squeeze roasted garlic from skins and mash with a fork. Stir garlic into risotto along with cheese, tomatoes, basil, and remaining ½ cup liquid. Cook 5 minutes over low heat. Serve at once.

281   PESTO CHICKEN AND SUMMER SQUASH RISOTTO

Prep: 10 minutes   Cook: 32 minutes   Serves: 4

Prepared pesto is one of my favorite convenience foods.

4½ cups chicken broth,
   preferably reduced-
   sodium
1½ cups dry white wine
¾ pound skinless, boneless
   chicken breasts, cut into
   1-inch chunks
½ teaspoon salt
½ teaspoon freshly ground
   pepper

2 tablespoons olive oil
1 small zucchini, cubed
1 small yellow crookneck
   squash, cubed
1½ cups Arborio rice
½ cup prepared or homemade
   pesto
¼ cup diced pimiento

1. In a medium saucepan, bring broth and wine to a simmer. Meanwhile, season the chicken with salt and pepper. In a large saucepan, heat olive oil and cook chicken over medium heat, stirring until golden, about 5 minutes. Add zucchini and crookneck squash and the rice. Reduce heat to medium-low and cook, stirring constantly, 2 minutes.

2. Add 5½ cups of simmering broth and wine to rice. Simmer, uncovered, stirring often, until rice is nearly tender, about 20 minutes. Add pesto, pimiento, and remaining ½ cup liquid. Cook 5 minutes, stirring, over low heat.

282   CHICKEN AND SHRIMP IN LEMON RICE

Prep: 15 minutes   Cook: 29 to 32 minutes   Serves: 6

This is an elegant dish for buffet entertaining. Just add a big tossed salad and a basket of French rolls.

1 pound skinless, boneless
   chicken breasts, cut into
   1-inch chunks
½ teaspoon freshly ground
   pepper
¼ cup olive oil
1 medium red bell pepper,
   chopped
3 large garlic cloves, crushed
   through a press
1½ cups converted long-grain
   white rice

¼ to ½ teaspoon crushed hot
   red pepper
1½ cups chicken broth
1 cup bottled clam juice
½ cup dry white wine
1½ tablespoons lemon juice
1 teaspoon grated lemon zest
6 ounces snow peas, trimmed
   and halved if large (about
   2 cups)
½ pound medium shrimp,
   shelled and deveined

1. Season chicken with pepper. In a large frying pan, heat olive oil over medium-high heat. Add chicken and cook, stirring, until golden, about 3 minutes. With a slotted spoon, remove chicken to a plate.

2. Add bell pepper and garlic to drippings in pan. Reduce heat to medium-low and cook, stirring often, until slightly softened, about 2 minutes. Add rice and cook, stirring, 1 minute. Stir in hot pepper, chicken broth, clam juice, wine, and lemon juice. Bring to a boil, cover, reduce heat to medium-low, and cook 18 minutes.

3. Gently stir lemon zest into rice. Arrange snow peas and shrimp on top, pushing them lightly into rice. Place chicken over shrimp. Cover and simmer until rice is tender, shrimp are pink and curled, and chicken is white throughout, 5 to 8 minutes.

283   HOPPIN' CHICKEN JOHN
Prep: 20 minutes   Cook: 37 minutes   Serves: 4 to 6

Hoppin' John, a mix of highly seasoned rice and black-eyed peas, is a Southern culinary good luck charm. Adding chicken adds to the good fortune of those who enjoy the dish.

½ **pound thick-sliced bacon, diced**
6 **skinless, boneless chicken thighs (about 1 pound)**
2 **large onions, chopped**
2 **celery ribs, chopped**
3 **garlic cloves, crushed through a press**
4 **cups cooked black-eyed peas, thawed frozen or drained canned**

1 **cup converted white rice**
2 **cups chicken broth**
1 **bay leaf**
½ **teaspoon salt**
½ **teaspoon freshly ground pepper**
1 **tablespoon cider vinegar**

1. In a large Dutch oven, cook bacon over medium heat until crisp, about 5 minutes. Remove to paper towels with a slotted spoon. Pour off all but 3 tablespoons of drippings. Cook chicken in drippings over medium-high heat, turning, until golden brown all over, about 7 minutes. Remove chicken to a plate.

2. Add onions, celery, and garlic to drippings in pan. Reduce heat to medium and cook, stirring often, until vegetables are softened, about 5 minutes. Add black-eyed peas, rice, broth, bay leaf, salt, pepper, and 2 cups water. Bring to a boil; reduce heat to medium-low.

3. Return chicken back to pan along with any juices that have accumulated on plate. Cover and simmer until rice is tender and chicken is cooked through, about 20 minutes.

4. Remove and discard bay leaf. Gently stir in vinegar and bacon and serve.

284   ROSEMARY CHICKEN AND WHITE BEANS
Prep: 10 minutes   Cook: 32 to 37 minutes   Serves: 4

8   chicken drumsticks (about
    2 pounds)
½   teaspoon salt
¼   teaspoon freshly ground
    pepper
2   teaspoons dried rosemary
2   tablespoons olive oil,
    preferably extra-virgin
1   medium onion, chopped
1   celery rib, thinly sliced

4   garlic cloves, crushed
    through a press
1   cup dry white wine
1   (16-ounce) can white beans,
    drained
1   (14½-ounce) can stewed
    tomatoes
½   teaspoon Tabasco or other
    hot sauce

1. Season chicken with half of salt and pepper and 1 teaspoon of rosemary. Heat olive oil in a large frying pan over medium-high heat. Add chicken and cook, turning occasionally, until browned all over, about 7 minutes. Remove to a plate.

2. Add onion, celery, and garlic to pan. Reduce heat to medium and cook, stirring occasionally, until vegetables are softened, about 5 minutes. Stir in wine, beans, tomatoes, and remaining rosemary. Return chicken to the pan along with any juices that have accumulated on plate.

3. Cover and simmer until chicken is tender with no trace of pink near bone, 20 to 25 minutes. Season with Tabasco and remaining salt and pepper before serving.

285   HARVEST CHICKEN SUPPER
Prep: 15 minutes   Cook: 50 to 52 minutes   Serves: 4 to 6

A 6¼-ounce box of wild and long-grain rice mix can be substituted for the wild rice here. If you do so, increase the broth to 3½ cups and add the packet of herbs in place of the herbs in the recipe.

1   chicken (about 3 pounds),
    cut into 8 pieces
½   teaspoon salt
¼   teaspoon freshly ground
    pepper
2   tablespoons vegetable oil
1   medium butternut squash
    (about 1¼ pounds),
    peeled, seeded, and cut
    into 1-inch chunks

1   medium onion, chopped
1   cup wild rice
2½   cups chicken broth,
    preferably reduced-
    sodium
1   teaspoon crumbled dried
    leaf sage
½   teaspoon dried thyme
¼   cup chopped parsley

1. Season chicken with salt and pepper. Heat oil in a large frying pan over medium-high heat. Add chicken and cook, turning once or twice, until browned, about 7 minutes. Remove to a plate.

2. Add squash and onion to drippings in pan. Reduce heat to medium and cook, stirring occasionally, until onion is softened, 3 to 5 minutes. Stir in rice, then add broth, sage, and thyme. Return chicken to pan along with any juices that have accumulated on plate.

3. Bring to a boil, reduce the heat to low, cover, and cook until rice is tender, liquid is absorbed, and chicken is cooked through, about 40 minutes. Stir in parsley and serve.

286 SPICY CHICKEN WITH LENTILS AND GARBANZO BEANS

Prep: 10 minutes   Cook: 1 hour 17 minutes   Serves: 4 to 6

To get just the amount of vegetables that you need, buy them from the salad bar in the supermarket. Mix and match the vegetables, using about 4 cups total.

1 chicken (about 3 pounds), cut into 8 pieces
½ teaspoon salt
¼ teaspoon freshly ground pepper
½ teaspoon cayenne
2 tablespoons olive oil
1 medium onion, chopped
1 cup sliced carrots
2 garlic cloves, crushed through a press
2 teaspoons curry powder
1 (14½-ounce) can stewed tomatoes

2 cups chicken broth
1 cup broccoli florets
1 cup cauliflower florets
1 cup lentils, rinsed and picked over
1 cup sliced zucchini or crookneck squash (about 4 ounces)
1 (10-ounce) can garbanzo beans, drained (about 1 cup)

1. Preheat oven to 375°F. Season chicken with salt, pepper, and half of cayenne. In a large Dutch oven, cook chicken in olive oil over medium-high heat, turning, until browned, about 7 minutes. Remove to a plate.

2. Add onion, carrots, and garlic to drippings in pan. Reduce heat to medium and cook, stirring, until vegetables are tender, about 5 minutes. Stir in curry powder, remaining cayenne, stewed tomatoes, and broth. Bring to a boil. Add broccoli, cauliflower, and lentils. Return chicken to pan along with any juices that have accumulated on plate.

3. Cover and bake for 45 minutes. Stir in zucchini and garbanzo beans. Cover and bake 20 minutes longer.

287 ST. PATRICK'S DAY CHICKEN
Prep: 20 minutes   Cook: 55 minutes   Serves: 4 to 6

1 chicken (about 3 pounds),
    cut into 8 pieces, skin
    removed
¾ teaspoon salt
½ teaspoon freshly ground
    pepper
2 tablespoons vegetable oil
1 large onion, cut into 6
    wedges
1 medium head of green
    cabbage (about
    1½ pounds), cut
    into 6 wedges

2 medium turnips, peeled and
    quartered
3 carrots, peeled and cut into
    2-inch lengths
½ pound small red potatoes,
    scrubbed
2 cups chicken broth,
    preferably reduced-
    sodium
1 bay leaf
1½ teaspoons dried thyme

1. Season chicken with ½ teaspoon salt and ¼ teaspoon pepper. In a large Dutch oven, heat oil and cook chicken over medium-high heat, turning once or twice, until browned, about 7 minutes. Remove from pan. Add onion, cabbage, turnips, and carrots to drippings and cook, stirring often, until lightly browned, about 8 minutes. Sprinkle lightly with remaining salt and pepper. Return chicken to pot and add potatoes, broth, bay leaf, and thyme. Stir to mix.

2. Reduce heat to medium-low and simmer, covered, stirring occasionally, until vegetables are tender, about 40 minutes. Discard bay leaf. Serve chicken and vegetables with the broth.

288 CHICKEN WITH SAUSAGES AND LENTILS
Prep: 10 minutes   Cook: 59 minutes   Serves: 4 to 6

½ pound Italian sausage, cut
    into 4 to 6 pieces
½ cup dry red or white wine
1 chicken (about 3 pounds),
    cut into 8 pieces
  Salt and freshly ground
    pepper
1½ tablespoons olive oil

1 medium onion, chopped
1 carrot, chopped
1 red bell pepper, chopped
1½ teaspoons dried marjoram
3 cups chicken broth
1 cup lentils, rinsed and
    picked over

1. In a small frying pan over medium heat, cook sausage in wine, uncovered, turning often, until liquid evaporates, about 5 minutes. Remove from heat.

2. Season chicken with salt and generously with pepper. In a large Dutch oven, heat olive oil and cook chicken and sausage in 2 batches over medium-high heat, turning often, until both are browned, about 7 minutes per batch. Remove chicken and sausage to a platter.

3. Add onion, carrot, and bell pepper to pan. Cook over medium heat, stirring occasionally, until vegetables are softened, about 5 minutes. Stir in marjoram, broth, and lentils.

4. Return chicken and sausage to pan along with any juices that have accumulated on platter. Cover and simmer over medium-low heat, until lentils are tender and most of the liquid is absorbed, about 35 minutes.

---

289 WILD MUSHROOM AND CHICKEN RISOTTO

Prep: 15 minutes   Cook: 32 minutes   Serves: 4

Any combination of wild mushrooms, fresh or reconstituted dried, can be used. Even a combination of cultivated and wild mushrooms will do, though the flavor will be less intense.

4½ cups chicken broth, preferably reduced-sodium
1 cup dry white wine
½ cup Madeira or dry sherry
1 pound skinless, boneless chicken thighs, cut into 1-inch chunks
½ teaspoon salt
½ teaspoon freshly ground pepper

3 tablespoons butter
½ pound sliced wild mushrooms, such as porcini, shiitake, and/or cremini (about 3 cups)
¼ cup finely chopped shallots
1½ cups Arborio rice
⅓ cup grated Parmesan cheese
¼ cup chopped flat-leaf parsley

1. In a medium saucepan, bring broth, wine, and Madeira to a simmer. Meanwhile, season chicken with salt and pepper. In a large saucepan, melt butter over medium heat. Add chicken, mushrooms, and shallots and cook, stirring often, until chicken is golden and mushrooms are just softened, about 5 minutes. Add rice and cook, stirring, 2 minutes.

2. Add 5½ cups of simmering liquid. Cook over medium-low heat, uncovered, stirring often, until rice is nearly tender, about 20 minutes. Stir in remaining ½ cup liquid, cheese, and parsley. Reduce heat to low and cook 5 minutes, stirring constantly. Serve at once.

290   TURKISH CHICKEN AND BULGUR PILAF

Prep: 20 minutes   Cook: 47 minutes   Serves: 4

Bulgur is cracked wheat, a full-flavored, nutty grain that is a staple in the kitchens of the Eastern Mediterranean.

1   chicken (about 3 pounds), cut into 8 pieces
½   teaspoon salt
¼   teaspoon freshly ground pepper
2   tablespoons olive oil
1   medium onion, chopped
1   green bell pepper, chopped
1   medium eggplant (about 1 pound), peeled and cut into 1-inch chunks

½   teaspoon ground cinnamon
¼   teaspoon crushed hot red pepper
⅛   teaspoon ground cloves
3   tablespoons tomato paste
2¼   cups chicken broth, preferably reduced-sodium
1   cup bulgur (cracked wheat)

1. Season chicken with salt and pepper. In a large Dutch oven, heat olive oil over medium-high heat. Add chicken and cook, turning, until browned, about 7 minutes. Remove to a plate.

2. Add onion, bell pepper, and eggplant to drippings in pan, reduce heat to medium, and cook, stirring often, until softened, about 5 minutes. Stir in cinnamon, hot pepper, cloves, tomato paste, and 1 cup broth. Return chicken to pan along with any juices that have accumulated on plate. Cover, reduce heat to medium-low, and cook 15 minutes.

3. Stir in bulgur and remaining 1¼ cups broth. Simmer, covered, until bulgur is tender and liquid is absorbed, about 20 minutes.

291   MUSTARD CHICKEN WITH VEGETABLES AND HOMINY

Prep: 15 minutes   Cook: 50 minutes   Serves: 6

3   pounds chicken legs, thighs, and drumsticks, separated, skin removed if desired
¼   teaspoon salt
⅛   teaspoon freshly ground pepper
2   tablespoons vegetable oil
2   garlic cloves, crushed through a press

2   teaspoons dried thyme
1   teaspoon dried summer savory
2   cups chicken broth
1   (1-pound) bag frozen mixed stew vegetables
1   (16-ounce) can hominy or posole, drained
2   tablespoons grainy Dijon mustard

1. Season chicken with salt and pepper. In a large Dutch oven, heat oil over medium-high heat. Add chicken in 2 batches and cook, turning, until browned, about 7 minutes per batch. Stir in garlic, thyme, and savory and cook 1 minute. Add broth, vegetables, and hominy.

2. Reduce heat to medium-low, cover, and cook until chicken is tender with no trace of pink near bone, about 35 minutes. Stir in mustard and season with additional salt and pepper to taste before serving.

---

292   MOROCCAN CHICKEN AND COUSCOUS
Prep: 20 minutes   Cook: 49 to 54 minutes   Serves: 4 to 6

Couscous, a tiny precooked pasta, is a staple in the Moroccan kitchen.

½ teaspoon crushed saffron
    threads or turmeric
1½ cups chicken broth,
    preferably reduced-
    sodium
2 tablespoons olive oil
1 chicken (about 3 pounds),
    cut into 8 pieces
1 large onion, chopped
2 carrots, coarsely chopped
2 garlic cloves, crushed
    through a press

1 teaspoon ground ginger
1 teaspoon hot paprika
¾ teaspoon ground cumin
¼ teaspoon cayenne
⅓ cup chopped cilantro
1 cup couscous
¼ cup lemon juice
2 teaspoons grated lemon zest
¾ cup sliced pimiento-stuffed
    olives
½ cup slivered almonds,
    preferably toasted

1. Stir saffron into broth; set aside. In a large Dutch oven, heat oil over medium-high heat. Add chicken in 2 batches and cook, turning, until browned, about 7 minutes per batch. Remove to a plate.

2. Add onion, carrots, and garlic to drippings in pan. Reduce heat to medium and cook, stirring often, until onion is softened, about 5 minutes. Stir in ginger, paprika, cumin, cayenne, reserved broth, and half of cilantro. Return chicken to pan along with any juices that have accumulated on plate. Reduce heat to medium-low, cover, and simmer until chicken is tender, 25 to 30 minutes. Remove chicken to a platter and cover to keep warm.

3. Stir couscous, lemon juice, lemon zest, olives, almonds, and remaining cilantro into liquid in pan. Cover and let stand over very low heat 5 minutes. Fluff with a fork. Serve with chicken.

293   DOUBLE BROCCOLI AND CHEESY CHICKEN CASSEROLE

Prep: 10 minutes   Cook: 42 to 44 minutes   Serves: 4

½ pound rotelle
8 skinless chicken drumsticks
¼ teaspoon salt
¼ teaspoon freshly ground pepper
2 tablespoons vegetable oil
1 cup frozen pearl onions, thawed
3 medium carrots, peeled and sliced

2 cups milk
1 (10¾-ounce) can cream of broccoli soup
1 cup grated Cheddar cheese (4 ounces)
3 cups small broccoli florets
½ cup seasoned dry bread crumbs
2 tablespoons butter, melted

1. In a large pot of boiling salted water, cook pasta until tender but still firm, about 10 to 12 minutes. Drain and turn into a buttered 2-quart casserole or baking dish.

2. Meanwhile, season chicken with salt and pepper. In a large frying pan, heat oil over medium-high heat. Add chicken and cook, turning, until browned all over, about 7 minutes. With tongs, transfer chicken to baking dish.

3. Add onions and carrots to frying pan. Cook, stirring often, until vegetables are lightly browned, 5 to 7 minutes. Add milk and bring to a simmer, scraping up browned bits from bottom of pan. Stir in soup and return to a simmer. Pour over chicken in baking dish. Add broccoli and stir to combine all ingredients.

4. Toss bread crumbs with melted butter and sprinkle over the top of the casserole. Bake, uncovered, until bubbly and lightly browned on top and chicken juices run clear when pricked, about 30 minutes.

294 CHICKEN AND WILD MUSHROOM TETRAZZINI

Prep: 25 minutes   Cook: 46 to 49 minutes   Serves: 6

Here's an excellent dish for using up leftover cooked chicken. Since you can assemble it hours ahead, it's great for a party or a potluck supper.

½ pound spaghetti
3 tablespoons butter
1 onion, chopped
1 large celery rib, chopped
6 ounces fresh wild
     mushrooms, such as
     shiitake or cremini, sliced
3 tablespoons flour
2 cups chicken broth
½ cup half-and-half or light
     cream
1 teaspoon dried thyme
2½ cups bite-sized pieces of
     cooked chicken (about
     5 ounces)

1 (10-ounce) package frozen
     baby green peas
⅓ cup coarsely chopped jarred
     roasted red peppers
¼ cup plus 1 tablespoon grated
     Parmesan cheese
   Salt and freshly ground
     pepper
3 tablespoons plain dry bread
     crumbs

1. Preheat oven to 350°F. In a large pot of boiling salted water, cook spaghetti until tender but still firm, about 9 minutes; drain.

2. Meanwhile, in a large frying pan, melt butter over medium heat. Add onion and celery and cook, stirring occasionally, until softened, 3 to 5 minutes. Add mushrooms and cook until tender, about 5 minutes. Sprinkle on flour and cook, stirring, 1 to 2 minutes. Stir in broth, half-and-half, and thyme. Bring to a boil, stirring, until thickened, about 2 minutes. Stir in chicken, peas, roasted peppers, and ¼ cup of cheese. Season with salt and pepper to taste.

3. In a shallow 2½- or 3-quart casserole or baking dish, toss chicken and sauce with spaghetti. Combine bread crumbs and remaining 1 tablespoon cheese. Sprinkle over casserole.

4. Cover with foil and bake 20 minutes. Uncover and bake until casserole is heated through and bread crumbs are browned, about 15 minutes. (If a crustier top is desired, run briefly under a broiler.)

295 TACO LASAGNE
Prep: 15 minutes   Cook: 55 minutes   Stand: 10 minutes   Serves: 6

Suit your own heat barometer by using mild, medium, or hot salsa.

12 lasagna noodles (about
    12 ounces), either regular
    or no-cook
2 cups part-skim ricotta
    cheese (15-ounce
    container)
1 egg
⅓ cup chopped cilantro
½ teaspoon ground cumin
2 cups tomato sauce (16-ounce
    can)

3 cups sliced, cooked chicken
2 cups thick and chunky salsa
    (16-ounce jar)
2 cups shredded Monterey
    Jack cheese with chiles
    (8 ounces)
1 cup shredded Cheddar
    cheese (4 ounces)
2 cups diced cooked chicken
    (8 ounces)

1. Preheat oven to 350°F. Cook or prepare lasagna noodles as directed on the package. In a small bowl, whisk together ricotta cheese, egg, cilantro, and cumin. In a medium bowl, blend tomato sauce and salsa. Toss together Monterey Jack and Cheddar cheese.

2. To assemble lasagne, spread about ½ cup of tomato sauce over bottom of a 9x13-inch baking dish. Make a lengthwise layer of 4 noodles. Spread half of ricotta mixture over noodles. Layer on half of chicken. Sprinkle half of the cheese, then spoon one-third of remaining sauce over cheese. Make another layer using 4 noodles, remaining ricotta mixture, and half each of remaining cheese and sauce. Top with remaining noodles and cover with remaining sauce. Sprinkle remaining cheese on top. Cover pan with foil.

3. Bake 45 minutes. Uncover and bake 10 minutes longer. Let stand 10 minutes before cutting into squares to serve.

---

296 CHICKEN AND STUFFING SAN ANTONIO
Prep: 10 minutes   Cook: 59 minutes   Serves: 6

4 pounds chicken parts, skin
    removed
1 tablespoon chili powder
3 tablespoons vegetable oil
1 large onion, coarsely
    chopped
2 celery ribs, sliced
1 red bell pepper, coarsely
    chopped

1 (2-ounce) can chopped green
    chiles
2 cups chicken broth,
    preferably reduced-
    sodium
1 (8-ounce) package corn
    bread stuffing (4 cups)
3 tablespoons chopped
    cilantro

1. Preheat oven to 375°F. Sprinkle chicken with chili powder. In a large frying pan, heat oil over medium-high heat. Add chicken in 2 batches and cook, turning, until browned, about 7 minutes per batch. Remove chicken to a platter.

2. Add onion, celery, and bell pepper to drippings in pan. Reduce heat to medium and cook, stirring occasionally, until vegetables are softened, about 5 minutes. Stir in chiles and broth and bring to a boil. Add stuffing mix and toss to coat with liquid.

3. Spoon stuffing mixture into a 9x13-inch baking dish or other shallow 3-quart casserole. Arrange chicken pieces on stuffing, pushing down into mixture.

4. Cover dish with foil and bake until chicken juices run clear when pricked, about 40 minutes. Sprinkle with cilantro and serve.

---

297 BRAZILIAN CHICKEN AND QUINOA
Prep: 20 minutes   Cook: 45 to 52 minutes   Serves: 6

Quinoa is a wonderful, nutty grain that is indigenous to the Andes Mountains in South America. Combining fruits and meats is a South American tradition. This dish reflects both.

1 chicken (about 3 pounds), cut into 8 pieces, skin removed if desired
½ teaspoon salt
¼ teaspoon freshly ground pepper
2 tablespoons vegetable oil
1 medium onion, chopped
1 cup quinoa
1½ teaspoons ground coriander
1 teaspoon ground allspice

1 teaspoon ground cumin
¾ teaspoon ground ginger
2 cups chicken broth, preferably reduced-sodium
1 pound sweet potatoes, peeled and cut into ¾-inch cubes
⅓ cup quartered pitted prunes
⅓ cup quartered dried figs
⅓ cup quartered dried apricots

1. Season chicken with salt and pepper. In a large Dutch oven, cook chicken in oil over medium-high heat, turning, until browned, about 7 minutes. Transfer to a plate.

2. Add onion to drippings in pan. Reduce heat to medium and cook, stirring occasionally, until softened, 3 to 5 minutes. Stir in quinoa, coriander, allspice, cumin, and ginger. Add broth, sweet potatoes, prunes, figs, and apricots. Return chicken to pan along with any juices that have accumulated on plate.

3. Reduce heat to medium-low, cover, and simmer until chicken is tender with no trace of pink near bone and liquid is absorbed by quinoa, 35 to 40 minutes.

298 PRAIRIE CHICKEN AND CORN PUDDING
Prep: 20 minutes   Cook: 48 to 60 minutes   Serves: 8 to 10

Set out some sliced tomatoes, a tossed green salad, and a basket of crisp bread sticks along with this one-pot dish for a simple buffet supper.

4 tablespoons butter
¼ cup flour
3 cups half-and-half or light cream
1 cup chicken broth
6 eggs
1 tablespoon sugar
¾ teaspoon ground cumin
¾ teaspoon salt
½ teaspoon freshly ground pepper
¼ teaspoon cayenne
3 cups fresh or frozen corn kernels
2 cups coarsely chopped cooked chicken (about ½ pound)
1½ cups thinly sliced scallions
2 cups shredded Cheddar cheese (8 ounces)

1. Preheat oven to 350°F. In a large saucepan, melt butter over medium heat. Stir in flour to make a paste. Cook, stirring, for 1 to 2 minutes without allowing to color. Gradually whisk in half-and-half and broth. Bring to a boil, stirring, until sauce is thick and smooth, 2 to 3 minutes. Remove from heat.

2. In a medium bowl, whisk together eggs, sugar, cumin, salt, pepper, and cayenne. Whisk about half of sauce into eggs to warm them, then whisk mixture into remaining sauce in pan. In a generously greased 9x13-inch baking dish or other shallow 3-quart casserole, toss together corn, chicken, scallions, and cheese. Add sauce and stir gently but thoroughly to combine. Spread evenly in dish.

3. Bake until pudding is light golden brown and a knife inserted off center comes out clean, 45 to 55 minutes.

299 CHICKEN AND CHEDDAR BREAD PUDDING

Prep: 15 minutes   Stand: 15 minutes
Cook: 55 to 60 minutes   Serves: 6

You can assemble this savory bread pudding several hours before baking, which makes it a great informal supper or brunch.

10 slices of firm white bread, crusts removed	4 eggs
3 tablespooons butter, softened	2½ cups milk
2½ cups shredded Cheddar cheese (about 10 ounces)	1 tablespoon Dijon mustard
	2 teaspoons dry mustard
½ cup diced smoked ham	¼ teaspoon salt
2 cups diced smoked or cooked chicken (about ½ pound)	¼ teaspoon coarsely ground pepper

1. Spread one side of bread with butter and cut each slice into 3 strips. Lay half of bread strips in bottom of a buttered 1½-quart baking dish (8 inches square). Sprinkle half of cheese, ham, and chicken over bread. Make another layer with remaining bread, cheese, ham, and chicken.

2. Preheat oven to 350°F. In a mixing bowl, whisk together eggs, milk, Dijon mustard, dry mustard, salt, and pepper. Pour custard over bread, pushing bread down into milk to make sure it is saturated. Let stand 15 minutes.

3. Bake, uncovered, until pudding is evenly puffed and golden brown and a knife inserted off center comes out clean, 55 to 60 minutes. Cut into squares to serve.

300   CHORIZO AND CHICKEN CORN BREAD PUDDING

Prep: 15 minutes   Cook: 38 minutes   Serves: 6

If you can't get bulk chorizo sausage, remove casings from link sausage and crumble the meat. This is a deliciously rich whole meal corn bread that is wonderful served with a big spinach salad.

½   pound bulk chorizo or other garlicky sausage
1   medium green bell pepper, chopped
1   medium onion, chopped
1   cup yellow cornmeal
1   cup flour
1   tablespoon sugar
2   teaspoons cream of tartar
1   teaspoon baking soda
¾   teaspoon salt
½   teaspoon coarsely ground black pepper
3   eggs

1   cup sour cream or plain yogurt
½   cup milk
4   tablespoons butter, melted
2   cups coarsely chopped cooked chicken (about ½ pound)
4   ounces shredded Monterey Jack cheese with chiles (1 cup)
½   cup fresh or frozen corn kernels
1½   cups bottled chunky salsa

1. Preheat oven to 400°F. In a large frying pan, cook chorizo over medium heat, stirring often, until browned, about 5 minutes. Add bell pepper and onion to pan and cook, stirring occasionally, until softened, about 3 minutes. Pour off any excess fat.

2. In a large mixing bowl, whisk together cornmeal, flour, sugar, cream of tartar, baking soda, salt, and pepper. In another mixing bowl, whisk together eggs, sour cream, milk, and melted butter until well blended. Make a well in center of dry ingredients and add liquids all at once. Stir just until blended. Add chicken, cheese, corn, and chorizo. Stir only until blended; do not overmix.

3. Spoon evenly into a buttered 8x12-inch baking dish or other shallow 2½-quart casserole. Bake until golden brown and a knife inserted into center comes out clean, about 30 minutes. Cut warm pudding into squares. Serve with salsa.

Chapter 13

Chicken Light and Lean

Chicken is by nature one of the lower-fat ways to obtain complete proteins. Along with its great versatility, the low-fat properties of chicken are among the major reasons why consumption has soared in recent years.

Though the skin of the chicken contributes most of the fat, studies have shown that in dishes such as roasted chicken, in which the fat drips away, there is no greater fat content if the skin is discarded after cooking. Many people feel that the skin contributes to the flavor of the dish during cooking. Consequently, skin-on chicken can also be low in fat as long as the skin is removed before eating.

Skinless, boneless chicken breasts are now a supermarket staple, but the newest items in the chicken case are skinless chicken breasts, thighs, and even drumsticks on the bone. Cooking on the bone results in a richer flavor with no added fat. The problem with chicken cookery is often the fat that is sometimes added to a recipe to enhance flavor.

Throughout this book, a serious attempt has been made to keep fat content as low as possible. This chapter, in particular, however, presents a collection of recipes that use little or no added fat, replacing it with lots of power-packed flavor ingredients, such as herbs, spices, fruits, and aromatic vegetables. Skillet cooking is done in very little oil or other fat, but using a nonstick frying pan will help, too. Finally, for best results, use peak ingredients, from fresh produce to dried herbs and spices.

301　POACHED CHICKEN IN LEMON-TARRAGON BROTH

Prep: 5 minutes　Cook: 12 to 15 minutes　Serves: 4

This is a master recipe for poached boneless chicken breasts. Vary the herbs to your taste and substitute wine for the lemon juice, if you wish. The chicken can be served warm in its cooking broth or refrigerated and used for salads or sandwiches, with the broth kept reserved for another use.

4　skinless, boneless chicken breast halves	1　teaspoon grated lemon zest
½　teaspoon freshly ground pepper	1　tablespoon chopped fresh tarragon or 1 teaspoon dried
¼　teaspoon salt	4　thin lemon slices
1½　cups chicken broth	4　sprigs of fresh tarragon or parsley
¼　cup lemon juice	

1. Season chicken with pepper and salt. Place chicken in a frying pan or saucepan just large enough to hold it in a single layer. Pour in broth and lemon juice, adding water if necessary to barely cover chicken. Sprinkle with lemon zest and chopped tarragon.

2. Cover pan and bring just to a boil. Reduce heat to medium-low, cover, and simmer until chicken is white throughout but still juicy, 12 to 15 minutes.

3. Serve chicken and broth ladled into shallow soup bowls. Garnish with lemon slices and tarragon sprigs.

302　DEVILED CHICKEN BREASTS

Prep: 10 minutes　Cook: 12 to 15 minutes　Serves: 6

A mustard crumb coating protects and flavors the delicate chicken. While I like to use whole wheat bread crumbs, regular white will also do.

¼　cup grainy Dijon mustard	½　teaspoon freshly ground pepper
¼　cup low-fat mayonnaise	6　skinless, boneless chicken breast halves
1　tablespoon chopped fresh dill or ¾ teaspoon dried	Lemon wedges
1　garlic clove, minced	Sprigs of fresh dill or parsley, for garnish
1½　cups whole wheat bread crumbs (from about 3 slices of bread)	

1. Preheat the oven to 450°F. Lightly grease a baking sheet or coat with non-stick cooking spray. In a shallow bowl, whisk together mustard, mayonnaise, dill, and garlic. Stir together bread crumbs and pepper and spread on a plate or sheet of waxed paper. Use your hands to flatten chicken to an even thickness.

2. Dip chicken into mustard mixture, then dredge in crumbs, turning to coat completely. Place in a single layer on prepared baking sheet.

3. Bake until chicken is white throughout and coating is golden and crisp, 12 to 15 minutes. Serve hot, garnished with lemon wedges and dill sprigs.

303 STEAMED MOROCCAN CHICKEN

Prep: 10 minutes   Cook: 20 to 25 minutes   Stand: 5 minutes
Serves: 4

Here, the highly seasoned broth used to steam the chicken doubles as the liquid for cooking the couscous.

2 cups chicken broth, preferably reduced-sodium
½ cup dry white wine
½ teaspoon salt
1 large garlic clove, crushed through a press
1 (1-inch) piece lemon peel, yellow part only
1 cinnamon stick, broken in half
6 whole peppercorns

4 whole allspice berries
4 whole coriander seeds
2 thin slices of fresh ginger
4 skinless, boneless chicken breast halves
2 slender carrots, peeled and thinly sliced
1 cup couscous
½ cup thinly sliced scallions
Salt and freshly ground pepper

1. In a deep saucepan or bottom of a steamer, combine broth, wine, and salt. In a piece of cheesecloth or a spice bag, tie together garlic, lemon peel, cinnamon stick, peppercorns, allspice, coriander, and ginger. Add to broth. Insert a steamer rack into pan and arrange chicken and carrots on rack. Cover tightly and bring just to a boil. Cook over medium heat, until chicken is white throughout and carrots are tender, 15 to 20 minutes. Transfer chicken to a carving board and place carrots in a bowl. Cover both with foil to keep warm. Remove spice bag from broth; measure and reserve 1¼ cups broth.

2. Place couscous in a heatproof serving bowl. Bring reserved broth to a boil and pour over couscous. Cover bowl and let stand 5 minutes, until liquid is absorbed. Add cooked carrots and scallions to couscous and toss with a fork to fluff up.

3. Slice chicken and arrange in a fan shape over warm couscous. Season with salt and pepper to taste and serve.

304   DILLED CHICKEN DIJON EN PAPILLOTE
Prep: 20 minutes   Cook: 10 to 12 minutes   Serves: 4

Parchment paper is the traditional wrap for presenting foods "en papillote," but aluminum foil also works well. This elegant-sounding cooking method is simply steaming in the oven, which seals in flavors and moisture —excellent for low-fat chicken cookery. Serve in the wrap and allow each person to slit open the pretty package.

1 **pound thinly sliced chicken breast cutlets**	2 **small leeks (white part only), thinly sliced**
2 **tablespoons Dijon mustard**	2 **teaspoons olive oil, preferably extra-virgin**
2 **tablespoons chopped fresh dill**	
½ **teaspoon freshly ground pepper**	

1. Preheat oven to 425°F. Cut 4 pieces of parchment paper or aluminum foil into 12x15-inch rectangles. Fold in half from short end and cut out large half hearts along folds, like valentines. When unfolded, hearts should measure about 14 inches wide and 12 inches long.

2. Divide chicken among hearts, placing on one side of hearts. Spread mustard over chicken, then sprinkle on dill, pepper, leeks, and olive oil. Fold hearts over and crimp edges neatly to seal completely.

3. Place on a baking sheet and bake until parchment is puffed and lightly browned and chicken is cooked through, 10 to 12 minutes. (Open one packet and check to be sure chicken is cooked through.) Serve at once.

305   POACHED CHICKEN ORIENTAL
Prep: 15 minutes   Cook: 13 to 15 minutes   Serves: 4

1 **large leek (white and pale green)**	3 **thin slices of fresh ginger**
1 **medium carrot**	¼ **teaspoon crushed hot red pepper**
1 **small red bell pepper**	4 **skinless, boneless chicken breast halves**
1 **small celery rib**	
2 **cups chicken broth, preferably reduced-sodium**	1 **teaspoon Asian sesame oil**
	2 **cups freshly cooked white or brown rice**
1 **cup dry white wine**	2 **tablespoons chopped cilantro or parsley**
2 **teaspoons soy sauce**	
4 **thin slices of lemon**	

1. Cut leek, carrot, bell pepper, and celery into thin (julienne) strips about ¼ x 1½ inches. In a frying pan or saucepan just large enough to hold chicken in a single layer, combine broth, wine, soy sauce, lemon slices, ginger, and hot pepper.

2. Add chicken and bring just to a boil. Reduce heat to medium-low, cover, and simmer 10 minutes. Add vegetable strips and simmer until chicken is white throughout and vegetables are crisp-tender, 3 to 5 minutes. Stir in sesame oil.

3. Divide rice among 4 shallow soup bowls. Top with chicken and ladle in broth and vegetables. Sprinkle with cilantro.

---

306 POACHED CHICKEN PRINTEMPS
Prep: 10 minutes   Cook: 18 to 20 minutes   Serves: 4

Bright green watercress is added at the end here, so that it just barely wilts. Use young, tender vegetables for the prettiest look.

2 cups chicken broth, preferaby reduced-sodium
1 cup dry white wine
2 tablespoons raspberry or white wine vinegar
1 tablespoon chopped fresh thyme or 1 teaspoon dried
½ teaspoon salt
½ teaspoon coarsely ground pepper
½ pound very small red potatoes or larger potatoes cut into 1-inch chunks, scrubbed

¼ pound baby carrots
4 skinless, boneless chicken breast halves
8 thin asparagus stalks, cut diagonally into 1½-inch lengths
¼ pound small sugar snap peas
¼ cup thinly sliced radishes
2 tablespoons minced fresh chives

1. In a large frying pan, combine broth, wine, vinegar, thyme, salt, and pepper. Add potatoes and carrots and boil chicken 5 minutes. Add cover, reduce heat to medium-low, and simmer 10 minutes.

2. Add asparagus and sugar snap peas. Continue to simmer, covered, until chicken is white throughout and vegetables are just tender, 3 to 5 minutes.

3. Serve vegetables and broth in shallow bowls. Sprinkle 1 tablespoon radishes and 1½ teaspoons chives on top of each serving.

307   NEAPOLITAN CHICKEN BAKED IN PAPER
Prep: 15 minutes   Cook: 10 to 12 minutes   Serves: 4

This low-fat technique seals in flavor and moisture. The explosion of aroma that occurs when the packet is slit open is tantalizing, so it's nice to present the packets intact to each diner.

1 **pound thinly sliced chicken breast cutlets**	2 **teaspoons extra-virgin olive oil**
1 **teaspoon dried Italian seasoning**	¼ **cup shredded fresh basil leaves**
¼ **teaspoon salt**	1 **small red bell pepper, thinly sliced**
¼ **teaspoon crushed hot red pepper**	1 **small yellow bell pepper, thinly sliced**
2 **garlic cloves, minced**	1 **small green bell pepper, thinly sliced**
2 **tablespoons balsamic vinegar**	

1. Preheat oven to 425°F. Cut 4 pieces of parchment paper or aluminum foil into 12x15-inch rectangles. Fold in half from short end and cut out large half hearts along folds, like valentines. When unfolded, hearts should measure about 14 inches wide and 12 inches long.

2. Divide chicken among hearts, placing on one side of each. Sprinkle with Italian seasoning, salt, hot pepper, garlic, vinegar, olive oil, basil, and red, yellow, and green bell peppers. Fold hearts over and crimp edges to seal completely.

3. Place packets on a baking sheet and bake until parchment is puffed and lightly browned and chicken is white throughout, 10 to 12 minutes. (Open one packet and check to be sure chicken is cooked through.) Serve at once.

308   SPICED YOGURT ROAST CHICKEN
Prep: 5 minutes   Stand: 15 minutes   Cook: 1 hour   Serves: 4

1 **whole chicken (about 3½ pounds)**	1 **teaspoon paprika**
⅓ **cup nonfat plain yogurt**	½ **teaspoon ground coriander**
1 **teaspoon lemon juice**	½ **teaspoon ground turmeric**
1 **garlic clove, minced**	½ **teaspoon salt**
1 **teaspoon ground cumin**	¼ **teaspoon cayenne**

1. Remove skin and all visible fat from chicken. Chop off and discard wings. Loosen skin of chicken, separating from meat without tearing. In a small bowl, stir together yogurt, lemon juice, garlic, cumin, paprika, coriander, turmeric, salt, and cayenne. Rub seasoned yogurt over surface and under skin of chicken. Tie legs together with kitchen string. Let chicken stand 15 minutes at room temperature.

2. Preheat oven to 350°F. Place chicken, breast side up, on a rack in a shallow pan. Roast to an internal temperature of 180°; juices from thigh should run clear when pricked near bone, about 1 hour.

3. Carve chicken. Remove skin before serving.

---

309   GRILLED CHICKEN FRA DIAVOLO
Prep: 10 minutes   Stand: 30 minutes   Cook: 15 to 16 minutes
Serves: 6

The term *fra diavolo* refers to a very spicy marinara sauce, traditionally served with lobster or other shellfish. I find that smoky grilled chicken has the character to stand up to the peppery sauce very nicely.

1 **tablespoon lemon juice**
4 **teaspoons olive oil,**
   preferably extra-virgin
4 **garlic cloves, minced**
1 **teaspoon dried Italian**
   seasoning
½ **teaspoon crushed hot red**
   pepper

1 **pound thinly sliced chicken**
   breast cutlets
3 **cups bottled low-fat**
   marinara sauce
½ **cup dry red wine**
1 **pound spaghetti**
½ **cup chopped parsley,**
   preferably flat-leaf

1. In a shallow dish, combine lemon juice, 1 tablespoon of olive oil, and half each of garlic, Italian seasoning, and hot pepper. Add chicken and rub all over with marinade. Let stand 30 minutes at room temperature or refrigerate up to 2 hours.

2. In a nonreactive medium saucepan, cook remaining garlic in remaining 1 teaspoon oil over medium heat until soft and fragrant, about 1 minute. Add remaining hot pepper along with marinara sauce and wine. Bring to a boil, reduce heat to medium-low, and simmer 5 minutes.

3. Prepare a medium-hot barbecue fire or preheat broiler. In a large pot of boiling salted water, cook spaghetti until tender but still firm, 9 to 10 minutes. Drain in a colander.

4. Meanwhile, grill or broil chicken, turning once, until white throughout, 5 to 7 minutes. Slice chicken and add to sauce along with parsley. Serve ladled over hot pasta.

310   GRILLED CHICKEN FILLETS WITH CANTALOUPE-LIME SALSA

Prep: 10 minutes   Stand: 15 minutes   Cook: 12 to 15 minutes
Serves: 4

This combination may sound strange, but the mild sweetness of cantaloupe, punctuated with tart lime, pairs beautifully with delicate chicken. Really ripe cantaloupe is probably the most fragrant of all fruits.

2 **cups coarsely chopped cantaloupe**
1 **medium red onion, chopped**
3 **tablespoons lime juice**
1 **teaspoon grated lime zest**

¼ **cup chopped cilantro**
¾ **teaspoon coarsely ground pepper**
4 **skinless, boneless chicken breast fillets (tenders)**
1½ **teaspoons olive oil**

1. Prepare a medium-hot barbecue fire or preheat broiler. In a mixing bowl, combine cantaloupe, onion, lime juice, lime zest, cilantro, and pepper. Toss to mix well. Let salsa stand 15 minutes at room temperature or refrigerate up to 2 hours.

2. Use your hand to flatten chicken to an even thickness. Rub with olive oil. Grill, turning once, until white throughout, 12 to 15 minutes.

3. Serve chicken with salsa spooned on top.

311   FIVE-SPICE GRILLED CHICKEN

Prep: 10 minutes   Stand: 30 minutes   Cook: 10 to 12 minutes
Serves: 4

The complexity of flavors provided by Chinese five-spice powder—a mix of fennel, anise, ginger, cinnamon, and cloves—imparts a subtle, sophisticated taste to this recipe. Several national brands now include this spice in their lines, though, of course, it can always be found in an Asian market.

2 **tablespoons soy sauce**
1 **tablespoon chicken broth**
1½ **teaspoons hot chili oil**
1 **tablespoon Chinese five-spice powder**

1 **large garlic clove, minced**
4 **skinless, boneless chicken breast halves**

1. In a shallow 2-quart dish, combine soy sauce, broth, hot oil, five-spice powder, and garlic. Use your hands to flatten chicken to an even thickness of about ½ inch. Place chicken in marinade and turn to coat both sides. Let stand 30 minutes at room temperature or refrigerate up to 3 hours, turning occasionally.

2. Prepare a medium-hot barbecue fire or preheat broiler. Coat grill rack with a nonstick vegetable spray. Grill chicken, turning once or twice, until white throughout, 10 to 12 minutes.

312 EASY LOW-FAT GRILLED CHICKEN ITALIANO

Prep: 5 minutes   Stand: 30 minutes   Cook: 25 to 35 minutes
Serves: 4

3 pounds skinless bone-in
   chicken breasts, thighs,
   or drumsticks

1 (8-ounce) bottle low-fat or
   fat-free Italian-seasoned
   vinaigrette dressing

1. Place chicken in a shallow dish. Pour vinaigrette over chicken. Cover and let stand 30 minutes at room temperature or refrigerate up to 6 hours.

2. Prepare a medium-hot fire in a barbecue grill or preheat broiler. Lightly oil grill rack or coat with a nonstick cooking spray. Remove chicken from marinade but do not pat dry. Reserve marinade. Grill or broil, skinned side down, 10 minutes. Turn and grill 5 minutes. Brush chicken with some of marinade and continue to grill, turning occasionally and brushing again, until chicken juices run clear when pricked with tip of a knife, 10 to 20 minutes longer. (Breast meat will take less time than thighs or drumsticks.) Stop basting about 5 minutes before chicken is done.

313 LEMON-ORANGE CHICKEN EN PAPILLOTE WITH TARRAGON AND VEGETABLES

Prep: 20 minutes   Cook: 10 to 12 minutes   Serves: 4

1 pound thinly sliced chicken
   breast cutlets
1 teaspoon grated lemon zest
1 teaspoon grated orange zest
1 teaspoon dried tarragon
½ teaspoon salt
½ teaspoon freshly ground
   pepper
1 tablespoon fresh lemon
   juice

1 tablespoon fresh orange
   juice
2 teaspoons olive oil,
   preferably extra-virgin
¼ pound snow peas, trimmed
2 carrots, peeled and cut into
   2½- by ¼-inch julienne
   strips
½ cup thinly sliced scallions

1. Preheat oven to 425°F. Cut 4 pieces of parchment paper or aluminum foil to 12x15-inch rectangles. Fold in half from short end and cut out large half hearts along folds, like valentines. When unfolded, hearts should measure about 14 inches wide and 12 inches long.

2. Divide chicken among hearts, placing on one side of each. Season chicken with lemon zest, orange zest, tarragon, salt, and pepper. Drizzle on lemon juice, orange juice, and olive oil. Scatter snow peas, carrots, and scallions over chicken. Fold hearts over and crimp edges to seal completely.

3. Place on a baking sheet and bake until parchment is puffed and lightly browned and chicken is cooked through, 10 to 12 minutes. (Open one packet and check to be sure chicken is cooked through.) Serve at once.

314 MARGARITA CHICKEN

Prep: 10 minutes   Stand: 30 minutes   Cook: 11 to 12 minutes
Serves: 4

Sugary grilled lime slices make a great edible garnish for this chicken, whose flavors echo the popular tequila cocktail. Serve with warm tortillas and a spinach salad.

3 tablespoons lime juice
2 tablespoons tequila
1 tablespoon chili powder
½ teaspoon dried oregano
½ teaspoon ground cumin
1½ teaspoons canola oil
4 skinless, boneless chicken breast halves

¼ teaspoon salt
⅛ teaspoon freshly ground pepper
8 thin slices of lime
1 teaspoon sugar

1. In a shallow 2-quart dish, combine lime juice, tequila, chili powder, oregano, cumin, and oil. Use your hands to flatten chicken to an even thickness of about ½ inch. Sprinkle lightly with salt and pepper. Place chicken in marinade and turn to coat both sides. Let stand 30 minutes at room temperature or up to 2 hours in refrigerator.

2. Prepare a medium-hot barbecue fire or preheat broiler. Coat grill rack with a nonstick vegetable spray. Grill or broil chicken, turning once, until cooked through, about 10 minutes.

3. Spray lime slices with nonstick vegetable spray and sprinkle with sugar. Grill or broil, turning once, until flecked with brown, 1 or 2 minutes. Use to garnish chicken.

315 FRUITED CHICKEN KEBABS

Prep: 15 minutes   Stand: 40 to 45 minutes   Cook: 12 minutes
Serves: 4

12 dried apricots
¾ cup dry white wine
2 tablespoons white wine vinegar
2 teaspoons olive oil, preferably extra-virgin
¼ cup chopped parsley
1 tablespoon chopped fresh oregano or 1 teaspoon dried

½ teaspoon cayenne
½ teaspoon salt
2 garlic cloves, minced
1 pound skinless, boneless chicken thighs or breasts, cut into 1½-inch chunks
1 large bell pepper, cut into 1½-inch squares

1. In a small nonreactive saucepan, bring apricots and wine to a simmer. Remove from heat, cover, and let stand 10 to 15 minutes to plump apricots.

2. In a shallow 2-quart dish, combine vinegar, olive oil, parsley, oregano, cayenne, salt, and garlic. Drain any remaining wine from apricots into marinade. Add chicken and turn to coat completely. Let stand at room temperature 30 minutes or cover and refrigerate up to 2 hours.

3. Prepare a medium-hot barbecue fire or preheat broiler. Coat grill rack with a nonstick vegetable spray. Thread chicken, apricots, and bell pepper onto 4 metal skewers, beginning and ending with apricots. Brush apricots and bell pepper with some of marinade.

4. Grill, turning once or twice and brushing with more marinade, until chicken is white throughout and peppers are just tender, about 12 minutes. Stop basting about 3 minutes before chicken is done. Serve directly from skewers.

316   SZECHUAN ORANGE CHICKEN
Prep: 20 minutes   Stand: 1 hour   Cook: 12 minutes   Serves: 4

While the strips of orange peel included in this marinade are not meant to be eaten, they are grilled right along with the chicken to maximize the flavor of the dish and add an extra touch of color to the plate. If you use bamboo skewers, be sure to soak them in water for at least 30 minutes first.

1 **orange**	1 **large garlic clove, minced**
2 **tablespoons soy sauce**	¾ **pound skinless, boneless**
1 **tablespoon rice vinegar**	**chicken breasts or thighs,**
2 **teaspoons minced fresh**	**cut into 1½-inch chunks**
ginger	8 **scallions, trimmed to leave**
1 **teaspoon Asian hot sesame**	**2 inches of green**
oil	2 **cups hot cooked rice**
¼ **teaspoon crushed hot red**	
pepper	

1. Use a swivel-bladed vegetable peeler or small sharp knife to cut off orange peel in 1-inch strips, taking care to peel only colored part. Squeeze 2 tablespoons juice from orange. In a shallow 2-quart dish, combine strips of orange peel, orange juice, soy sauce, vinegar, ginger, sesame oil, hot pepper, and garlic. Add chicken and turn to coat completely. Refrigerate 30 minutes, turning once. Add scallions to marinade and refrigerate 30 minutes longer.

2. Prepare a medium-hot barbecue fire or preheat broiler. Coat grill rack with a nonstick vegetable spray. Thread chicken, strips of orange peel, and scallions onto metal or soaked bamboo skewers. Grill or broil, turning once or twice, until chicken is white throughout and scallions and peel are lightly browned, about 12 minutes.

3. Serve chicken, orange peel, and scallions over rice.

317 LIGHT-AND-EASY CHICKEN TETRAZZINI
Prep: 10 minutes   Cook: 15 to 17 minutes   Serves: 4

Grating fresh Parmesan cheese on top of this skillet tetrazzini and using a lightened white sauce base with fresh herbs gives this old favorite a modern twist. Rotini pasta gives it a new look.

¾ **pound rotini or other short spiral pasta**
¾ **cup sun-dried tomato halves (1½ ounces)**
1 **tablespoon butter**
½ **pound fresh mushrooms, sliced (about 2½ cups)**
1 **cup thinly sliced scallions**
3 **garlic cloves, crushed through a press**
3 **tablespoons flour**
1 **teaspoon Italian seasoning**
½ **teaspoon freshly ground pepper**

1½ **cups chicken broth, preferably reduced-sodium**
¾ **cup skim milk**
2 **cups cubed cooked skinless chicken breast (about ½ pound)**
½ **cup chopped fresh basil**
3 **tablespoons dry sherry**
2 **tablespoons grated Parmesan cheese, preferably imported**

1. In a large pot of boiling salted water, cook pasta until tender but still firm, about 12 minutes; drain in a colander. Meanwhile, in a small heatproof bowl, cover dried tomatoes with boiling water. Let stand 10 minutes, until softened; drain. Thinly slice tomatoes.

2. In a large nonstick frying pan, melt butter over medium-low heat. Add mushrooms, scallions, and garlic, cover, and cook, stirring often, until mushrooms are softened, about 5 minutes. Add flour and cook, stirring, for 2 minutes. Add Italian seasoning and pepper, then whisk in broth and milk. Bring to a boil over medium heat, stirring, until sauce is thickened, 3 to 5 minutes.

3. Stir in chicken, basil, sherry, and sun-dried tomatoes. Simmer over medium-low heat, stirring often, 5 minutes. Toss sauce with pasta and cheese and serve.

318 CHICKEN AND THREE-BEAN CHILI
Prep: 15 minutes   Cook: 1 hour 7 minutes   Serves: 8 to 10

Here's a great big casserole to serve a crowd. Take it to your next potluck supper or block party or ladle it up in front of the VCR. Pass baked tortilla chips and an assortment of chili garnishes, if you like: chopped tomato, scallions, pickled jalapeños, and nonfat sour cream, for example.

2 large onions, chopped
1 large green bell pepper, chopped
1 tablespoon olive oil
1 cup chicken broth, preferably reduced-sodium
4 large garlic cloves, crushed through a press
1½ pounds skinless, boneless chicken thighs, cut into ¾-inch chunks
¼ cup chopped smoked ham
2 tablespoons chili powder
1½ teaspoons ground cumin
1 teaspoon dried oregano

½ teaspoon cayenne
½ teaspoon freshly ground pepper
2 (14½-ounce) cans stewed tomatoes, preferably Southwestern-style
1 (15-ounce) can black beans, drained
1 (15-ounce) can red kidney beans, drained
1 (15-ounce) can white or cannellini beans, drained
½ cup chopped cilantro or parsley
Salt

1. Preheat oven to 350°F. In a large Dutch oven, cook onion and bell pepper in olive oil and 2 tablespoons of broth, covered, over medium-low heat, stirring often, until onion is softened, about 5 minutes. Add garlic and cook, uncovered, 1 minute. Add chicken, ham, chili powder, cumin, oregano, and cayenne. Cook, stirring, 1 minute. Add remaining broth, stewed tomatoes, all 3 types of beans, and half of cilantro.

2. Cover chili and bake 50 minutes. Uncover and bake until slightly thickened, about 10 minutes.

3. Stir in remaining cilantro. Season with salt to taste before serving.

319 CHICKEN AND VEGETABLE TAGINE
Prep: 20 minutes   Chill: 3 hours   Cook: 40 to 45 minutes   Serves: 6

A tagine is a Moroccan stew that often begins by marinating some of the main ingredients in part of the aromatics used to flavor the recipe. Here, chicken on the bone is used because it adds even more character to the finished dish.

4 bone-in chicken breast halves, skinned
1 teaspoon ground cumin
½ teaspoon ground ginger
¼ teaspoon cayenne
¼ teaspoon ground cinnamon
1 teaspoon salt
1 large onion, coarsely chopped
4 garlic cloves, minced
½ cup orange juice
3 tablespoons lemon juice
1 teaspoon grated orange zest
¾ cup chopped parsley
½ cup chopped cilantro
2 cups chicken broth, preferably reduced-sodium
1 (14½-ounce) can stewed tomatoes
¼ cup chopped dates
1 small eggplant, peeled and cut into 1-inch cubes
1 medium zucchini, sliced ½ inch thick
½ teaspoon freshly ground pepper
3 cups cooked couscous

1. Season chicken with cumin, ginger, cayenne, cinnamon, and ½ teaspoon salt, rubbing spices into meat. Place chicken in a medium bowl. Add onion, garlic, orange juice, lemon juice, orange zest, and half each of parsley and cilantro. Cover and refrigerate 3 hours.

2. Transfer chicken with all of its marinade to a large flameproof casserole. Add broth and stewed tomatoes and bring to a boil. Reduce heat to medium-low, cover, and simmer 20 minutes.

3. Stir dates and eggplant into casserole and simmer 10 minutes. Add zucchini and simmer until tender, 10 to 15 minutes.

4. Stir in remaining parsley and cilantro. Season with remaining salt and pepper to taste. Serve ladled over couscous.

320 KASHA AND CHICKEN PILAF

Prep: 15 minutes   Cook: 20 to 21 minutes   Serves: 6 to 8

Kasha is roasted buckwheat, and it can be found in the rice section of large supermarkets and in health food stores. To bring out its nutty goodness, I toss it in the hot pan before adding the liquid.

1 medium onion, chopped
½ pound mushrooms, sliced
1 medium carrot, peeled and thinly sliced
1 celery rib, thinly sliced
1 tablespoon olive oil, preferably extra-virgin
3 cups chicken broth, preferably reduced-sodium
1 pound skinless, boneless chicken breast thighs or breasts, cut into 1-inch chunks

2 garlic cloves, crushed through a press
1 cup thawed frozen green peas
1½ cups kasha
¾ teaspoon ground coriander
½ teaspoon freshly ground pepper
Salt

1. In a large nonstick frying pan, combine onion, mushrooms, carrot, and celery in olive oil and ¼ cup of broth. Cover and cook over medium-low heat until vegetables are just softened, about 4 minutes. Add chicken and garlic and cook, covered, 3 minutes. Stir in peas and remove from heat.

2. Heat a large frying pan with a lid until a drop of water sizzles. Add kasha and cook over high heat, stirring constantly, until fragrant, 1 to 2 minutes. Stir in remaining chicken broth, coriander, pepper, cooked vegetables, and chicken.

3. Cover pan, reduce heat to medium-low, and simmer until kasha is tender and liquid is absorbed, about 12 minutes. Season with salt to taste and serve.

321 ROASTED ELEPHANT GARLIC AND CHICKEN PASTA

Prep: 10 minutes   Cook: 20 minutes   Serves: 4

Elephant garlic, which has enormous cloves, has a mild flavor and, when roasted, it takes on a pungent sweetness. Regular garlic will also work perfectly well: use 6 large cloves in place of the 4 elephant garlic cloves.

4 **elephant garlic cloves (about 1½ ounces), peeled**
4 **large shallots, peeled**
1 **tablespoon olive oil, preferably extra-virgin**
¾ **cup chicken broth, preferably reduced-sodium**
¾ **cup dry white wine**
1½ **teaspoons dried marjoram**

¾ **pound skinless, boneless chicken breasts, cut into 1-inch chunks**
¾ **pound penne**
½ **cup chopped flat-leaf parsley**
2 **tablespoons grated Romano cheese**
Salt and freshly ground pepper

1. Preheat oven to 450°F. Lay garlic and shallots on a piece of aluminum foil and drizzle with olive oil. Wrap to enclose completely. Roast until garlic is softened, about 20 minutes. Remove garlic and shallots from foil and finely chop or mash them both.

2. Meanwhile, in a nonreactive medium saucepan, bring broth, wine, and marjoram to a boil. Boil 3 minutes. Add chicken, reduce heat to medium-low, and simmer, uncovered, until chicken is white throughout, 8 to 10 minutes. Stir in roasted garlic and shallots.

3. In a large pot of boiling salted water, cook penne until tender but still firm, 10 to 12 minutes; drain. In a large serving bowl, toss hot pasta with chicken and sauce, parsley, cheese, and salt and pepper to taste.

Chapter 14

Wok Wonders

Since none of these recipes takes longer than 10 minutes to cook, this chapter could be subtitled "Instant Suppers." That is the nature of stir-frying, where a small amount of oil is heated in a wok or heavy frying pan over high heat and the food is cooked with constant stirring.

Most stir-fry ingredients are cut into small pieces and a sauce is usually added to finish the dish. Because the cooking time is so fast, it is important that all of the ingredients and the sauce be prepared ahead of time and set out within reach before the quick cooking begins.

All but one of these recipes call for skinless and boneless chicken parts; in most cases, breasts and thighs are interchangeable. Where an option is given, I've put my preference first. All of the recipes can be cooked either in a wok or a heavy frying pan about 12 inches in diameter, though in truth, the tossing around appropriate for high temperature stir-frying is much more easily—and neatly—accomplished in a wok.

In either case, to keep the chicken from sticking to the pan, be sure the oil is hot and almost smoking before beginning to cook.

Most of these dishes are best spooned over rice. Choose your favorite variety.

322 INDONESIAN CHICKEN AND CARROT STIR-FRY

Prep: 15 minutes   Cook: 6 minutes   Serves: 4

½ cup chicken broth
3 tablespoons smooth peanut butter
2 tablespoons soy sauce
2 tablespoons lime juice
1 or 2 jalapeño peppers, minced
2 tablespoons vegetable oil
¾ pound skinless, boneless chicken thighs or breasts, cut into thin strips

2 large garlic cloves, minced
2 medium carrots, thinly sliced on a diagonal
4 ounces snow peas (about 1 cup), trimmed and halved if large
¼ cup shredded fresh basil
¼ cup chopped roasted peanuts

1. In a small bowl, blend together broth, peanut butter, soy sauce, lime juice, and jalapeño pepper. Set sauce aside.

2. In a wok or large frying pan, heat oil over high heat. Add chicken and stir-fry 2 minutes. Add garlic and carrots and stir-fry 1 minute. Add snow peas and stir-fry 1 minute longer.

3. Add peanut butter sauce to wok, reduce heat to medium-low, and cook 2 minutes. Stir in basil. Serve at once, garnished with chopped peanuts.

323 CHICKEN, VEGETABLE, AND SHIITAKE MUSHROOM STIR-FRY IN OYSTER SAUCE

Prep: 10 minutes   Cook: 8 to 9 minutes   Serves: 6

1 cup chicken broth
⅓ cup Chinese oyster sauce
3 tablespoons dry sherry
1 tablespoon rice vinegar or white wine vinegar
1 tablespoon Asian sesame oil
1 tablespoon cornstarch
¼ cup vegetable oil
1 pound skinless, boneless chicken breasts or thighs, cut into thin strips

3 garlic cloves, minced
1 tablespoon minced fresh ginger
4 cups (about 8 ounces) mixed fresh vegetables, such as broccoli florets, sliced bell pepper, zucchini, carrot, and/or celery
½ pound shiitake mushrooms, stemmed, caps sliced

1. In a small bowl, stir together broth, oyster sauce, sherry, vinegar, sesame oil, and cornstarch. Set sauce aside.

2. In a wok or large frying pan, heat 2 tablespoons oil over high heat. Add chicken and stir-fry 3 minutes. Use a slotted spoon to remove from pan.

3. Add remaining 2 tablespoons oil, garlic, ginger, vegetables, and mushrooms to wok. Stir-fry 3 minutes. Return chicken to pan. Stir sauce briefly to blend cornstarch and add to wok. Cook, stirring, until vegetables are crisp-tender and sauce thickens, 2 to 3 minutes. Serve at once.

---

324 SWEET-AND-SOUR CHICKEN
Prep: 10 minutes   Cook: 9 to 10 minutes   Serves: 6

Bottled sweet-and-sour sauce makes this Chinese restaurant favorite a breeze to make at home.

⅓ cup cornstarch
½ teaspoon salt
½ teaspoon freshly ground
    pepper
2 egg whites, beaten until
    frothy
1 pound skinless, boneless
    chicken thighs or breasts,
    cut into 1-inch chunks
5 tablespoons vegetable oil
1 large onion, cut into
    12 wedges
1 large green bell pepper, cut
    into 1-inch squares

1 (5-ounce) can sliced water
    chestnuts, drained
1 medium tomato, seeded and
    cut into 1-inch chunks
1 (8-ounce) can pineapple
    chunks in juice, juice
    reserved
1 cup bottled sweet-and-sour
    sauce
1 tablespoon rice vinegar or
    cider vinegar

1. Combine cornstarch, salt, and pepper in a plastic bag. A few pieces at a time, dip chicken in beaten egg whites, then shake in cornstarch-filled bag to coat.

2. In a wok or large frying pan, heat ¼ cup of oil and stir-fry chicken over medium-high heat until golden brown and crisp, 4 to 5 minutes. Use a slotted spoon to remove chicken from pan.

3. Add remaining 1 tablespoon oil to wok and stir-fry onion and bell pepper over high heat 2 minutes. Add water chestnuts, tomato, pineapple chunks and juice, sweet-and-sour sauce, and vinegar. Cook 2 minutes. Return chicken to pan and cook 1 minute, until heated through.

325 DOUBLE GINGER CHICKEN AND SCALLION STIR-FRY

Prep: 10 minutes   Cook: 5 to 6 minutes   Serves: 4

There is a double hit of ginger here, giving both hot and sweet character to the dish.

1 cup chicken broth
1 tablespoon soy sauce
2 teaspoons cornstarch
2 teaspoons Chinese hot chili oil
3 tablespoons vegetable oil
1 pound skinless, boneless chicken breasts or thighs, cut into thin strips
2 garlic cloves

3 tablespoons minced fresh ginger
1 bunch scallions, thinly sliced lengthwise, then cut into 2-inch lengths
2 tablespoons chopped crystallized ginger
2 tablespoons chopped cilantro (optional)

1. In a small bowl, combine broth, soy sauce, cornstarch, and chili oil. Stir to dissolve cornstarch. Set sauce aside.

2. In a wok or large frying pan, heat vegetable oil over high heat. Add chicken and stir-fry until chicken is just white, 2 to 3 minutes. Add garlic, ginger, and scallions. Stir-fry 1 minute.

3. Stir sauce briefly to blend cornstarch. Add to wok and cook, stirring, until sauce thickens, about 2 minutes. Serve at once, garnished with crystallized ginger and cilantro, if desired.

326 ORANGE CHICKEN

*Prep: 15 minutes   Stand: 30 minutes   Cook: 5 to 6 minutes
Serves: 4*

2 garlic cloves, minced
3 tablespoons soy sauce
1 tablespoon grated orange zest
2 teaspoons dark Asian sesame oil
¼ teaspoon crushed hot red pepper
¾ pound skinless, boneless chicken breasts or thighs, cut into thin strips

2 teaspoons cornstarch
½ cup orange juice
2 tablespoons peanut or other vegetable oil
1 tablespoon minced fresh ginger
6 ounces sugar snap peas, trimmed (about 2 cups)
1 red bell pepper, cut into thin strips
½ cup sliced scallions

1. In a small bowl, combine garlic, soy sauce, orange zest, sesame oil, and hot pepper. Place chicken in a shallow dish and coat with half of garlic-soy mixture. Cover and refrigerate 30 minutes to 1 hour. Stir cornstarch and orange juice into remaining garlic mixture. Reserve for sauce.

2. In a wok or large frying pan, heat oil over high heat. Add chicken and stir-fry 2 minutes. Add ginger, peas, and bell pepper. Stir-fry until pepper is crisp-tender and chicken is white throughout, 2 to 3 minutes. Add scallions and reserved sauce and cook, stirring, 1 minute. Serve at once.

327 THAI HOT CHICKEN NOODLE SALAD

Prep: 15 minutes   Stand: 10 to 15 minutes
Cook: 7 minutes   Serves: 4

Nam pla is Thai fish sauce, a common seasoning ingredient and condiment in the Thai kitchen. It is available at Asian markets and in many large supermarkets.

½ **pound Asian rice noodles or capellini**
¼ **cup nam pla (Thai fish sauce)**
3 **tablespoons lime juice**
2 **tablespoons sugar**
1 **tablespoon soy sauce**
1 **teaspoon grated lime zest**
3 **tablespoons peanut or other vegetable oil**
2 **garlic cloves, minced**
1 **jalapeño pepper, minced**

½ **pound chicken breast fillets, thinly sliced**
½ **pound shiitake mushrooms, stemmed, caps thinly sliced**
⅓ **cup thinly sliced scallions**
½ **pound kale, shredded**
8 **cups shredded romaine lettuce**
⅓ **cup chopped cilantro**
¼ **cup chopped roasted peanuts**

1. If using Asian rice noodles, place in a bowl and cover with boiling water. Let stand 10 to 15 minutes to soften. If using capellini, cook and drain according to package directions.

2. In a small bowl, combine nam pla, lime juice, sugar, soy sauce, and lime zest. Set sauce aside.

3. In a wok or large frying pan, heat oil over high heat. Add garlic, jalapeño, and chicken and stir-fry 1 minute. With a slotted spoon, remove from wok. Add mushrooms and scallions to wok and stir-fry 2 minutes. Add kale and stir-fry until wilted, about 2 minutes. Return chicken to pan. Add sauce and cook 2 minutes.

4. Toss chicken and sauce with noodles. Serve on a bed of lettuce, with cilantro and peanuts sprinkled on top.

328 LEMON CHICKEN AND ASPARAGUS STIR-FRY

Prep: 10 minutes   Cook: 5 minutes   Serves: 4

1 **pound skinless, boneless chicken breasts, cut into thin strips**	¾ **pound slender asparagus spears, cut diagonally into 1½-inch pieces**
¼ **teaspoon salt**	1 **cup reduced-sodium chicken broth**
⅛ **teaspoon freshly ground pepper**	1½ **tablespoons lemon juice**
1 **tablespoon ground coriander**	½ **cup thinly sliced scallions**
3 **tablespoons vegetable oil**	2 **teaspoons grated lemon zest**

1. Season chicken with salt, pepper, and coriander.

2. In a wok or large frying pan, heat oil over high heat. Add chicken and stir-fry 2 minutes. Add asparagus and stir-fry 1 minute. Add broth and cook 2 minutes, or until chicken is white throughout and asparagus is crisp-tender. Stir in lemon juice, ¼ cup of scallions, and 1 teaspoon of lemon zest. Serve at once, garnished with remaining scallions and lemon zest.

329 CURRIED CHICKEN AND APPLE STIR-FRY

Prep: 10 minutes   Cook: 6 minutes   Serves: 4 to 6

Use whatever tart red apples are available in your area. I like to serve this quick curry over wild rice or a mix of long-grain white and wild rice.

½ **cup apple cider**	¼ **cup vegetable oil**
2 **tablespoons soy sauce**	1 **pound skinless, boneless chicken breasts or thighs, cut into thin strips**
1½ **tablespoons Calvados or brandy**	
2 **tablespoons cider vinegar**	1 **large celery rib, thinly sliced**
2 **teaspoons cornstarch**	1 **large tart red apple, cored and thinly sliced**
½ **teaspoon ground coriander**	
¼ **teaspoon cayenne**	½ **cup coarsely chopped walnuts**
2 **teaspoons curry powder**	

1. In a small bowl, stir together cider, soy sauce, Calvados, vinegar, cornstarch, coriander, cayenne, and 1 teaspoon of curry powder. Set sauce aside.

2. Season chicken with remaining 1 teaspoon curry powder. In a wok or large frying pan, heat 2 tablespoons of oil over high heat. Add chicken and stir-fry 2 minutes. With a slotted spoon, remove chicken from pan.

3. Add remaining 2 tablespoons of oil to wok. Add celery and apple and stir-fry 2 minutes. Return chicken to pan. Stir sauce briefly to blend cornstarch, add, and cook, stirring, until thickened, about 2 minutes. Stir in walnuts and serve.

330   TANGERINE ALMOND CHICKEN
Prep: 15 minutes   Cook: 5½ minutes   Serves: 4

1 cup chicken broth
½ cup tangerine juice
2 tablespoons soy sauce
1 tablespoon rice wine
   vinegar
1 tablespoon cornstarch
1 pound skinless, boneless
   chicken breasts or thighs,
   cut into thin strips
1 teaspoon ground cumin

¼ teaspoon cayenne
3 tablespoons vegetable oil
⅓ cup slivered almonds
1 tablespoon grated tangerine
   zest
1 large garlic clove
2 small tangerines, sectioned
   and seeded
½ cup thinly sliced scallions

1. In a small bowl, combine broth, juice, soy sauce, vinegar, and corn-starch. Stir to dissolve cornstarch. Set sauce aside.

2. Season chicken with cumin and cayenne. In a wok or large frying pan, heat oil over high heat. Add chicken and stir-fry 2 minutes. Add almonds and stir-fry 1 minute. Add tangerine zest and garlic and stir-fry 30 seconds. Stir broth mixture briefly to blend cornstarch. Add, along with tangerines and scallions. Cook, stirring, until sauce thickens, about 2 minutes. Serve at once.

331   GARLIC CHICKEN WITH ZUCCHINI AND CHOW MEIN NOODLES
Prep: 10 minutes   Cook: 5 minutes   Serves: 4

½ cup chicken broth
2 tablespoons soy sauce
1 tablespoon dry sherry
2 tablespoons Chinese oyster
   sauce
1 teaspoon cornstarch
2 tablespoons vegetable oil
¾ pound skinless, boneless
   chicken thighs, cut into
   1-inch chunks

1 cup thinly sliced scallions
1 medium zucchini, halved
   lengthwise and thinly
   sliced
6 garlic cloves, finely chopped
1 jalapeño pepper, minced
2 cups chow mein noodles

1. In a small bowl, stir together broth, soy sauce, sherry, oyster sauce, and cornstarch. Set sauce aside.

2. In a wok or large frying pan, heat oil over medium-high heat. Add chicken and stir-fry 2 minutes. Add zucchini, garlic, jalapeño, and ½ cup of scallions. Stir-fry 1 minute. Stir sauce to blend cornstarch, add, and cook, stirring, until thickened, about 2 minutes.

3. Serve spooned over chow mein noodles. Sprinkle remaining scallions on top.

332   PACIFIC RIM PINEAPPLE CHICKEN
Prep: 15 minutes   Stand: 1 hour   Cook: 8½ minutes   Serves: 4

½ cup apricot nectar or
    pineapple juice
2 tablespoons rice wine
    vinegar
1 tablespoon brown sugar
1 tablespoon soy sauce
1 tablespoon grated fresh
    ginger
¼ cup plus 2 tablespoons
    chopped fresh mint
1 pound skinless, boneless
    chicken breasts or thighs,
    cut into strips

2 teaspoons cornstarch
3 tablespoons vegetable oil
4 ounces sugar snap peas
    (about 1½ cups), trimmed
1 red bell pepper, cut into thin
    strips
1 garlic clove, minced
2 tablespoons canned
    chopped green chiles
1 papaya, peeled, seeded, and
    cut into 1-inch chunks

1. In a shallow dish, combine apricot nectar, vinegar, brown sugar, soy sauce, ginger, and ¼ cup mint. Add chicken and stir to coat completely. Cover and refrigerate 1 hour, stirring once or twice. Remove chicken from marinade. Stir cornstarch into marinade and set it aside.

2. In a wok or large frying pan, heat oil over high heat. Add chicken and stir-fry 2 minutes. Add sugar snap peas and bell pepper and stir-fry 1 minute. Add garlic and stir-fry 30 seconds. Stir marinade to blend cornstarch. Add with chiles and papaya. Simmer 5 minutes, stirring often. Serve garnished with remaining 2 tablespoons chopped mint.

333   SESAME CHICKEN AND SNOW PEA STIR-FRY
Prep: 15 minutes   Cook: 8½ minutes   Serves: 4

1 cup chicken broth
1½ tablespoons soy sauce
1 tablespoon hoisin sauce
2 teaspoons cornstarch
2 teaspoons Asian sesame oil
1 pound skinless, boneless
    chicken breast fillets,
    thinly sliced crosswise
3 tablespoons sesame seeds
3 tablespoons vegetable oil

1 yellow bell pepper, cut into
    thin strips
6 ounces snow peas (about
    1½ cups), trimmed and
    halved if large
1 garlic clove, minced
½ teaspoon crushed hot red
    pepper
⅓ cup chopped red onion

1. In a small bowl, combine broth, soy sauce, hoisin sauce, cornstarch, and sesame oil. Stir to mix well. Set sauce aside.

2. Sprinkle chicken with sesame seeds to coat lightly, patting them in with your hands to help them stick. Cut chicken crosswise into ½-inch strips.

3. In a wok or large frying pan, heat oil over high heat. Add chicken and stir-fry 2 minutes. Use a slotted spoon to remove from wok.

4. Add bell pepper to wok and stir-fry 1 minute. Add snow peas and stir-fry 1 minute. Add garlic and hot pepper and stir-fry 30 seconds. Stir sauce briefly to blend cornstarch, add, and cook, stirring, until thickened, about 2 minutes. Return chicken to pan and cook until white, about 2 minutes longer. Serve at once, garnished with red onion.

---

334 SHREDDED CHICKEN AND VEGETABLE STIR-FRY

Prep: 15 minutes   Cook: 7 minutes   Serves: 4 to 6

Other vegetables, such as broccoli, snow peas, asparagus, and zucchini, can replace equal amounts of the vegetables listed in this basic stir-fry recipe. Serve over steamed white rice.

¾ **cup thinly sliced chicken breast cutlets**
1 **cup chicken broth**
2 **tablespoons soy sauce**
1 **tablespoon rice vinegar or white wine vinegar**
1 **tablespoon dry sherry**
2 **teaspoons cornstarch**
3 **tablespoons peanut or vegetable oil**
1 **tablespoon minced fresh ginger**
2 **garlic cloves, minced**

¼ **to ½ teaspoon crushed hot red pepper**
1 **medium yellow summer squash (about 6 ounces), cut into matchstick pieces**
1 **red bell pepper, cut into very thin strips**
¼ **pound green beans, thinly sliced lengthwise**
½ **cup canned baby corn**
2 **cups sliced bok choy (about 4 ounces)**
½ **cup thinly sliced scallions**

1. Thinly slice chicken crosswise across grain. In a small bowl, combine broth, soy sauce, vinegar, sherry, and cornstarch.

2. In a wok or large frying pan, heat oil. Add chicken and stir-fry 3 minutes over medium-high heat. Use a slotted spoon to remove from pan. Add ginger, garlic, hot pepper, squash, bell pepper, and green beans and stir-fry 1 minute. Add corn and bok choy and stir-fry 1 minute. Return chicken to wok. Stir sauce briefly to blend cornstarch and add to wok. Cook, stirring, until sauce thickens, about 2 minutes. Transfer chicken and vegetables with sauce to a serving dish. Sprinkle scallions on top.

335 STIR-FRIED CHICKEN LIVERS AND PEARL ONIONS

Prep: 15 minutes   Cook: 10 to 12 minutes   Serves: 4

A recipe from Chinese cooking expert Ken Hom inspired me to try stir-frying chicken livers. The nutty flavor of quinoa would be nice with this dish, as would brown rice.

- 2 cups fresh or frozen pearl onions (about 8 ounces)
- ½ cup chicken broth
- ¼ cup Madeira or dry sherry
- 2 tablespoons teriyaki sauce
- 2 teaspoons cornstarch
- 1 teaspoon Chinese five-spice powder

- 1 pound chicken livers, cut into ¾- to 1-inch pieces
- ¼ teaspoon salt
- ⅛ teaspoon freshly ground pepper
- 3 tablespoons vegetable oil
- 2 tablespoons chopped parsley

1. In a medium saucepan of boiling salted water, cook onions until half-done, about 5 minutes. Drain and pat dry on paper towels.

2. In a small bowl, stir together broth, Madeira, teriyaki sauce, cornstarch, and ½ teaspoon of five-spice powder. Set sauce aside. Season chicken livers with salt, pepper, and remaining ½ teaspoon five-spice powder.

3. In a wok or large frying pan, heat oil over high heat. Add chicken livers and stir-fry 1 minute. Add onions and stir-fry until livers are browned and onions are golden, 2 to 3 minutes.

4. Stir sauce to blend cornstarch, add to wok, and simmer until thickened, 2 to 3 minutes. Serve at once, garnished with parsley.

---

336 CHICKEN AND BROCCOLI STIR-FRY ITALIANO

Prep: 15 minutes   Cook: 11 to 13 minutes   Serves: 4

Pasta may have its origins in the Orient, but we know it best from Italy. This recipe blends the two.

- ¾ pound orecchiette (little ears) or butterflies
- 3 tablespoons peanut or other vegetable oil
- ½ pound skinless, boneless chicken thighs, cut into ¾-inch cubes
- 4 cups broccoli florets
- 1 red bell pepper, cut into strips

- 2 garlic cloves, minced
- 1 teaspoon dried Italian herb seasoning
- ½ teaspoon crushed hot red pepper
- 1¼ cups chicken broth
- ¼ cup rice wine or dry marsala
- ⅓ cup grated Parmesan cheese
- ½ cup toasted pine nuts

1. In a large pot of boiling salted water, cook pasta until tender but still firm, 11 to 13 minutes. Drain in a colander.

2. Meanwhile, in a wok or large frying pan, heat oil over high heat. Add chicken and stir-fry 2 minutes. Add broccoli and bell pepper and stir-fry 2 minutes. Add garlic, Italian seasoning, and hot pepper and stir-fry 15 seconds. Add broth and wine. Cover and cook 2 minutes. Uncover and cook 2 minutes.

3. Add drained pasta to wok and toss to coat with sauce. Add cheese and toss again. Sprinkle with pine nuts and serve.

---

337 PEANUT CHICKEN NOODLE STIR-FRY
Prep: 15 minutes   Cook: 5 to 6 minutes   Serves: 4 to 6

The richness of the peanut butter is nicely balanced with the lime juice.

3 **garlic cloves**	3 **tablespoons vegetable oil**
⅔ **cup chunky peanut butter**	1 **pound skinless, boneless**
⅓ **cup lime juice**	**chicken thighs, cut into**
3 **tablespoons soy sauce**	**thin strips**
½ **teaspoon crushed hot red**	1 **red bell pepper, cut into thin**
pepper	**strips**
1 **cup chicken broth**	⅔ **cup chopped scallions**
¾ **pound vermicelli**	¼ **cup chopped cilantro**
6 **ounces snow peas (about**	
2 cups), trimmed and	
halved if large	

1. With machine on, toss garlic into feed tube of a food processor. Add peanut butter, lime juice, soy sauce, and hot pepper and process until blended. Pour broth through feed tube slowly and process until smooth. Set sauce aside.

2. In a large pot of boiling salted water, cook vermicelli until just tender, 5 to 6 minutes, adding snow peas to water during last 30 seconds of cooking. Drain pasta and snow peas into a colander.

3. While pasta is cooking, heat oil in a wok or large frying pan over high heat. Add chicken and stir-fry 2 minutes. Add bell pepper and stir-fry until chicken is white throughout and pepper is crisp-tender, 2 to 3 minutes longer. Remove wok from heat.

4. Add noodles, snow peas, and peanut sauce to wok. Toss gently to combine. Serve noodles with scallions and cilantro sprinkled on top.

Chapter 15

All Ground Up

Ground chicken, like ground turkey, is a wonderful hamburger alternative. Because it is softer than ground beef, I've found that adding some bread crumbs gives ground chicken the body it needs to make good burgers and meat loaves. In chili or pasta sauces, it can usually be substituted measure for measure for ground beef, pork, or veal.

These days, ground chicken is widely available in the supermarket and is often a mix of white and dark meat—the latter a plus for extra flavor. Depending upon the blend, some chicken skin may also be added to give a little fat to the mix. If you wish to make really lean ground chicken, grind your own from skinless, boneless chicken breasts. Cut the breasts into chunks, then pulse in a food processor just until ground. Be careful, though, or the chicken will be pureed to a paste in no time. This is desirable for recipes such as the chicken and vegetable terrine, but will lack good texture for burgers.

Use these recipes as your guide, but experiment with substituting ground chicken for beef in your own favorite recipes as well.

---

338 CHICKEN-STUFFED PEPPERS
Prep: 10 minutes   Cook: 45 minutes   Serves: 4

This is a modern adaptation of one of my favorite childhood suppers. Serve over egg noodles.

4 small green bell peppers	**1 teaspoon dried oregano**
1 pound ground chicken	**½ teaspoon dried marjoram**
¾ cup fresh bread crumbs	**½ teaspoon salt**
1 small onion, chopped	**¼ teaspoon freshly ground**
1 large garlic clove, minced	**pepper**
1 egg	**4 cups marinara sauce**

1. Cut tops off peppers and remove seeds and ribs. In a mixing bowl, use your hands to gently but throroughly combine ground chicken, bread crumbs, onion, garlic, egg, oregano, marjoram, salt, and pepper. Divide stuffing in 4 parts and fill pepper cavities, mounding and rounding tops.

2. In a nonreactive saucepan just large enough to hold peppers, bring marinara sauce to a simmer. Add peppers, cover pot, and simmer over medium-low heat until peppers are tender and filling is white throughout, about 45 minutes.

339   DILLED CHICKEN BURGERS

Prep: 10 minutes   Cook: 12 to 15 minutes   Serves: 4

Served open face, these are rather like a Scandinivian sandwich.

¼ cup sour cream
2 tablespoons mayonnaise
2 tablespoons Dijon mustard
1 pound ground chicken
1 egg, lightly beaten
1 cup fresh whole wheat
  bread crumbs
½ cup chopped scallions

¼ cup chopped fresh dill or
  2 teaspoons dried
½ teaspoon salt
¼ teaspoon freshly ground
  pepper
4 thick slices of whole wheat
  bread
4 leaves of red leaf lettuce

1. Prepare a medium-hot fire in a grill. Lightly oil grill rack or coat with non-stick vegetable spray.

2. In a small bowl, stir together sour cream, mayonnaise, and 1 tablespoon of mustard. Cover mustard sauce and refrigerate. In a mixing bowl, combine chicken, egg, bread crumbs, scallions, dill, salt, pepper, and remaining 1 tablespoon mustard. Mix with your hands to blend well. Form into 4 patties, each about 3 inches in diameter.

3. Grill chicken patties, turning once, until white throughout but still juicy, about 12 to 15 minutes. About 2 minutes before chicken is done, grill bread, turning once until lightly toasted.

4. To serve, spread mustard sauce on toast. Add lettuce and then burgers.

340   TUSCAN CHICKEN PATTIES

Prep: 10 minutes   Cook: 12 to 15 minutes   Serves: 6

Grilled Italian bread with tomato and basil is the classic bruschetta. Add a grilled chicken patty and it turns into a whole meal.

3 tablespoons olive oil,
  preferably extra-virgin
1 tablespoon balsamic
  vinegar
1 large garlic clove, minced
¼ teaspoon crushed hot red
  pepper
1½ pounds ground chicken
½ cup seasoned dry bread
  crumbs

¾ teaspoon salt
½ teaspoon freshly ground
  pepper
6 slices of mozzarella cheese
6 slices of Italian bread, cut
  ¾ inch thick
6 thin slices of sweet onion
6 slices of tomato
12 fresh basil leaves

1. Prepare a medium-hot fire in a barbecue grill. In a small bowl, combine olive oil, vinegar, garlic, and hot pepper. In a large mixing bowl, combine chicken, bread crumbs, salt, and pepper. Mix with your hands to blend well. Form into 6 patties, each about 4 inches in diameter.

2. Grill patties, turning once, until white throughout but still juicy, about 12 to 15 minutes. About 2 minutes before patties are done, top with cheese slices to melt. Grill bread until lightly toasted on both sides, about 1 minute. Liberally brush one side of grilled bread with flavored oil.

3. Place onion and tomato slices on brushed sides of toasts. Drizzle with any remaining oil. Add patties, then basil leaves, and serve.

341   CHICKEN SALISBURY STEAK
Prep: 10 minutes   Cook: 18 to 22 minutes   Serves: 4

The original version is named for Dr. J. H. Salisbury, who in the late nineteenth century recommended eating beef three times per day. We like his recipe but prefer chicken these days.

1 **pound ground chicken**	1 **egg white**
¾ **cup fresh bread crumbs**	3 **tablespoons flour**
¼ **cup chopped parsley**	1 **tablespoon butter**
¼ **cup minced onion**	1 **tablespoon vegetable oil**
1 **teaspoon dried thyme**	6 **ounces fresh mushrooms,**
½ **teaspoon salt**	**sliced**
½ **teaspoon freshly ground**	½ **cup dry white wine**
pepper	¾ **cup chicken broth**
2 **teaspoons Worcestershire**	
sauce	

1. In a large mixing bowl, use your hands to lightly but throroughly combine chicken, bread crumbs, parsley, onion, thyme, salt, pepper, Worcestershire, and egg white. Form into 4 patties, each about ½ inch thick. Spoon about 2 tablespoons of flour onto a small plate. Dredge patties in flour to coat lightly.

2. Heat butter and oil in a large frying pan over medium heat. Add patties and cook, turning once with a spatula, until browned outside and white throughout, 10 to 13 minutes. Remove patties to a platter.

3. Add mushrooms to drippings in pan and cook over medium-high heat, stirring often, until softened, about 5 minutes. Stir in remaining flour and cook, stirring, 1 minute. Pour in wine and broth and bring to a boil, stirring, until thickened, 2 to 3 minutes. Season with additional salt and pepper to taste. Spoon sauce and mushrooms over chicken patties and serve at once.

342   CAJUN CHICKEN BURGERS
Prep: 10 minutes   Cook: 10 to 13 minutes   Serves: 6

Any extra seasoning mix you make here will keep on the shelf for a couple of months if you store it in a tightly covered jar.

1 **tablespoon paprika**	¾ **cup fresh bread crumbs**
1 **tablespoon chili powder**	1 **egg white**
1 **teaspoon onion powder**	2 **tablespoons vegetable oil or**
1 **teaspoon garlic powder**	**melted butter**
1 **teaspoon salt**	¼ **cup mayonnaise**
¾ **teaspoon black pepper**	1 **tablespoon Dijon mustard**
½ **teaspoon cayenne**	6 **sourdough sandwich rolls**
½ **teaspoon ground cumin**	6 **lettuce leaves**
1½ **pounds ground chicken**	6 **slices of tomato**

1. In a small dish, combine paprika, chili powder, onion powder, garlic powder, salt, pepper, cayenne, and cumin. In a medium bowl, use your hands to gently but thoroughly mix ground chicken, bread crumbs, and egg white. Form into 6 patties, each about ½ inch thick. Sprinkle patties liberally with spice blend, pressing in with palm of your hand.

2. In a large frying pan, heat oil over medium heat. Add patties and cook, turning once with a spatula, until browned outside and white throughout but still juicy, 10 to 13 minutes.

3. In a small dish, combine mayonnaise and mustard. Spread on cut sides of rolls. Assemble burgers with lettuce and tomato.

343   CHICKEN PATTIES AU POIVRE
Prep: 10 minutes   Cook: 10 to 12 minutes   Serves: 4

Coarsely grind pepper yourself or buy it in jars in the spice section of the supermarket.

1 **pound ground chicken**	1 **tablespoon flour**
⅔ **cup fresh bread crumbs**	2 **tablespoons butter**
3 **tablespoons minced shallots**	¼ **cup dry white wine**
¼ **cup plus 2 tablespoons**	¼ **cup chicken broth**
chopped parsley	½ **cup heavy cream**
½ **teaspoon dried thyme**	8 **slices of French bread,**
¼ **teaspoon grated nutmeg**	**lightly toasted**
¼ **teaspoon salt**	
1 **teaspoon coarsely ground**	
black pepper	

1. In a mixing bowl, use your hands to gently but thoroughly blend chicken, bread crumbs, shallots, ¼ cup chopped parsley, thyme, nutmeg, and salt. Form into 8 small patties, each about ½ inch thick. Sprinkle each patty with pepper, pressing in lightly. Dust patties with flour.

2. In a large frying pan, melt butter over medium heat. Add patties and cook, turning once with a spatula, until golden brown outside and white throughout, 6 to 7 minutes. Remove patties to a plate.

3. Add wine and broth to pan. Bring to a boil, stirring up browned bits clinging to bottom. Cook, stirring, 2 minutes. Add cream and boil, stirring often, until lightly thickened, 2 to 3 minutes.

4. Place patties on toast, spoon on sauce, and sprinkle remaining 2 tablespoons parsley on top.

---

344   CHICKEN PICADILLO
Prep: 15 minutes   Cook: 43 minutes   Serves: 8

I like this spicy Caribbean-style chopped meat stew for a buffet dish, since it is best made ahead and accompanied by steamed rice. Add a big green salad and a basket of warm corn bread for a great party meal.

2 **pounds ground chicken**	¼ **teaspoon ground allspice**
1 **large onion, chopped**	¼ **teaspoon ground cloves**
1 **large Italian frying pepper**	¼ **to ½ teaspoon cayenne, to**
or medium green bell	**taste**
pepper, chopped	1 **bay leaf**
1 **garlic clove, crushed**	½ **cup raisins**
through a press	1 **(16-ounce) can tomatoes in**
2 **tablespoons vegetable oil**	**juice**
2 **tablespoons chili powder**	¼ **cup orange juice**
1 **teaspoon salt**	3 **tablespoons cider vinegar**
1 **teaspoon dried oregano**	½ **cup slivered almonds**
½ **teaspoon ground cinnamon**	

1. In a large nonreactive saucepan, cook chicken, onion, pepper, and garlic in oil over medium heat, stirring, until chicken is white and onion is softened and pale gold, about 10 minutes.

2. Add chili powder and cook, stirring, 2 minutes. Stir in salt, oregano, cinnamon, allspice, cloves, and cayenne and cook 1 minute. Add bay leaf, raisins, tomatoes, orange juice, and vinegar. Break up tomatoes with back of a spoon. Cover pan and simmer over low heat 30 minutes. Remove and discard bay leaf.

3. Stir in almonds and serve immediately. Or let cool and refrigerate up to 24 hours. Reheat and stir in almonds just before serving.

345   CHICKEN AND BEAN BURRITOS
Prep: 20 minutes   Cook: 19 minutes   Serves: 4

2 tablespoons vegetable oil
¾ pound ground chicken
1½ tablespoons chili powder, to
taste
2 (14½-ounce) cans Mexican-
style stewed tomatoes

1 (15-ounce) can kidney
beans, drained
8 (7- or 8-inch) flour tortillas
¾ cup sour cream
2 cups shredded romaine
lettuce

1. In a large frying pan, heat oil over medium-high heat. Add chicken and cook, stirring, until white, about 8 minutes.

2. Add chili powder and cook, stirring, 1 minute. Measure out and reserve ¾ cup stewed tomatoes. Add remaining stewed tomatoes and beans to chicken. Simmer, uncovered, until thickened but not dry, about 10 minutes.

3. Wrap tortillas in microwave-safe plastic wrap and heat about 30 seconds in a microwave oven (or about 5 minutes wrapped in foil in a 350°F. conventional oven).

4. To serve, spoon filling into centers of tortillas. Roll up, folding ends in to keep filling inside tortillas. Eat out of hand or with a knife and fork, accompanied by sour cream, lettuce, and reserved stewed tomatoes as a garnish.

346   MINTED GRILLED CHICKEN BURGERS IN PITA POCKETS
Prep: 15 minutes   Cook: 12 to 15 minutes   Serves: 6

1½ pounds ground chicken
1 medium onion, chopped
¾ cup fresh bread crumbs
2 garlic cloves, crushed
through a press
¼ cup chopped fresh mint or
1½ teaspoons dried
1½ teaspoons ground cumin
½ teaspoon ground coriander

1 teaspoon salt
¾ teaspoon freshly ground
pepper
6 pita breads
2 medium tomatoes, seeded
and chopped
¼ cup chopped black olives
1 cup plain yogurt
Alfalfa or radish sprouts

1. Prepare a medium-hot fire in a barbecue grill. In a large mixing bowl, combine chicken, onion, bread crumbs, garlic, mint, cumin, coriander, salt, and pepper. Mix with your hands to blend well. Form into 6 oval patties, each about 4½ inches long and ½ inch thick.

2. Grill chicken patties, turning once, until white throughout but still juicy, about 12 to 15 minutes. About 2 minutes before burgers are done, warm pitas at edge of grill. Split pitas to make pockets, then insert a chicken patty into each. Add chopped tomato, olives, yogurt, and sprouts. Serve at once.

347   CHEESY CHICKEN CALZONES
Prep: 10 minutes   Cook: 25 minutes   Serves: 2 to 4

½ pound ground chicken	½ teaspoon dried thyme
¼ cup chopped onion	¼ teaspoon salt
1 garlic clove, crushed through a press	¼ teaspoon crushed hot red pepper
1 tablespoon olive oil	1½ cups marinara sauce
½ cup part-skim ricotta cheese	1 (10-ounce) tube refrigerated pizza dough
1 teaspoon dried oregano	

1. Preheat oven to 425°F. In a medium frying pan, cook chicken, onion, and garlic in olive oil over medium heat, stirring often, until chicken is white, about 10 minutes. Pour off any excess fat. Stir in ricotta cheese, oregano, thyme, salt, hot pepper, and ½ cup of marinara sauce. Let cool.

2. Unfold pizza dough and flatten to a 12-inch square. Cut into 4 even squares. Spoon filling into center of each square. Fold dough over filling to form triangles. Press edges together, then crimp with a fork. Make 3 slashes in each calzone to allow steam to escape. Set on a lightly oiled baking sheet.

3. Bake until rich golden brown, about 15 minutes. Heat remaining 1 cup marinara sauce and use as a dip for calzones.

348   SPAGHETTI AND CHICKEN MEATBALLS
Prep: 15 minutes   Cook: 30 minutes   Serves: 4

1 pound ground chicken	¼ teaspoon freshly ground pepper
1 egg, beaten	2 tablespoons grated Parmesan cheese plus extra as accompaniment
1 cup fresh bread crumbs	
¼ cup chopped parsley	
1 garlic clove, minced	
1 teaspoon dried oregano	4 cups marinara sauce
1 teaspoon dried basil	1 pound spaghetti
½ teaspoon salt	

1. In a mixing bowl, use your hands to mix gently but thoroughly chicken, egg, bread crumbs, parsley, garlic, oregano, basil, salt, pepper, and 2 table-spoons of Parmesan cheese. Form chicken mixture into meatballs about 1½ to 2 inches in diameter.

2. Pour marinara sauce into a large nonreactive saucepan and bring to a simmer over medium heat. Drop meatballs into simmering sauce. Partially cover pot, reduce heat to medium-low, and simmer, stirring gently, about 30 minutes, until meatballs are white throughout.

3. Meanwhile, in a large pot of boiling salted water, cook spaghetti until tender but still firm, 8 to 10 minutes. Drain into a colander. Serve meatballs and sauce over spaghetti. Pass additional grated cheese separately.

349 CHICKEN AND STUFFING LOAF

Prep: 10 minutes   Cook: 55 to 65 minutes   Stand: 10 minutes
Serves: 6

½ cup finely chopped celery
½ cup finely chopped onion
1 tablespoon vegetable oil
1½ pounds ground chicken
1 egg, beaten
¾ cup crushed herb-seasoned
    stuffing mix

¼ teaspoon freshly ground
    pepper
1 cup canned whole cranberry
    sauce
2 tablespoons prepared white
    horseradish

1. Preheat oven to 350°F. Lightly oil a 9x5-inch or 8x4-inch loaf pan. In a medium frying pan, cook celery and onion in oil over medium-low heat, stirring often, until softened, about 5 minutes. Let cool.

2. In a mixing bowl, use your hands to gently but thoroughly combine chicken, egg, stuffing mix, pepper, and cooked onion and celery. Spoon into loaf pan, patting top to even.

3. Bake 30 minutes. In a small bowl, blend cranberry sauce and horseradish. Spread over top of loaf and continue to bake until firm on top and white throughout but still juicy, 20 to 30 minutes longer. An instant-reading thermometer should register 165°. Let loaf stand 10 minutes before slicing 1 inch thick.

350 SPICY THREE-ALARM CHICKEN CHILI

Prep: 15 minutes   Cook: 31 to 36 minutes   Serves: 8

The amount of jalapeño peppers here determines the alarm bells of the chili. Serve spooned into flour or corn tortillas or over rice.

1½ pounds ground chicken
1 large onion, chopped
2 garlic cloves, crushed
    through a press
2 tablespoons vegetable oil
1½ tablespoons chili powder
1 teaspoon dried oregano
½ teaspoon ground cumin
1 (16-ounce) can plum
    tomatoes, drained

1½ cups chicken broth
1 (4-ounce) can chopped green
    chiles
1, 2, or 3 fresh or canned
    jalapeño peppers, seeded
    and chopped
¼ cup chopped cilantro

1. In a large saucepan, cook chicken, onion, and garlic in oil over medium heat until chicken is white and onion is softened and pale gold, about 10 minutes.

2. Add chili powder, oregano, and cumin and cook, stirring, 1 minute. Stir in tomatoes, broth, chopped chiles, and jalapeño(s), breaking up tomatoes with back of a spoon. Simmer over medium-low heat, stirring occasionally, until chili is slightly thickened, 20 to 25 minutes.

351 CHICKEN AND VEGETABLE TERRINE

Prep: 15 minutes   Cook: 1½ to 1¾ hours   Stand: 45 minutes
Chill: 4 hours   Serves: 8

For an elegant summer dish, serve this sophisticated terrine chilled with a mustardy mayonnaise or pesto sauce.

1½ **pounds skinless, boneless**	1 **small red bell pepper,**
chicken breasts, cut into	**chopped**
2-inch chunks	1 **cup finely diced baked ham**
1 **egg**	1½ **teaspoons salt**
2 **cups cold heavy cream**	½ **teaspoon grated nutmeg**
1 **(10-ounce) package frozen**	¼ **teaspoon cayenne**
peas and carrots, thawed	¼ **teaspoon freshly ground**
⅓ **cup chopped scallions**	**black pepper**

1. Preheat oven to 350°F. Place chicken in a food processor and add egg. With machine on, add cream gradually through feed tube. Continue to process about 45 seconds to make a smooth, thick puree. Transfer to a medium bowl. Stir in peas and carrots, scallions, bell pepper, ham, salt, nutmeg, cayenne, and black pepper.

2. Pack into a buttered 9x5x3-inch loaf pan. Lay a sheet of buttered waxed paper over chicken mixture, then cover pan tightly with foil. Place in a large baking pan and pour in enough hot water to reach halfway up sides of loaf pan.

3. Bake 1½ to 1¾ hours, until an instant-reading thermometer registers 165°, loaf is firm, and juices run clear when pricked.

4. Let cool at room temperature 45 minutes. Drain off any liquid. Place another loaf pan on top of loaf and fill with cans to weight terrine and make it denser. Refrigerate at least 4 hours or up to 2 days. To serve, drain off any accumulated liquid, unmold, and cut into ½-inch slices.

352   ZITI WITH EASY CHICKEN BOLOGNESE SAUCE

Prep: 15 minutes   Cook: 28 minutes   Serves: 4

1   pound ground chicken
1   large onion, chopped
1   large green bell pepper, chopped
2   garlic cloves, crushed through a press
2   tablespoons olive oil
1½   teaspoons dried oregano
1½   teaspoons dried basil
¼   teaspoon crushed hot pepper

1   (28-ounce) can plum tomatoes, juices reserved
1   (8-ounce) can tomato sauce
½   cup dry red or white wine
Pinch of sugar
Salt and freshly ground pepper
1   pound ziti or other tubular pasta
Grated Parmesan cheese

1. In a large saucepan, cook chicken, onion, bell pepper, and garlic in olive oil over medium heat, stirring often, until chicken is white and vegetables are softened, about 8 minutes.

2. Add oregano, basil, hot pepper, tomatoes with their juices, tomato sauce, wine, and sugar. Simmer, uncovered, over medium-low heat, stirring often and breaking up tomatoes with back of a spoon, 20 minutes.

3. Meanwhile, in a large pot of boiling salted water, cook ziti until tender but still firm, 11 to 13 minutes. Drain into a colander.

4. To serve, spoon sauce over ziti. Pass cheese separately.

Chapter 16

A Bird of Your Own

Game hens are not wild game or baby chickens, nor are they necessarily from Cornwall. They are lovely little birds of between 1 and 1½ pounds that will serve one or two people quite nicely. In addition to boasting a flavor likened by many to old-fashioned, farm-raised chickens, they make a smashing presentation on any dinner plate and cook far faster than their bigger cousins. These attributes make game hens a perennial favorite for small dinner parties.

Game hens are sold whole, halved, and quartered. My favorite is quartered since the pieces are easiest to grill or broil. I like to prepare them with a simple herb glaze and then serve them at room temperature for a fancy picnic or tailgate party, though in this chapter you'll find all sorts of flavors to suit all types of tastes. Halves are well suited to baking or grilling, and they make a dramatic plate presentation, needing only a little rice or vegetable and an herb sprig for a special effect. When cooking whole hens, shop for the smallest size—those that weigh about a pound each.

Game hens are roasted at a high heat to ensure a richly browned exterior in a relatively short time. As with chicken, they are done when the thigh juices run clear when pricked with a knife tip. (An instant-reading thermometer is not as reliable here since there is very little depth for inserting the gauge.)

If you haven't tried game hens in some time, now is the time to renew acquaintance with the prettiest little bird on the block.

353   HOT-AS-HADES BROILED GAME HENS

Prep: 10 minutes   Cook: 25 minutes   Serves: 4

2 tablespoons dry white wine	¼ teaspoon salt
1 tablespoon olive oil	⅛ teaspoon crushed hot red
1 tablespoon lemon juice	pepper
1 teaspoon Tabasco or other	Pinch of cayenne
hot sauce	2 Cornish game hens,
1 large garlic clove, crushed	quartered
through a press	

1. Preheat broiler. In a small bowl, stir together wine, olive oil, lemon juice, Tabasco, garlic, salt, hot pepper, and cayenne.

2. Place hens on a broiler pan, skin side up, and brush with some of sauce. Broil about 6 inches from heat 10 minutes. Turn, brush with more sauce, and broil 10 minutes. Turn and brush again with remaining sauce. Broil until juices run clear when pricked with a knife tip, about 5 minutes longer.

354   BROILED GAME HENS AND SPICED APPLES

Prep: 10 minutes   Cook: 27 minutes   Serves: 4

2 Cornish game hens,	Salt and freshly ground
quartered	pepper
2 tablespoons olive oil	¼ cup dry white wine
½ teaspoon ground cloves	2 tablespoons crabapple jelly
2 tart apples, cut into ½-inch-	
thick slices	

1. Preheat broiler. Use your hands to flatten hen quarters somewhat. In a small bowl, stir together olive oil and cloves. Brush or rub all sides of hens and apples with flavored oil. Season hens and apples lightly with salt and pepper. In a small saucepan, cook wine and jelly over medium heat, stirring to melt jelly, about 2 minutes. Remove from heat and reserve crabapple glaze.

2. Place hens on a broiler pan, skin side down, and broil about 6 inches from heat 10 minutes. Turn and brush with some of glaze. Broil 10 minutes. Turn and brush again. Brush apple slices with glaze and add to pan. Broil 3 minutes. Turn hens and apples over and brush again. Broil until apples are glazed and softened and hen juices run clear when thigh is pricked with a knife tip, about 2 minutes.

3. Serve hens garnished with broiled apple slices.

355 ROSEMARY GRILLED GAME HENS
Prep: 10 minutes   Stand: 30 minutes   Cook: 40 minutes   Serves: 4

Other herbs work just as well in this basic grilled game hen recipe. I like to use halved hens, or even quarters, as they cook far more evenly and are thus easier than attempting to grill a whole hen.

2 **Cornish game hens, halved**	1 **tablespoon olive oil**
4 **teaspoons chopped fresh**	**Salt and freshly ground**
rosemary or 1½ teaspoons	**pepper**
dried	**Fresh rosemary sprigs, for**
1 **garlic clove, crushed**	**garnish**
through a press	

1. Use your hands to flatten hen halves somewhat. Loosen skin of hens and rub rosemary and garlic under skin, spreading as much as possible with your fingers without tearing skin. Let hens stand 30 minutes at room temperature.

2. Prepare a medium fire in a barbecue grill or preheat broiler. Rub hen halves with olive oil and season generously with salt and pepper. Grill or broil, turning once, until skin is richly browned and juices run clear when thigh is pricked with a knife tip, about 40 minutes.

3. Serve garnished with rosemary sprigs.

356 GINGER-HONEY HENS
Prep: 10 minutes   Cook: 35 minutes   Serves: 6

3 **Cornish game hens,**	3 **tablespoons dry white wine**
quartered	1 **tablespoon white wine**
½ **teaspoon salt**	**vinegar**
¼ **teaspoon freshly ground**	1 **tablespoon butter**
pepper	1 **tablespoon grated fresh**
3 **tablespoons honey**	**ginger**

1. Preheat oven to 450°F. Use your hands to flatten hen quarters somewhat. Season with salt and pepper. Place in a shallow roasting pan, skin side up. Roast 10 minutes.

2. Meanwhile, make glaze. In a small nonreactive saucepan, combine honey, wine, vinegar, butter, and ginger, heating and stirring to melt butter.

3. After hens have roasted 10 minutes, turn and brush with some of glaze. Roast 10 minutes. Turn again and brush liberally with more of glaze. Roast until juices run clear when pricked with a knife tip, about 15 minutes longer.

357 ROASTED LEMON AND OREGANO GAME HENS

Prep: 15 minutes   Cook: 45 minutes   Serves: 4

¼ cup chopped flat-leaf parsley
1 tablespoon dried oregano
1 tablespoon grated lemon zest
3 garlic cloves, crushed through a press
¾ teaspoon salt

¾ teaspoon freshly ground pepper
2 teaspoons lemon juice
1 cup plain yogurt
2 Cornish game hens, halved
2 tablespoons olive oil
Parsley sprigs and lemon slices, for garnish

1. Preheat oven to 425°F. In a small bowl, combine parsley, oregano, lemon zest, crushed garlic, salt, and pepper. Stir about half of garlic-herb paste, along with lemon juice, into yogurt. Use your fingers to loosen skin on hens. Rub remaining paste under skin, spreading it as much as possible without tearing skin. Brush hens with olive oil. Season lightly with additional salt and pepper.

2. Place, skin side up, in a shallow roasting pan and roast 15 minutes. Turn hens over. Reduce oven temperature to 400° and roast 20 minutes. Turn again and roast until hens are cooked through and thigh juices run clear when pricked with a knife tip, about 10 minutes.

3. Serve hen halves garnished with parsley and lemon. Spoon yogurt sauce alongside.

358 BOURBON BARBECUED HENS

Prep: 10 minutes   Cook: 40 minutes   Serves: 4

While perfect for the backyard barbecue, these hens can also be broiled with excellent results.

⅓ cup bottled chili sauce
2 tablespoons bourbon
1 tablespoon molasses
2 teaspoons soy sauce

2 Cornish game hens, quartered
1 tablespoon vegetable oil

1. Prepare a medium fire in a barbecue grill or preheat broiler. In a small nonreactive saucepan, simmer chili sauce, bourbon, molasses, and soy sauce over medium-low heat 5 minutes. Use your hands to flatten hen quarters somewhat.

2. Rub hens with oil. Grill or broil, skin side down, 10 minutes. Turn, brush with some of sauce, and grill 10 minutes. Turn and brush liberally with more sauce. Grill or broil until skin is crisp and browned and juices run clear when pricked with a knife tip, about 15 minutes longer.

359   CHÈVRE ROASTED GAME HENS
Prep: 5 minutes   Cook: 45 minutes   Serves: 4

The slightly gamy flavor of Cornish hens stands up well to the assertiveness of goat cheese. If desired, a good herbed cheese spread, such as boursin, can be substituted for the chèvre.

2 Cornish game hens, halved	**Salt and freshly ground**
3 ounces soft herbed chèvre	**pepper**

1. Preheat oven to 400°F. Loosen skin of hens with your fingers. Rub cheese under skin, spreading as much as possible without tearing skin. Season hens lightly with salt and pepper.

2. Place hen halves, skin side up, in a shallow roasting pan. Roast 10 minutes. Reduce oven temperature to 375° and continue to roast until juices run clear when pricked with a knife point, about 35 minutes longer.

360   SMOKED APPLE–THYME GAME HENS
Prep: 5 minutes   Cook: 2½ hours   Serves: 4

If you don't have a smoker, you can convert a covered grill into a good facsimile. Be sure to keep the fire constant, but not too hot. You'll need four to six handfuls of applewood or other wood chips for this recipe.

4 Cornish game hens, halved	**¼ teaspoon freshly ground**
2 tablespoons chopped fresh	**pepper**
thyme or 2 teaspoons	**3 tablespoons apple jelly**
dried leaf thyme	**3 tablespoons dry white wine**
½ teaspoon salt	

1. Soak wood chips in cold water for at least 30 minutes. Prepare a home smoker according to manufacturer's directions. Or prepare a medium indirect charcoal fire in a covered grill by pushing hot coals to one side of grill so that hens can be placed on grill away from direct heat. Just before cooking, toss about one-third of the chips onto fire. If using a gas grill, follow manufacturer's instructions for grill smoking.

2. Loosen skin on hen halves and rub half of thyme under skin, spreading as much as possible without tearing skin. Season hens with salt and pepper. Place hens, breast side up, on smoker rack or grill rack away from coals. Cover smoker or grill and smoke 2 hours, adding more wood chips about halfway through smoking time.

3. While hens are smoking, make glaze by heating jelly, wine, and remaining thyme in a small nonreactive saucepan, stirring until jelly melts. After 2 hours of smoking, brush hens with glaze and smoke 15 minutes. Brush again and smoke to an internal temperature of 180°F.; thigh juices should run clear when pricked with a knife tip. This will take about 15 minutes longer, for a total of about 2½ hours smoking time.

361 APRICOT MUSTARD–GLAZED GAME HENS

Prep: 10 minutes   Cook: 35 minutes   Serves: 6

3 Cornish game hens,
   quartered
¼ teaspoon salt
½ teaspoon freshly ground
   pepper

¼ cup Dijon mustard
3 tablespoons apricot
   preserves
1 tablespoon vegetable oil
1 tablespoon lemon juice

1. Preheat oven to 450°F. Use your hands to flatten hen quarters somewhat. Season lightly with salt and generously with pepper. Place in a shallow roasting pan, skin side up. Roast 10 minutes.

2. Meanwhile, make glaze. In a small saucepan, heat together mustard, preserves, oil, and lemon juice. After hens have roasted 10 minutes, turn and brush with some of glaze. Roast 10 minutes. Turn again and brush with glaze. Roast until juices run clear when pricked with a knife tip, about 15 minutes longer.

362 GAME HENS WITH CUMBERLAND SAUCE

Prep: 10 minutes   Cook: 35 minutes   Serves: 6

This is a simplified version of a classic British sweet-and-sour sauce for game. The hens can be served warm or at room temperature for an autumn picnic or tailgate party.

1 cup port wine
¼ cup fresh orange juice
¼ cup red currant jelly
2 tablespoons grainy Dijon
   mustard

1 tablespoon red wine vinegar
1 teaspoon grated orange zest
6 Cornish game hens,
   quartered

1. In a nonreactive saucepan, bring wine, orange juice, and jelly to a simmer, stirring to melt jelly. Simmer until reduced by one-third, about 4 minutes. Remove from heat and stir in mustard, vinegar, and orange zest. Set sauce aside. (Sauce can be made a day ahead and refrigerated.)

2. Preheat oven to 450°F. Use your hands to flatten hen quarters somewhat. Place in a shallow roasting pan, skin side up. Brush with some of sauce and roast 10 minutes. Turn, brush again, and roast 10 minutes. Roast, turning and brushing one more time, for a total of 35 minutes roasting time.

3. Serve hot or at room temperature.

363   BURNISHED HENS
Prep: 10 minutes   Cook: 36 to 37 minutes   Serves: 6

Worcestershire sauce stains these hens to a burnished golden brown color, which is especially lovely if you serve them with bright vegetables, such as green beans and sautéed cherry tomatoes.

1 tablespoon olive oil	1 tablespoon Dijon mustard
2 tablespoons chopped shallots	¼ teaspoon freshly ground black pepper
2 tablespoons Worcestershire sauce	3 Cornish game hens, quartered
2 tablespoons apricot preserves	

1. Preheat oven to 450°F. In a small saucepan, heat olive oil and cook shallots over medium-low heat until softened, 1 to 2 minutes. Add Worcestershire sauce, preserves, mustard, and pepper, stirring to melt preserves.

2. Use your hands to flatten hen quarters somewhat. Place in a shallow roasting pan, skin side up. Brush with some of sauce and roast 10 minutes. Turn, brush again, and roast 10 minutes. Turn and brush again, then roast until juices run clear when pricked with a knife tip, about 15 minutes longer.

364   CURRIED ORANGE GAME HENS
Prep: 10 minutes   Cook: 35 minutes   Serves: 6

3 Cornish game hens, quartered	1½ teaspoons curry powder
¼ cup orange marmalade	½ teaspoon salt
1½ tablespoons olive oil	¼ teaspoon freshly ground black pepper
1 tablespoon lemon juice	⅛ teaspoon cayenne

1. Preheat oven to 450°F. Use your hands to flatten hen quarters somewhat. Place in a shallow roasting pan, skin side up. Roast 10 minutes.

2. Meanwhile, make glaze. In a small saucepan, heat together marmalade, olive oil, lemon juice, curry powder, salt, pepper, and cayenne, stirring to melt marmalade. After hens have roasted 10 minutes, turn and brush with some of glaze. Roast 10 minutes. Turn again and brush liberally with glaze. Roast until juices run clear when pricked with a knife tip, about 15 minutes longer.

365 THANKSGIVING FOR TWO
Prep: 20 minutes   Cook: 1 hour 4 to 20 minutes   Serves: 2

When there are two for Thanksgiving, a whole hen for each makes for a bountiful and beautiful meal.

1¼ cups chicken broth
 1 cup packaged dry corn
     bread stuffing mix
 ¼ cup coarsely chopped fresh
     cranberries
 ¼ cup coarsely chopped
     pecans

 2 whole Cornish game hens
 1 tablespoon butter
 3 tablespoons Madeira or dry
     sherry
     Salt and freshly ground
     pepper
 2 teaspoons flour

1. Preheat oven to 400°F. Bring ½ cup of broth to a simmer. In a medium bowl, pour hot broth over stuffing mix. Add cranberries and pecans and stir to mix well. Stuff hens with as much stuffing as possible. (Any extra can be roasted in a small pan alongside hens for about 30 minutes.)

2. Place hens in a shallow roasting pan, breast side up. In a small pan, melt butter and stir in 1 tablespoon of Madeira. Brush hens with Madeira butter. Season lightly with salt and pepper. Roast 15 minutes. Reduce oven temperature to 350° and continue to roast, basting occasionally with pan juices, until juices run clear when pricked with a knife tip, 45 minutes to 1 hour longer.

3. Remove hens from pan and pour off all but 1 tablespoon pan drippings. Stir flour into drippings in roasting pan and cook over medium-high direct heat 1 to 2 minutes. Whisk in remaining ¾ cup broth and 2 tablespoons Madeira. Cook, stirring, until sauce is lightly thickened, about 3 minutes. Season with salt and pepper to taste. Pass sauce separately.

Index

Acknowledgments

This book is for my three sons, Dave, Jeff, and Matt, who would all eat chicken 365 days every year (and who did this year). It is also for my husband, Scott, who steadfastly supports all my endeavors, samples my recipes, and never chickens out.

My thanks also to Susan Wyler and Susan Friedland—two better editors a writer could never hope to have.

I am also grateful to Anne Salisbury and the folks at Perdue Farms, Incorporated, for their generous supplies of all cuts of chicken and game hens for recipe development and testing.